TAHITI
-POLYNESIA
HANDBOOK

EXCHANGE RATES

(as of mid-1989; subject to change)

One French Franc	=	18.18	Pacific Francs
One U.S. Dollar	=	118	Pacific Francs
One Australian Dollar	=	89	Pacific Francs
One Canadian Dollar	=	98	Pacific Francs
One New Zealand Dollar	=	69	Pacific Francs
One West German D.M.	=	60	Pacific Francs
100 Japanese Yen	=	83	Pacific Francs
One Pound Sterling	=	187	Pacific Francs

As this appalling ocean surrounds the verdant land,
so in the soul of man there lies one insular Tahiti,
full of peace and joy, but encompassed by
all the horrors of the half-known life.
God help thee! Push not off from that isle,
thou canst never return.

Herman Melville

TAHITI
-POLYNESIA
HANDBOOK

DAVID STANLEY

PUBLICATIONS, INC.

TAHITI-POLYNESIA HANDBOOK

Please send all comments,
corrections, additions,
amendments, and critiques to:

DAVID STANLEY
c/o MOON PUBLICATIONS, INC.
722 WALL STREET
CHICO CA 95928, USA

Published by
  Moon Publications, Inc.
  722 Wall Street
  Chico, California 95928, USA

Printed by
  Colorcraft Ltd.

Printing History
  1st edition—September 1989

Library of Congress Cataloging in Publication Data

Stanley, David.
  Tahiti-Polynesia handbook

  Bibliography: p. 209
  Includes index.
  1. French Polynesia—Description and travel.
  I. Title.
  DU870.S73   1989   996.2   89-12091
  ISBN 0-918373-33-6

Printed in Hong Kong

Cover photograph courtesy of Tahiti Tourist Board

CONTENTS

LIST OF MAPS

MAP SYMBOLS

LIST OF CHARTS

PHOTO AND ILLUSTRATION CREDITS

ABBREVIATIONS

A$—Australian dollars
a/c—air conditioned
BBQ—barbecue
C—centigrade
d—double
EEZ—Exclusive
  Economic Zone
f.—CFP (Pacific francs)
I.—island
Is.—islands

km—kilometer
kph—kilometers per hour
LDS—Latter-day Saints
  (Mormons)
min.—minutes
MV—motor vessel
no.—number
NZ—New Zealand
OW—one way
pp—per person

RT—round trip
s—single
SPF—South Pacific
  Forum
t—triple
tel.—telephone
U.S.—United States
US$—U.S. dollars
WW II—World War Two
YHA—Youth Hostel Assn.

IS THIS BOOK OUT OF DATE?

Travel writing is like trying to take a picture out the side of *le truck*: time frustrates the best of intentions. Things change fast—you'll understand how hard it is for us to keep up. So if something in *Tahiti-Polynesia Handbook* seems out of date, please let us hear about it. Did anything lead you astray or inconvenience you? In retrospect, what sort of information would have made your trip easier? Please share your discoveries with us and we'll share them with others. Everything will be carefully field-checked, but your lead could help us zero in on some fascinating aspect which might otherwise be overlooked. Please be as precise and accurate as you can, however. Notes made on the scene are far better than later recollections. Write comments into your copy of *Tahiti-Polynesia Handbook* as you go along, then send us a summary when you get home. If this book helped you, please help us make it even better. Address your letters to:

David Stanley
c/o Moon Publications
722 Wall Street
Chico, CA 95928 USA

ACKNOWLEDGEMENTS

Two of the people who contributed most to *Tahiti-Polynesia Handbook* were editor Deke Castleman and book designer Asha Johnson. Mapmaker/illustrator Louise Foote supervised the mapping, assisted by Alexandra Foote and Robert Race. Christa Jorgensen proofread the galleys, while Mark Morris helped Christa do the indexing. Todd Clark and Nancy Kennedy did the camera work and pasted up the boards. Moon's art director Dave Hurst designed the cover and spec'd the color pages. Bette, Bill, Cindy, Darcy, Donna, Lucinda, Magnus, Mark, Michelle, Rick, Robert K., and Taran all contributed in their own ways.

Special thanks to Cao Hyacinth and Patrick Robson of the Tahiti Tourist Board, to the French Government Tourist Offices in Chicago and New York, to the Consulate General of France in San Francisco, to Madame Jacques Brel for kind permission to reproduce *Les Marquises,* to Agnes Charriaud, Claudine de Vos, and Marie-France Boeve for help in transcribing the song's words, to Canadian yachties Jean and Scott Thompson for a detailed report on the Marquesas and Tuamotus, to Kik Velt for bicycling tips, to Persis Sturges for help in updating Polynesian air routes, and to Phil Esmonde of the South Pacific Peoples Foundation of Canada for a big box of resources.

I'm deeply grateful to Bengt Danielsson of Papehue, Tahiti, who read and corrected the entire manuscript. Dr. Danielsson arrived in Tahiti-Polynesia in 1947 aboard Thor Heyerdahl's famous raft *Kon Tiki.* During the next ten years, he and his French wife, Marie Therese, carried out anthropological field work in the Tuamotu, Marquesas, and Society islands. Later Bengt served as director of Sweden's National Museum of Ethnology before returning to Tahiti for good in 1971. Some of his numerous publications are listed in the Booklist herein. If *Tahiti-Polynesia Handbook* displays any historical accuracy it's due to the very thorough check Bengt did; remaining inadequacies are the responsibility of the author.

Thanks too to the following readers who took the trouble to write us letters about their trips: Allen Ashby, Ann Baker, Lucy Barefoot, John E. Beaumont, Anne Beck, Walter Bersinger, Robert and Phyllis Bisordi, Mark Chaffey, Scott Coffman, Mary T. Crowley, E. Desurvire, Glenn B. Fried, A. Grobmeier, Guynette, Alvina Hart, Thomas Helin, Robert Kennington, Stacy Kunz-Ciulik, Greg La Shelle, Sandy Lukacs, Chris McLowerty, Pat Pautu, Richard J. Pierce, Marie-France Philip, Gerry Phillips, Richard Phinney, Joel Rea, Rolf Reinstrom, Steve Schein, Denise and Fariua Tehiva, and Michael A. Zenft. Their help is most appreciated!

Bengt Danielsson

FOREWORD

"All my life I had longed to go to the South Seas. These very words had magic in them, conjuring up primordial memories of palms and coral reefs and sun-drenched sands, of fruits and flowering trees, of women warm in welcome, of peace and isolation, and of a shore where the struggle for existence is unknown."

Thus writes Cecil Lewis, an ordinary, average American, who before the Second World War managed to realize his dream and consequently published an enthusiastic account of the happy months he spent in Tahiti and the other Society Islands.

The dream is not dead. But as most South Sea travelers today will sadly discover, the "native" villages they find along their crowded paths are often human zoos, where the athletic guitar players and graceful hula dancers are paid performers, professional natives so to say, with a bank account, a car, and a TV set at home.

So there is a general belief that there is nothing left of the "real" South Seas. Fortunately, this is not altogether true. During the forty years I have lived in Tahiti, I have received a steady stream of visitors, who are all appalled by the traffic jams, concrete buildings, and frantic life in and around Papeete, and therefore eager to learn the exact location of the primitive, unspoilt island paradises they have been dreaming of, and which do exist in the remote archipelagoes of Tahiti-Polynesia, or French Polynesia, as the colony is officially named.

It has always surprised me that none of the previous guidebooks have supplied this badly needed information, and I am very happy to see that my friend David Stanley has at long last filled this gap and has thus taken a heavy burden off my shoulders. Fortunately, this does not mean, however, that there is nothing in this new-style up-to-date handbook about the central, more sophisticated islands, like Tahiti, Moorea, Raiatea, and Bora Bora.

Actually, this blend of old and new, Polynesian and European cultural elements found today in varying degrees in the majority of the 118 islands is as interesting and fascinating as the "pure" traditional life-style in the outer islands. Whereas few other travel guides take notice of these changes, the readers of this handbook will also find much information about all these social, economic, and political consequences due to the long exposure of a stone-age people with a simple subsistence economy and strong family and community solidarity to our Western type of individualistic and commercial civilization.

There are also pertinent notices about the regional differences in French Polynesia which, in fact, consists of five distinct archipelagoes, inhabited by native peoples, speaking separate Polynesian tongues and having different cultural traditions.

The last but not the least important feature of this unique handbook is the complete, detailed, and accurate practical information it offers the users about where to stay and what to pay—as well as equally useful advice about how to avoid being overcharged for goods and services.

With sincere congratulations for your fortunate choice of handbook, I guarantee you a happy sojourn, wish you warmly welcome to my islands and extend to you the traditional greeting, corresponding to a Hawaiian aloha, which in Tahitian is pronounced

AROHA

Papehue, Tahiti

Bengt Danielsson

INTRODUCTION

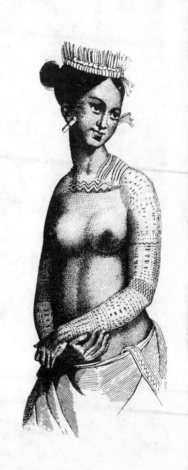

Tarita co-starred with Marlon Brando in the 1962 MGM film Mutiny on the Bounty

the Tahitian fleet preparing to attack Moorea, 1774 (after William Hodges)

INTRODUCTION

Legendary Tahiti, isle of love, has long been the vision of "la Nouvelle Cythere," the earthly paradise. Explorers Wallis, Bougainville, and Cook told of a land of spellbinding beauty and enchantment, where the climate was delightful, hazardous insects and diseases unknown, and the islanders, especially the women, among the handsomest ever seen. Rousseau's "noble savage" had been found! A few years later, Fletcher Christian and Capt. Bligh acted out their drama of sin and retribution here.

The list of famous authors who came and wrote about these islands reads like a high-school literature course: Herman Melville, Robert Louis Stevenson, Pierre Loti, Rupert Brooke, Jack London, W. Somerset Maugham, Charles Nordhoff and James Norman Hall (the Americans who wrote *Mutiny on the Bounty*), among others. Exotic images of uninhibited dancers, fragrant flowers, and pagan gods fill the pages. Here, at least, life was meant to be enjoyed.

The most unlikely P.R. man of them all was a once-obscure French painter named Paul Gauguin, who transformed the primitive color of Tahiti and the Marquesas into powerful visual images seen around the world. When WW II shook the Pacific from Pearl Harbor to Guadalcanal, rather than bloodcurdling banzais and saturation bombings, Polynesia got a U.S. serviceman named James A. Michener, who added Bora Bora to the legend. Marlon Brando arrived in 1961 on one of the first jets and, along with thousands of tourists and adventurers, has been coming back ever since.

Trouble In Paradise

In the early '60s, President Charles de Gaulle transferred France's atomic testing program from Algeria to Polynesia. Since then over 150 nuclear explosions, 44 of them in the atmosphere, have rocked the Tuamotus, spreading contamination as far as Peru and New Zealand.

POLYNESIA AT A GLANCE

	POPULATION (1988)	AREA (hectares)
WINDWARD ISLANDS	140,341	118,580
Tahiti	131,309	104,510
Moorea	8,801	12,520
LEEWARD ISLANDS	22,232	38,750
Huahine	4,479	7,480
Raiatea	8,560	17,140
Tahaa	4,005	9,020
Bora Bora	4,225	1,830
Maupiti	963	1,140
AUSTRAL ISLANDS	6,509	14,784
Rurutu	1,953	3,235
Tubuai	1,846	4,500
TUAMOTU ISLANDS	11,754	72,646
Rangiroa	1,305	7,900
Manihi	429	1,300
GAMBIER ISLANDS	620	4,597
MARQUESAS ISLANDS	7,358	104,930
Nuku Hiva	2,100	33,950
Hiva Oa	1,671	31,550
TAHITI-POLYNESIA	188,814	354,287

TAHITI-POLYNESIA

The official French attitude to its Pacific colonies has changed little since 1842 when Admiral Du Petit-Thouars sailed into Papeete harbor and forced young Queen Pomare IV to sign a request for a French protectorate. In the 1960s-70s, as independence blossomed across the South Pacific, France tightened its strategic grip on Tahiti-Polynesia.

New mineral wealth has been discovered on the seabed and the arms race is far from over. Deadly plutonium, with a radioactive half-life of 24,000 years, could now be leaking into the sea from dumps and cracks at the French facilities on Moruroa.

THE LAND

Tahiti-Polynesia consists of five great archipelagos, the Society, Austral, Tuamotu, Gambier, and Marquesas islands. The Society Is. are subdivided into the Windwards or *Iles du Vent* (Tahiti, Moorea, Maiao, Tetiaroa, and Mehetia), and the Leewards or *Iles Sous Le Vent* (Huahine, Raiatea, Tahaa, Bora Bora, Maupiti, Tupai, Maupihaa/Mopelia, Manuae/Scilly, and Motu One/Bellingshausen). Together the 35 islands and 83 atolls of Tahiti-Polynesia total only 3,543 sq km in land area, yet they're scattered over 5,030,000 sq km of the southeastern Pacific, from the Cook Is. in the west to Pitcairn in the east. Though Tahiti-Polynesia is only half the size of Corsica in land area, if Papeete were Paris then the Gambiers would be in Romania and the Marquesas near Stockholm.

There's a wonderful geological diversity to these islands midway between Australia and South America—from the dramatic, jagged volcanic outlines of the Society and Marquesas islands to the 400-meter-high hills of the Australs and Gambiers and the low coral atolls of the Tuamotus. All of the Marquesas are volcanic islands, while the Tuamotus are all coral islands or atolls. The Societies and Gambiers include both volcanic and coral types.

Tahiti, just over 4,000 km both from Auckland and Honolulu, is not only the best known of the islands, but also the largest (1,045 sq km) and highest (2,241 meters). Bora Bora and Maupiti are noted for their combination of high volcanic peaks within low coral rings. Rangiroa is one of the world's largest coral atolls. Makatea is an uplifted atoll. In the Marquesas, precipitous and sharply crenelated mountains rise hundreds of meters, with craggy peaks, razor-back ridges, plummeting waterfalls, deep fertile valleys, and dark broken coastlines pounded by surf. Compare them to the pencil-thin strips of yellow reefs, green vegetation, and white beaches enclosing the transparent Tuamotu lagoons. In all, Tahiti-Polynesia offers some of the most varied and spectacular scenery in the entire South Pacific.

Darwin's Theory Of Atoll Formation
The famous formulator of the theory of evolution surmised that atolls form as high volcanic islands subside into lagoons. The original island's fringing reef grows into a barrier reef as the volcanic portion sinks. When the last volcanic material finally disappears below sea level, the coral rim of the reef/atoll remains to indicate how big the island once was.

Of course, all this takes place over thousands, perhaps millions, of years, but deep down below every atoll is the old volcanic core, as any nuclear tester worth his contamination knows. Darwin's theory is well illustrated at Bora Bora, where a high volcanic island remains inside the rim of Bora Bora's barrier reef; this island's volcanic core is still sinking imperceptibly at the rate of one cm a century. Return to Bora Bora in about a million years and all you'll find will be a coral atoll like Rangiroa or Manihi.

Plate Tectonics
High or low, all of the islands have a volcanic origin best explained by the "Conveyor Belt Theory." A crack opens in the sea floor and

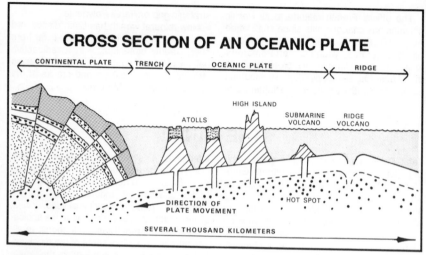

CROSS SECTION OF AN OCEANIC PLATE

CONTINENTAL PLATE | TRENCH | OCEANIC PLATE | RIDGE

HIGH ISLAND

ATOLLS

SUBMARINE VOLCANO   RIDGE VOLCANO

DIRECTION OF PLATE MOVEMENT

HOT SPOT

SEVERAL THOUSAND KILOMETERS

volcanic material escapes upward. A submarine volcano builds up slowly until the lava finally breaks the surface, becoming a volcanic island. The Pacific Plate moves northwest approximately 10 cm a year; thus, over geologic eons the volcano disconnects from the hot spot or crack from which it emerged. As the old volcanoes disconnect with the crack, new ones appear to the southeast, and the older islands are carried away from the cleft in the Earth's crust from which they were born.

The island then begins to sink under its own weight, perhaps only one cm a century, but erosion also cuts into the volcano, by this time extinct. In the warm clear waters a living coral reef begins to grow along the shore. As the island subsides, the reef continues to grow upward. In this way a lagoon forms between the reef and the shoreline of the slowly sinking island. This barrier reef marks the old margin of the original island.

As the hot spot shifts southeast, in an opposite direction to the sliding Pacific Plate (and shifting magnetic pole of the Earth), the process is repeated, time and again, until whole chains of islands ride the blue Pacific. Weathering is most advanced on the composite islands and atolls at the northwest ends of the Society, Austral, Tuamotu, and

Marquesas chains. Maupiti and Bora Bora with their exposed volcanic cores are the oldest of the larger Society Islands. The Tuamotus have eroded almost to sea level; the Gambier Islands originated out of the same hot spot and volcanic peaks remain inside a giant atoll reef. In every case, the islands at the southeast end of the chains are the youngest.

By drilling into the Tuamotu atolls, scientists have proven their point conclusively: the coral formations are about 350 meters thick at the southeast end of the chain, 600 meters thick at Hao near the center, and 1,000 meters thick at Rangiroa near the northwest end of the Tuamotu Group. Clearly Rangiroa, where the volcanic rock is now a kilometer below the surface, is many millions of years older than the Gambiers, where a volcanic peak still stands 482 meters above sea level.

Island-building continues at an active undersea volcano called MacDonald 50 meters below sea level at the southeast end of the Australs. The crack spews forth about a cubic mile of lava every century and someday MacDonald too will poke its smoky head above the waves. The theory of plate tectonics, or the sliding crust of the Earth, seems proven in Tahiti-Polynesia.

Life Of An Atoll

A circular or horseshoe-shaped coral reef bearing a necklace of sandy, slender islets *(motus)* of debris thrown up by storms, surf, and wind is known as an atoll. Atolls can be up to 100 km across, but the width of dry land is usually only 200-400 meters from inner to outer beach. The central lagoon can measure anywhere from one to 50 km in diameter; huge Rangiroa Atoll is 77 km long. Entirely landlocked lagoons are rare; passages through the barrier reef are usually found on the leeward side. Most atolls are no higher than four to six meters.

A raised or elevated atoll is one that has been pushed up by submarine volcanic activities to become a coral platform. Raised atolls have steep oceanside cliffs and are often known for their huge sea caves. The only raised atoll in Tahiti-Polynesia is crescent-shaped Makatea in the northwestern corner of the Tuamotu group. It is 100 meters high, seven km long, and 4.5 km wide. Soil derived from coral is extremely poor in nutrients, while volcanic soil is known for its fertility. Dark-colored beaches are formed from volcanic material; the white beaches of travel brochures are entirely coral-based.

A new danger facing the atolls of Oceania is the "greenhouse effect," a gradual warming of Earth's environment due to fuel combustion leading to the melting of the polar ice caps. This phenomena threatens to raise sea levels from 0.2 to 1.4 meters by the year 2030, reducing the supply of drinking water and the growing area for food crops. Entire populations could be forced to evacuate and in time whole archipelagos may be flooded.

CORAL REEFS

To understand how a basalt volcano becomes a limestone atoll, it's necessary to know a little about the growth of coral. Coral reefs cover some 200,000 sq km worldwide, between 35 degrees north and 32 degrees south latitude. A reef is created by the accumulation of millions of tiny calcareous skeletons left by long generations of tiny coral polyps. Though the skeleton is usually white, the living polyps are of many different colors.

They thrive in clear salty water where the temperature never drops below 20 degrees C. They must also have a base not over 25 meters from the surface on which to form. The coral colony grows slowly upward on the consolidated skeletons of its ancestors until it reaches the low-tide mark, after which development extends outward on the edges of the reef. Sunlight is critical for coral growth. Colonies grow quickly on the ocean side due to clearer water and a greater abundance of food. A strong healthy reef can grow four to five cm a year. Fresh or cloudy water inhibits coral growth, which is why villages and ports all across the Pacific are located at the reef-free mouths of rivers.

Polyps extract calcium carbonate from the water and deposit it in their skeletons. All reef-building corals also contain limy encrustations of microscopic algae within their cells. The algae, like all green plants, obtain their energy from the sun, and contribute this energy to the growth of the reef's skeleton. As a result, corals behave (and look) more like plants than animals, competing for sunlight just as terrestrial plants do. Some polyps are also carnivorous, and supplement their energy by capturing small planktonic animals at night with minute stinging tentacles. A small piece of coral is a colony composed of large numbers of polyps.

Coral Types

Corals belong to the phylum *Cnidaria,* a broad group of stinging creatures which includes hydroids (polyps), soft corals, sea anemones, sea fans, and jellyfish *(medusae).* Only those types with hard skeletons are considered true corals. The order *Madreporia,* such as brain, honeycomb, or mushroom corals, have external skeletons and are important reef builders. The *Octorallians,* such as fan corals, black corals, and sea whips, have internal skeletons. The fire corals belong to the order *Milleporina* and are recognized by their smooth, velvety surface and yellowish brown color. The stinging toxins of this last group can easily penetrate the

human skin and cause swelling and painful burning that can last up to an hour. The many varieties of soft, colorful anemones gently waving in the current might seem inviting to touch, but beware! Many are also poisonous.

The corals, like most other forms of life in the Pacific, colonized the ocean from the fertile seas of Southeast Asia. Thus the number of species declines as you move east. Over 600 species of coral make their home in the Pacific, compared to only 48 in the Caribbean. The diversity of coral colors and forms is endlessly amazing. This is our most unspoiled environment, a world of almost indescribable beauty.

Exploring A Reef

Until you've explored a good coral reef, you haven't experienced one of the greatest joys of nature. Dive shops throughout the region rent scuba and snorkeling gear, so do get into the clear, warm waters around you. Be careful, however, and know the dangers. Practice snorkeling in the shallow water; don't head into deep water until you're sure you've got the hang of it. Breathe easily; don't hyperventilate.

When snorkeling on a fringing reef, beware of deadly currents and undertows in channels which drain tidal flows. Observe the direction the water is flowing before you swim into it. If you feel yourself being dragged out to sea through a reef passage, try swimming across the current rather than against it. If you can't resist the pull at all, it may be better to let yourself be carried out. Wait till the current diminishes, then swim along the outer reef face until you find somewhere to come back in. Or use your energy to attract the attention of someone on shore. Most beach drownings occur in such situations, so try not to panic.

Snorkeling on the outer edge or drop-off of a reef is thrilling for the variety of fish and corals, but only attempt it on a very calm day. Even then it's best to have someone on shore or standing on the edge of the reef (at low tide) to watch for occasional big waves which can take you by surprise and smash you into the rocks. Also, beware of unperceived currents outside the reef—you may not get a second chance.

A far better idea is to limit your snorkeling to the protected inner reef and leave the open waters to the scuba diver. They know their waters and are able to show you the most amazing things in perfect safety. Dive centers are operating on Tahiti, Moorea, Tetiaroa, Raiatea, Bora Bora, Rangiroa, and Manihi. Rangiroa and Manihi offer the best diving, followed by Bora Bora and Moorea. Diving is possible year-round, with marinelife most profuse from July to November. All scuba divers must have a medical report from their doctor indicating that they are in good physical condition. Divers should bring their certification card, buoyancy compensator, and regulator. Many of the scuba operators listed in this book offer resort courses for beginning divers. The main constraint is financial: snorkeling is free, while scuba diving varies from f.4000-6500 a dive.

Conservation

Coral grows very slowly: by breaking off pieces you can destroy in a few minutes what took decades to form. We recommend that you not remove seashells, coral, plantlife, or marine animals from the sea. In a small way, you are upsetting the delicate balance of nature, and coral is much more beautiful underwater anyway! This is a particular problem along shorelines frequented by large numbers of tourists who can completely strip a reef in very little time. If you'd like a souvenir, content yourself with what you find on the beach. In many places coral reefs are protected by law. We also recommend that you think twice about purchasing jewelry or souvenirs made from coral or seashells.

There's an urgent need for stricter government regulation of the marine environment. As consumerism and industrialism spread, once-remote areas become subject to the problems of pollution and overexploitation. As a visitor, don't hesitate to practice your conservationist attitudes.

CLIMATE

The hot and humid summer season runs from Nov. to April. The climate is somewhat cooler and drier the rest of the year. The refreshing southeast tradewinds blow consistently from May to Aug., varying to easterlies from Sept. to December. The northeast trades from Jan. to April coincide with the hurricane season.

The tradewinds are caused by hot air rising near the equator, which then flow toward the poles at high altitude. Cooler air drawn toward the vacuum is deflected to the west by the rotation of the Earth. Tahiti-Polynesia's proximity to the intertropical convergence on the equator or "doldrum zone"—where the most heated air is rising—explains the seasonal shift in the winds from northeast to southeast. The tradewinds cool the islands and offer clear sailing for mariners, making May to Oct. the most favorable season to visit.

Hurricanes are relatively rare, although they do hit the Tuamotus and occasionally Tahiti. From Nov. 1980 to May 1983 an unusual wave of eight hurricanes and two tropical storms battered the islands. A hurricane would only inconvenience a visitor staying at

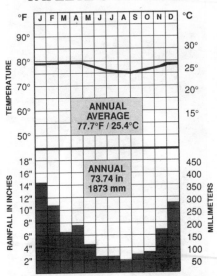

PAPEETE'S CLIMATE

ANNUAL AVERAGE
77.7°F / 25.4°C

ANNUAL
73.74 in
1873 mm

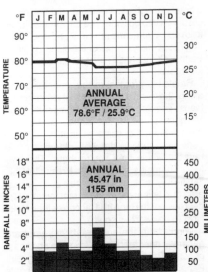

ATUONA'S CLIMATE

ANNUAL AVERAGE
78.6°F / 25.9°C

ANNUAL
45.47 in
1155 mm

a waterspout during a tropical cyclone or
hurricane

a hotel, though campers and yachties might
get blown into oblivion. The days immediately
following a hurricane are clear and dry. Tahiti-
Polynesia enjoys some of the cleanest air on
Earth—air that hasn't blown over a continent
for weeks.

Rainfall is greatest in the mountains and
along the windward shores of the high islands. The Societies are far damper than the
Marquesas. In fact, the climate of the Marquesas is erratic: some years the group experiences serious drought, others it could
rain the whole time you're there. The low-
lying Tuamotus get the least rainfall of all.
Tahiti-Polynesia encompasses such a vast
area that latitude is an important factor: at 27
degrees south Rapa Iti is far cooler than Nuku
Hiva (nine degrees south).

Winds from the southeast (maramu) are
generally drier than those from the northeast
or north. The northeast winds often bring rain:
Papenoo on the northeast side of Tahiti gets

twice as much as rain-shadowed Punaauia.
The annual rainfall is extremely variable but
the humidity is generally high, reaching 98%.
In the evening the heat of the Tahiti afternoons is replaced by soft, fragrant mountain
breezes called hupe, which drift down to the
sea.

FLORA AND
LAND-BASED FAUNA

The variety of species encountered in the
Pacific islands declines as you move away
from the Asian mainland. Island birdlife is
more abundant than land-based fauna, but
still reflects the decline in variety from west to
east. The flora, too, manifests this phenomenon. Although some species may have
spread across the islands by means of floating seeds or fruit, wind and birds were probably more effective. The microscopic spores
of ferns, for example, can be carried vast
distances by the wind. In the coastal areas of
Tahiti most of the plants now seen have been
introduced by man.

Here in Polynesia the air is sweet with the
bouquet of tropical blossoms such as burst-
ing bougainvillea, camelia, frangipani, ginger,
orchids, poinsettia, and pitate jasmine. The
fragrant flowers of the Polynesian hibiscus
(purau) are yellow, not red or pink as on the
Chinese hibiscus. A useful tree, the soft wood
of the hibiscus is used for house and canoe
construction, the bast fiber to make cordage
and mats. The national flower, the delicate,
heavy-scented tiare Tahiti (Gardenia tahitien-
sis), can have anywhere from six to nine
white petals. It blooms year-round, but especially from Sept. to April. In his Plants and
Flowers of Tahiti Jean-Claude Belhay writes:
"The tiare is to Polynesia, what the lotus is to
India: a veritable symbol." Follow local cus-
tom by wearing this blossom or a hibiscus
behind your left ear if you're happily taken,
behind your right ear if you're still available.

Tahiti-Polynesia's high islands support a
great variety of plantlife, while the low islands
are restricted to a few hardy, drought-re-
sistant species such as coconut and pan-

danus palm. On the atolls taro, a root vegetable with broad heart-shaped leaves, must be cultivated in deep organic pits. Rainforests fill the valleys and damp windward slopes of the high islands, while brush and thickets grow in more exposed locations. *Mape* (Tahitian chestnut) grows along the streams. Other trees you'll encounter include almond, candlenut, casaurina (ironwood), flamboyant, barringtonia, *purau* (wild hibiscus), pistachio, and rosewood. Mountain bananas *(fei)* grow wild in the high country. Along the coast fruits such as avocado, banana, custard apple, guava, grapefruit, lime, lychee, mango, orange, papaya, pineapple, watermelon, and a hundred more are cultivated.

Mangroves can occasionally be found along some high-island coastal lagoons. The cable roots of the saltwater-tolerant mangroves anchor in the shallow upper layer of oxygenated mud, avoiding the layers of hydrogen sulphide below. The tree provides shade for tiny organisms dwelling in the tidal mudflats—a place for birds to nest and fish or shellfish to feed and spawn. The mangroves also perform the same task as landbuilding coral colonies along the reefs. As sediments are trapped between the roots, the trees extend farther into the lagoon—creating a unique natural environment.

Of the 90 species of birds in Tahiti-Polynesia, 59 are found in the Society Islands, of which 33 are native. Among the seabirds are the white-tailed tropicbirds, brown and black noddies, white and crested terns, petrels, and boobies. The *itatae* (white tern), often seen flying about with its mate far from land, lays a single egg in the fork of a tree without any nest. The baby terns can fly soon after hatching. Its call is a sharp ke-ke-yek-yek. The *oio* (black noddy) nests in colonies, preferably in palm trees, building a flat nest of dead leaves, sticks, and stems. It calls a deep cra-cra-cra. The hopping Indian mynah bird *(Acridotheres tristis)* with its yellow beak and feet was introduced from Indonesia at the turn of the century to control insects. Today these noisy, aggressive birds are ubiquitous feeding on fruit trees and forcing the native finches and blue-tinged doves out of their habitat.

The Polynesians brought with them chickens, dogs, pigs, and rats. Captain Cook introduced cattle, horses, and goats; Capt. Wallis left behind cats. Whalers dropped more goats off in the Marquesas. Giant African snails *(Achatina fulica)* were brought to Tahiti from Hawaii in the 1960s by a local policeman fond of fancy French food. He tried to set up a "snail farm" with the result that some escaped, multiplied, and now crawl wild destroying the vegetation. Dogs and roosters add to the sounds of the night.

The Giant African Snail (Achatina fulica) *was introduced to many Pacific islands during or just after WW II, perhaps deliberately as a wartime survival food or maybe by accident. Each individual has both male and female organs, and can lay up to 500 eggs at a time. This scavenger is considered an agricultural pest and possible carrier of disease. Rats and coconut crabs help control their numbers.*

MARINELIFE

Polynesia's richest store of life is found among the fishes of the lagoons and open sea, including angelfish, bonito, butterflyfish, eels, groupers, harpfish, jacks, mahi mahi, mullets, parrotfish, sharks, soldierfish, stingrays, surgeonfish, swordfish, trumpetfish, tuna, and countless more. It's believed that most Pacific marine organisms evolved in the triangular area bounded by New Guinea, the Philippines, and the Malay Peninsula. This "Cradle of Indo-Pacific Marinelife" includes a wide variety of habitats and has remained stable through several geological ages. From this cradle the rest of the Pacific was colonized.

Sharks

The danger from sharks has been exaggerated. Of some 300 different species, only 28 are known to have attacked humans. Most dangerous are the white, tiger, hammerhead, and blue sharks. Fortunately, all inhabit deep water, far from the coasts. Sometimes, however, attracted by wastes thrown overboard, they follow ships into port and create problems. An average of 50 shark attacks a year occur worldwide, so considering the number of people who swim in the sea, your chances of being involved are pretty slim. In Tahiti-Polynesia shark attacks are extremely rare.

Sharks are not dangerous where food is abundant, but they can be very nasty far offshore. You're always safer if you keep your head underwater (with a mask and snorkel), and don't panic if you see a shark—you might attract it. Even if you do, usually they're only curious, so look them straight in the eye, and slowly back off. Sharks are attracted by shiny objects (a knife or jewelry), bright colors (especially yellow and red), urinating, spearfishing, blood, and splashing: divers should ease themselves into the water. Sharks have poor eyesight and often mistake the white palms and soles of a bather's hands and feet for small fish.

Never swim alone if you suspect the presence of sharks. If you see one, get out of the water calmly and quickly, and go elsewhere (unless you're with someone knowledgeable, such as a local divemaster). Sharks normally stay outside the reef, but ask local advice. White beaches are safer than dark and clear water safer than murky. Avoid swimming in places where sewage or edible wastes enter the water, or fish have just been cleaned. Recent studies indicate that sharks, like most other creatures, are territorial. Thus an attack could be a shark's way of warning someone to get out of his backyard. Over half the victims of these incidents are not eaten, but merely wounded. Let common sense be your guide, not blind fear or carelessness.

Barracuda

Swimmers need not fear an attack by barracuda. In these lush tropical waters where marinelife abounds, barracudas can find a lot more tasty food. Most cases of barracuda attack are provoked: a spearfisherman shoots one in the tail, another is attracted by the spearfisherman's catch, or a third is simply startled by chance. Still, if you see a barracuda, it's wise to swim away from it; in turn, it will usually swim away from you.

Sea Urchins

Sea urchins (living pin cushions) are common in tropical waters. The black variety is the

The sea urchin feeds on seaweed and uses tubular feet on its underside for locomotion. The long protective spines do not always protect it from hungry snails and fish.

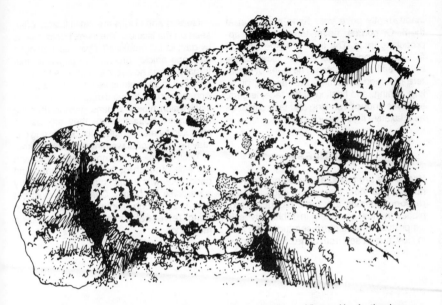

The highly camouflaged stonefish (Synanceia verrucosa) rests on reef flats waiting for the chance to strike small fish. The deadly venom in the stonefish's dorsal fins causes excruciating pain and even death to anyone who happens to step on one.

most dangerous: their long sharp quills can go right through a snorkeler's fins. Even the small ones, which you can easily pick up in your hand, can pinch you if you're careless. They're found on rocky shores and reefs, never on clear sandy beaches where the surf rolls in.

Most sea urchins are not poisonous, though quill punctures are painful and can become infected if not treated. The pain is caused by an injected protein which you can eliminate by holding the injured area in a pail of very hot water for about 15 minutes. This will coagulate the protein, eliminating the pain for good. If you can't heat water, soak the area in vinegar or urine for a quarter hour. Remove the quills if possible, but being calcium they'll decompose in a couple of weeks anyway—not much of a consolation as you limp along in the meantime. In some places sea urchins are a favorite delicacy: the orange or yellow meat is delicious with lemon and salt.

Others

Although jellyfish, stonefish, crown-of-thorns starfish, cone shells, eels, and poisonous sea snakes are hazardous, injuries resulting from any of these are rare. Gently apply methylated spirit, alcohol, or urine (but not water, kerosene, or gasoline) to areas stung by jellyfish. Treat the wound by holding it, along with an opposite foot or hand, in water as hot as you can stand for 30 minutes (the opposite extremity prevents scalding due to numbness). Harmless sea cucumbers (beche-de-mer) punctuate the lagoon shallows. Stonefish also rest on the bottom and are hard to see due to camouflaging; if you happen to step on one their dorsal fins inject a painful poison which burns like fire in the blood. Fortunately stone fish are not common.

Never pick up a live cone shell; some varieties have a deadly stinger dart coming out from the pointed end. Eels hide in reef crevices by day; most are dangerous only if you inadvertently poke your hand or foot in at them. Of course, never tempt fate by approaching them. The flesh of some types of fish is also poisonous, so ask local advice before eating your catch. The signs of *ciguatera* (seafood poisoning) are nausea, prickling, itching, and tingling of the face, fingers, and toes. Induce vomiting and take castor oil as a laxative if you're unlucky.

REPTILES

Sea turtles are facing extinction due to overhunting and the harvesting of eggs. For this reason, importing any turtle product is prohibited in most countries. In Tahiti-Polynesia it's prohibited to capture sea turtles on land in Nov. and at sea from June to January.

Geckos and skinks are small lizards often seen on the islands. The skink hunts insects by day; its tail breaks off if you catch it, but a new one quickly grows. The gecko is nocturnal and has no eyelids. Adhesive toe pads enable it to pass along vertical surfaces, and it changes color to avoid detection. Unlike the skink which avoids humans, geckos often live in people's homes where they eat insects attracted by electric lights. Its loud ticking call may be a territorial warning to other geckos.

Tahiti-Polynesia has no snakes. This, and the lack of leeches, poisonous plants, and dangerous wild animals, makes the country a paradise for hikers. Centipedes exist but their bite, though painful, is not lethal. The main terrestial hazards are dogs and mosquitos.

the double-hulled sailing canoe Hokule'a

HISTORY

THE POLYNESIANS

Discovery And Settlement

Thousands of years ago the early Polynesians set out from Southeast Asia on a migratory trek which would lead them to make the "many islands" of Polynesia their home. Great voyagers, they sailed their huge double-hulled canoes far and wide, steering with huge paddles and pandanus sails. To navigate they read signs from the sun, stars, currents, swells, winds, clouds, and birds. The first Polynesian islands settled were Tonga and Samoa; the oldest known dwelling site on Tongatapu dates from 1200 B.C. Around the time of Christ they pushed out into the eastern half of the Pacific from this primeval area remembered as Havaiki.

About A.D. 300 they reached the Marquesas from Samoa, and somewhere around A.D. 500 they sailed on from the Marquesas to Hawaii and Easter Island. They were on the Society Islands by 800 and sailed from there to the Cooks and New Zealand around 1000, completing the occupation of the Polynesian triangle. These were planned voyages of colonization carrying all the plants and animals needed to continue their way of life. To show how it was done a group of Hawaiians led by American anthropologist Ben Finney sailed the recreated canoe *Hokule'a* from Hawaii to Tahiti and back in 1976 and 1980, without modern navigational instruments.

The Polynesians lived from fishing and agriculture, using tools made from stone, bone, shell, and wood. The men were responsible for planting, harvesting, fishing, cooking, house and canoe building; the women tended the fields and animals, gathered food and fuel, prepared food, and made *tapa* clothes and household items. Both males and females worked together in family or community groups, not as individuals. The Polynesians lost the art of pottery making during their long stay in Havaiki and had to cook their food in underground ovens *(umu)*. It was *tapu* for men and women to eat together so two earth ovens had to be prepared

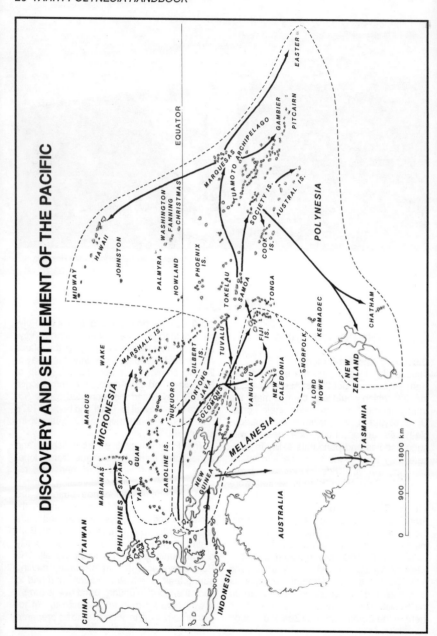

DISCOVERY AND SETTLEMENT OF THE PACIFIC

each time. Breadfruit, taro, yams, sweet potatoes, bananas, and coconuts were cultivated. Pigs, chickens, and dogs were also kept for food, but the surrounding sea yielded the most important source of protein.

Numerous taboos regulated Polynesian life, such as prohibitions against taking certain plants or fish which were in danger of extinction. Land was collectively owned by families and tribes, and there were nobles and commoners. The chiefly families controlled the land worked collectively by commoners and took its produce, but redistribution customs were well defined. Large numbers of people could be mobilized for public works or war.

Canoes were made of planks stitched together with sennit and caulked with gum from breadfruit trees. Clothing consisted of *tapa* (bark cloth). Both men and women wore a belt of pandanus leaves or *tapa* when at work, and during leisure a skirt which reached to their knees. Ornaments were of feathers, whale or dolphin teeth, and flowers. Both sexes were artfully tattooed using candlenut oil and soot. For weapons there were clubs, spears, and slings. Archery was practiced only as a game to determine who could shoot farthest. Spear throwing, wrestling, boxing, kite flying, surfing, and canoe racing were popular sports. Polynesian music was made with nasal flutes and cylindrical sharkskin or hollow slit drums. Their dancing is still appreciated today.

The museums of the world possess many fine stone and wood *tikis* in human form from the Marquesas Islands where the decorative sense was highly developed. Sculpture in the Australs was more naturalistic and only here were female *tikis* common. The Tahitians showed less interest in the plastic arts, but excelled in the social arts of poetry, oratory, theater, music, song, and dance. Life on the Tuamotus was a struggle for existence and objects had utilitarian functions. Countless Polynesian cult objects were destroyed in the early 19th century by over-zealous missionaries.

Prior to European contact three hereditary classes structured the Society Islands: high

a tattooed Marquesan woman from Dumont d'Urville's Voyage au Sud Pole *(1846)*

chiefs *(arii)*, lesser chiefs *(raatira)*, and commoners *(manahune)*. A small slave class *(titi)* also existed. The various *arii* tribes controlled wedge-shaped valleys and their authority was balanced. None managed to gain permanent supremacy over the rest. Two related forces governed Polynesian life: *mana* and *tapu*. *Mana* was a spiritual power of which the gods and high chiefs had the most and the commoners the least. In this rigid caste system marriage or even physical contact between persons of unequal *mana* was forbidden. Children resulting from sexual relations between the classes were killed. Our word "taboo" originated from the Polynesian *tapu*. Early missionaries would often publicly violate the taboos and smash the images of the gods to show that their *mana* had vanished.

Religion centered around a cult place with a stone altar called a *marae*. Here priests prayed to the ancestors or gods and conducted all the significant ceremonies of Polynesian life. An individual's social position was determined by his family connections and the recitation of one's genealogy confirmed it. Members of the Raiatea-based Arioi Society traveled through the islands performing ritual

a chief mourner before a cadaver, 1773 (after William Hodges)

copulation and religious rites. The fertility god Oro had descended on a rainbow to Bora Bora's Mount Pahia where he found a beautiful *vahine*. Their child was the first Arioi. In their pursuit of absolute *free* love the Arioi killed their own children and shared husbands/wives. Human sacrifices took place on important occasions on a high chief's *marae*. Cannibalism was rife in the Marquesas, and also practiced in the Tuamotus.

Archaeology

The first archaeological survey of Tahiti-Polynesia was undertaken in 1925 by Professor Kenneth P. Emory of Honolulu's Bernice P. Bishop Museum. Emory's successor, Professor Yosihiko Sinoto of the same museum, has carried out extensive excavations and restorations in the area since 1960. In 1962, at a 9th century graveyard on Maupiti's Motu Paeao, Emory and Sinoto uncovered artifacts perfectly matching those of the New Zealand Maoris. A few years later at Ua Huka in the Marquesas Sinoto discovered a coastal village site dating from A.D. 300, the oldest

yet found in Eastern Polynesia. Sinoto was responsible for the restoration of the Maeva *maraes* on Huahine and many historical *marae* on Tahiti, Moorea, Raiatea, and Bora Bora. During construction of the Bali Hai Hotel on Huahine in 1973-77 Sinoto's student diggers located 10 flat hand clubs of the *patu* model previously considered only to exist in New Zealand, plus a 1,000-year-old sewn double canoe.

EUROPEAN CONTACT

European Exploration

While the Polynesian history of the islands goes back at least 1,700 years, the European period only began in the 16th century when the Magellan expedition sailed past the Tuamotus and Mendana visited the Marquesas. Quiros saw the Tuamotus in 1606, as did the Dutchmen Le Maire and Schouten in 1616 and Roggeveen in 1722. But it was not until 18 June 1767 that Captain Samuel Wallis on the HMS *Dolphin* happened upon Tahiti. He and most of his contemporary explorers were in search of *Terra Australis Incognita,* a mythical southern landmass thought to balance the northern hemisphere.

At first the Tahitians attacked the ship, but after experiencing the receiving end of gunfire they decided to be friendly. Eager to trade, they loaded down the Englishmen with pigs, fowl, and fruit. Iron was in the highest demand, and Tahitian women lured the sailors to exchange nails for love. Consequently, to prevent the ship's timbers from being torn asunder for the nails, no man was allowed on shore except in parties strictly for food and water. Wallis sent ashore a landing party which named Tahiti "King George III Island," turned some sod, and hoisted the Union Jack. A year later the French explorer Louis-Antoine de Bougainville arrived on the east coast, unaware of Wallis' discovery, and claimed Tahiti for the King of France.

Wallis and Bougainville only visited briefly, leaving it to Capt. James Cook to really describe Polynesia to Europeans. Cook visited "Otaheite" four times, in 1769, 1773, 1774, and 1777. His first three-month visit was to observe the transit of the planet Venus across the face of the sun. The second and third were in search of the southern continent, while the fourth was to locate a northwest passage between the Pacific and Atlantic oceans. Some of the finest artists and scientists of the day accompanied Capt. Cook.

Their explorations added the Leeward Islands, two Austral islands, and a dozen Tuamotu islands to European knowledge. Cook wrote that to the Leewards, "as they lie contiguous to each other, I gave the names of Society Islands." Later the name was extended to the Windward Islands. On Tahiti Cook met a high priest from Raiatea named Tupaia who had an astonishing knowledge of the Pacific and could name dozens of islands. He drew Cook a map which included the Cook Is., the Marquesas, and perhaps also some Samoan islands!

In 1788 Tahiti was visited for six months by HMS *Bounty* commanded by Lieutenant William Bligh with orders to collect young breadfruit plants for transportation to the West Indies. The famous mutiny did not take place at Tahiti as some travel brochures infer, but in Tongan waters. Bligh, one of the top mariners of the 18th century, managed to escape 6,500 km to Dutch Timor in an open boat, so in 1791 the HMS *Pandora* came to Tahiti in search of the *Bounty* mutineers, intending to take them to England for trial. They captured 14 survivors of the 16 who had elected to stay on Tahiti when Fletcher Christian and eight others left for Pitcairn. Although glamorized by Hollywood, the mutineers helped destroy traditional Tahitian society by acting as mercenaries for rival chiefs.

By the early 19th century ruffian British and American whalers were fanning out over the

Captain Cook and his officers sharing a meal with Tahitians

Omai, a native of Huahine, accompanied Capt. Cook's second expedition to England in 1774 and immediately became the talk of London. For many Europeans he epitomized the "noble savage" but, to those who came to know him, he was a sophisticated man with a culture of his own.

Pacific. Other ships traded with the islanders for sandalwood, beche-de-mer, and mother-of-pearl, as well as the usual supplies. They brought with them smallpox, measles, influenza, tuberculosis, scarlet fever, and venereal disease which devastated the unprepared Polynesians. Slave raids, alcohol, and European firearms did the rest.

Kings and Missionaries

In 1797 the ship *Duff* dropped off 18 male English missionaries and their wives on Tahiti. By this time Pomare, chief of the area adjoining Matavai Bay, had become powerful through the use of European tools, firearms, and mercenaries. He welcomed the missionaries but would not be converted. Infanticide, sexual freedom, and human sacrifices continued. By 1800 all but five of the original 18 had left Tahiti disappointed.

In 1803 Pomare I died and his despotic son, Pomare II, attempted to conquer the entire island. After initial success he was forced to flee to Moorea in 1808. Missionary Henry Nott went with him and in 1812 Pomare II turned to him for help in regaining his lost power. Though the missionaries refused to baptize Pomare II himself because of his heathen and drunken habits, his subjects on Moorea became nominal Christians. In 1815 this "Christian king" managed to regain Tahiti and overthrow paganism. The eager missionaries then enforced the Ten Commandments and dressed the Tahitian women in "Mother Hubbard" costumes—dresses which covered their bodies from head to toe. Henceforth singing anything but hymns was banned, dancing proscribed, and all customs which offended puritanical sensibilities wiped away. "Morality police" terrorized the confused Tahitians in an eternal crusade against sin. Even the wearing of flowers in the hair was prohibited.

In *Omoo* (1847) Herman Melville comments: "Doubtless, in thus denationalizing the Tahitians, as it were, the missionaries were prompted by a sincere desire for good; but the effect has been lamentable. Supplied with no amusements, in place of those forbidden, the Tahitians, who require more recreation than other people, have sunk into a listlessness, or indulge in sensualities, a hundred times more pernicious than all the games ever celebrated in the Temple of Tanee."

COLONIALISM

The Rape Of Polynesia

Upon Pomare II's death from drink at age 40 in 1821, the crown passed to his infant son, Pomare III, but he passed away in 1827. At this junction the most remarkable Tahitian of the 19th century, Aimata, half-sister of Pomare II, became Queen Pomare IV. She was to rule Tahiti, Moorea, and part of the Austral and Tuamotu groups for half a century until her death in 1877, a barefoot Tahitian Queen

1. vegetation, Bora Bora (D. Stanley); **2.** a house on Moorea (Phil Esmonde)

1. Lake Vaihiria, Tahiti (D. Stanley); **2.** Maupiti (D. Stanley); **3.** a *motu* (Tahiti Tourist Board photo by Tini Colombel); **4.** Hanavave, Fatu Hiva, Marquesas Is. (Tahiti Tourist Board)

the ceding of Matavai, Tahiti, to English missionaries in 1797

Victoria. She allied herself closely with the London Missionary Society (LMS). When two French-Catholic priests, Honore Laval and Francois Caret, arrived on Tahiti in 1836 from their stronghold at Mangareva (Gambier Islands), she expelled them promptly.

This affront brought a French frigate to Papeete in 1838, demanding $2000 compensation and a salute to the French flag. Although the conditions were met, the Queen and her chiefs wrote to England appealing for help, but none came. A second French gunboat returned and threatened to bombard Tahiti unless its missionaries were given free entry. Back in Mangareva Laval pushed forward a grandiose building program which wiped out 80% of the population of the Gambiers from overwork.

A French consul named Moerenhout was appointed to Queen Pomare in 1838. In Sept. 1842, while the Queen and George Pritchard, the English consul, were away, he tricked a few local chiefs into signing a petition asking to be brought under French "protection." This demand was immediately accepted by French Admiral DupetitThouars who was in league with Moerenhout. In Nov. 1843 the Queen's red and white flag was hauled down, and Tahiti was officially declared a French protectorate. Queen Pomare fled to Raiatea a few months later and Pritchard was deported to England in March 1844, bringing Britain and France to the brink of war. The Tahitians resisted as best they could for three years: old French forts and war memorials recall the struggle.

A French Protectorate

At the beginning of 1847 when Queen Pomare realized that no British assistance was forthcoming, she and her people reluctantly accepted the French protectorate. As a compromise the British extracted a promise from the French not to annex the Leeward Is., so Huahine, Raiatea, and Bora Bora remained independent. The French had taken possession of the Marquesas in 1842, even before imposing a protectorate on Tahiti. French missionaries then attempted to convert the Tahitians to Catholicism, but only in the Marquesas were they successful.

Queen Pomare tried to defend the interests of her people as best she could, but much of her nation was dying: between the 18th century and 1926 the population of the Marquesas fell from 80,000 to only 2,000. In 1776 Capt. Cook estimated the population of Tahiti to be 70,000. By 1829 it had dropped to 8,568 and a low of 7,169 was reached in 1865. The name *Pomare* means "night cough" from *po,* night, plus *mare,* cough, because Pomare I's infant daughter died of tuberculosis in 1792. Pomare V, the final, degenerate member of the line, was more interested in earthly pleasures than the traditions upheld by his mother. In 1880, with

tomb of King Pomare V, Tahiti: *Pomare V's mother died in 1877 after reigning for 50 troubled years during which she was exhorted to accept a French protectorate over her Polynesian kingdom. A less heroic figure than his mother, King Pomare V (above left), the fifth and last of his name to hold the throne, took over a luckless dynasty and also took to drink. He was particularly fond of Benedictine and although the distinctive symbol enshrined forever atop his pylon-shaped mausoleum at Arue appears to be a massive Benedictine bottle it is actually a Grecian vase. He died in 1891, an unhappy man.*

French interests at work on the Panama Canal, a smart colonial governor convinced him to sign away his kingdom for a 5000-franc-a-month pension.

Tahiti-Polynesia then became the full French colony it is today, the "Etablissements francais de l'Oceanie." In 1957 the name was changed to "Polynesie Francaise." The most earthshaking event between 1880 and 1960 was a visit by two German cruisers, the *Scharnhorst* and *Gneisenau,* which shelled Papeete on 22 Sept. 1914. (Both were subsequently sunk by the British at the Battle of the Falkland Islands.) On 2 Sept. 1940 the colony declared its support for the Free French side and the Americans arrived to establish a base on Bora Bora soon after Pearl Harbor. Polynesia remained cut off from occupied metropolitan France until the end of the war. Tahitians served with the Pacific battalion in North Africa and Italy.

RECENT HISTORY

The early 1960s were momentous times for Polynesia. Within a few years MGM filmed *Mutiny on the Bounty,* an international airport opened on Tahiti, and the French began testing their atomic bombs. After Algeria became independent in July 1962 the French decided to move their Sahara nuclear testing facilities to the Tuamotus. In 1963, when all local political parties protested the invasion of Polynesia by thousands of French troops and technicians sent to establish a nuclear test center, President Charles de Gaulle simply outlawed political parties. The French set off their first atmospheric nuclear explosion at Moruroa on 2 July 1966. In 1974, 44 bombs later, international protests forced the French to switch to underground tests which still continue today. Over the years the territorial assembly of Tahiti-Polynesia has adopted numerous resolutions asking the French government to halt the testing, without response.

The spirit of the time is best summed up in the life of one man, Pouvanaa a Oopa, an outspoken WW I hero from Huahine. In 1949 he became the first Polynesian to occupy a seat in the French Chamber of Deputies. In 1957 he was elected vice-president of the Government Council. A dedicated proponent of independence, Pouvanaa was arrested in 1958 on trumped-up charges of arson, eventually sentenced to an eight-year prison term, and exiled by the French government. He was not freed until 1968. In 1971 he won the "French" Polynesia seat in the French Senate, a post he held until his death in early 1977. Tahitians refer to the man as *metua* (father) and his statue stands in front of Papeete's Territorial Assembly.

Pouvanaa's successors, John Teariki (now deceased) and Francis Sanford (since retired), were also defenders of Polynesian autonomy and opponents of nuclear testing. Their combined efforts convinced the French government to grant Polynesia a new statute with a slightly increased autonomy in 1977.

Nuclear Issues
The entire nuclear fuel cycle is carried out in the Pacific region, from uranium mining in Australia right through to dumping the end product—radioactive wastes—in the ocean. Over 250 nuclear devices have been exploded in the area since 1945, an average of over six a year for 40 years, more than half of them by France. French testing continues unabated in a lonely corner of Tahiti-Polynesia. Today, an estimated 10,000 nuclear warheads are stored at various island bases around the Pacific or deployed on naval vessels. The U.S. alone has 517 military bases in the Pacific, the French 15, the Soviets 10.

the Tahitian independence leader Pouvanaa a Oopa (1895-1977)

Today, three Pacific states, Belau, Vanuatu, and New Zealand, are world leaders in the struggle against nuclear imperialism. In 1979 the Republic of Belau became the first constituted nuclear-free zone in the world by a 92% referendum vote. Vanuatu and New Zealand have banned nuclear warships from their shores. And in 1985 member states of the South Pacific Forum signed a treaty declaring their territories a zone free of nuclear testing and dumping. (France, the U.S., and Britain, have refused to ratify the treaty.) The fact that the nuclear age began in their backyard at Hiroshima, Nagasaki, Bikini, and Enewetak has not been lost on the islanders. They see few real benefits coming from nuclear power, only deadly dangers.

Greenpeace
In July 1985 French General Directorate for Foreign Security (DGSE) agents planted terrorist bombs on the Greenpeace ship *Rainbow Warrior* as it lay anchored at Auckland, New Zealand. Greenpeace photographer Fernando Pereira drowned in the sinking. Top officials in the French government who ordered the killing and the two agents who

NON A LA BOMBE EN POLYNESIE

actually planted the bombs have never been brought to trial.

By chance two other DGSE agents were captured by N.Z. police, tried, and sentenced to 10 years imprisonment. A year later France tried to block butter and mutton exports to Europe to blackmail New Zealand into allowing the convicted saboteurs, Major Alain Mafart and Captain Dominique Prieur, to serve a three-year term of exile at the French military base on Hao in the Tuamotus in lieu of jail, promising they would stay there until their sentences were complete. French Prime Minister Chirac brought both home to Paris in 1987 a year before their terms expired.

The bombing was intended to prevent the ship from sailing to Moruroa to commemorate the 40th anniversary of Hiroshima there. The French also feared that the Greenpeace environmentalists intended to carry doctors to Mangareva for a survey which might uncover the serious health problems they have thus far successfully covered up. The French attack couldn't stop a five-boat "peace flotilla"

which formed a floating picket line off Moruroa in Oct. 1985. The ketch *Vega,* which deliberately breached the 12-nautical-mile limit, was seized by a French warship.

Analysis
Tahiti-Polynesia is part of a worldwide chain of French colonies including Kerguelen, Guyana, Martinique, Guadeloupe, Mayotte, New Caledonia, Wallis and Futuna, Reunion, and St. Pierre and Miquelon, under the DOM-TOM (Ministry of Overseas Departments and Territories). France spends 16 billion French francs a year to maintain this system, a clear indicator it's something totally different from colonial empires of the past, which were based on economic exploitation, not investment. A closer analogy is the American network of military bases around the world, which serve the same purpose—projecting power. What is at stake is French national prestige.

These conditions totally contradict what has happened elsewhere in the South Pacific. Over the past 20 years the British have voluntarily withdrawn from their Pacific colonies, at the same time that the French have been digging in. This created the anachronism of a few highly visible bastions of white colonialism in the midst of a sea of English-speaking independent nations. When French officials summarily rejected all protests against their nuclear testing and suppression of independence movements, even going to the extreme of employing state terrorism to stop a protest vessel from leaving New Zealand, most Pacific islanders were outraged. Their subsequent boycotts of French goods and anti-French statements have only exacerbated the situation.

What must be accepted is that there's a place for France in the Pacific. It's no longer possible to turn the clock back to 1842 or 1767. In fact, in almost every Pacific microstate the basis for complete autodependence simply doesn't exist. But France must be convinced that its interests in the Pacific are better served by emphasizing social, cultural, and economic matters, and not outright political and military domination.

By continuing its nuclear testing, uncontrolled immigration, and military build-ups, France risks a bitter independence struggle with the Tahitians. This may well lead to either New Caledonia-style chaos or the dismemberment of the country, plus continuing universal condemnation and a black image in the region. By stopping the testing and granting full internal self-government to its colonies, France would quickly be accepted as a good neighbor throughout the Pacific, as it was before 1963 when de Gaulle exported *la bombe.* (The commentary above was inspired by Jean Chesneaux's article "France in the Pacific: Global Approach or Respect for Regional Agendas?" in Vol. 18, No. 2, 1986, of the *Bulletin of Concerned Asian Scholars.)*

GOVERNMENT

In 1885 an organic decree created the colonial system of government which remained in effect until the proclamation of a new statute in 1958, making Tahiti-Polynesia an overseas territory. In 1977, when Francis Sanford, Polynesia's representative in the French Parliament, threatened to launch an independence campaign, the French granted the territory partial internal self-government. A new local-government statute passed by the French parliament and promulgated on 6 Sept. 1984 gave only slightly more powers to the Polynesians; the constitution of the Republic of France remains the supreme law of the land. There have been requests to the United Nations Special Committee of 24 that the territory be reinscribed on its priority list of states awaiting decolonization, as New Caledonia was in 1986.

A Territorial Assembly elects the president of the government, who chooses his 10 ministers. The Territorial Assembly controls and has to pay for public works, sports, health, social services, and primary education. Only the French government can dissolve the assembly. The 41 assembly members are elected from geographical constituencies, with 22 seats from Tahiti/Moorea and 19 seats from the rest of the territory. One vote in the Tuamotus has the weight of three on Tahiti and many constituencies have been gerrymandered. French soldiers and civil servants can vote in local elections the day they arrive in the territory, and there are thousands of them.

The territory is represented in Paris by two elected deputies, a senator, and a social and economic councilor. The French government, through its high commissioner and assisted by a secretary general of his choice, retains control over defense, foreign affairs, money, justice, immigration, the police, the civil service, foreign trade, TV and radio broadcasting, international communications, secondary education, and the municipal councils. As may be seen, the high commissioner has considerable power. He can also dissolve the Territorial Assembly or refer its decisions to an administrative tribunal.

Tahiti-Polynesia is divided into 48 communes, each with an elected Municipal Council which chooses a mayor from its ranks. These elected bodies, however, are controlled by appointed French civil servants who run the five administrative subdivisions. The administrators of the Windward, Tuamotu-Gambier, and Austral subdivisions are based at Papeete, while the headquarters of the Leeward Is. administration is at Uturoa, and the Marquesas Is. is at Taiohae.

pro-independence
demonstrators at the
High Commissioner's
gate in Papeete

Politics

In 1984 the pro-nuclear, anti-independence mayor of Pirae, Gaston Flosse, leader of the neo-Gaullist **Tahoeraa Huiraatira** (Popular Union), became the first elected president of newly "autonomous" Tahiti-Polynesia. In the 1986 territorial elections Flosse's party won a majority of assembly seats, but a year later Flosse resigned as president to devote his full time to the post of French Secretary of State for the South Pacific. With the defeat of the Chirac government in 1988 Flosse found himself out in the cold politically. Flosse's reputation for fixing government contracts while in office earned him the title "Mr. Ten Percent" from the Paris newspaper *Liberation.*

In Dec. 1987 Tahoeraa deputy leader Alexandre Leontieff broke with Flosse and formed a coalition government with other Tahoeraa defectors and several smaller parties. In the 1988 elections to select Polynesia's two representatives to the 577-member French National Assembly, Flosse was defeated in the heavily Catholic eastern constituency by Emile Vernaudon, charismatic leader of the anti-nuclear **Aia Api** (New Land Party). The predominantly Protestant western constituency elected the autonomist mayor of Papeete, Jean Juventin, of the **Here Aia Te Nunaa Ia Ora** as its deputy. Juventin favors independence in association with France and

is opposed to nuclear testing. Daniel Millaud of *Ea Api,* Tahiti-Polynesia's senator from 1980-89, is a strong advocate of full internal self-government.

The pro-independence movement is split into many factions. The most outspoken group in favor of immediate and complete independence is the **Tavini Huiraatira No Te Ao Maohi** (Polynesian Liberation Front) formed in 1978 by Faaa mayor Oscar Temaru. Temaru won 14% of the vote in the 1988 election for a western National Assembly deputy. **Ia Mana Te Nunaa** (Let the People Take the Power) was founded in 1975 to campaign for land redistribution and an independent nuclear-free socialist state. Jacqui Drollet, secretary-general of the party, serves as Minister of Health in the territorial coalition government.

The most radical of the pro-independence groups is the **Te Taata Tahiti Tiama** (Independent Tahitians' Party), led by Pouvanaa a Oopa's nephew Charlie Ching. The French have made something of a martyr of Ching by repeatedly jailing him on dubious charges. Another well-known independence leader is Tetua Mai, imprisoned by the French when he formed a provisional government. The *independentistes* are strongest in Papeete, weakest in the Tuamotus and Marquesas—areas heavily dependent on French aid.

ECONOMY

Government Spending

The inflow of people and money since the early 1960s has substituted consumerism for subsistence. Except for tourism and cultured pearls, the economy of Tahiti-Polynesia is now totally dominated by French government spending. The French government contributes very little to the territorial budget, but it finances departments and services under the direct control of the high commissioner (defense, foreign affairs, police, justice, immigration, information, foreign trade, international communications, labor, finance, postal services, television, higher education, and the 200-nautical-mile Exclusive Economic Zone).

The colonial government spends between 80 and 90 billion Pacific francs in the territory each year, two-thirds of it on the military. Much of the rest goes into inflated salaries for 2,200 expatriot French civil servants. Posts in the colonies are much sought after among French officials for the high salaries and benefits, exotic location, lack of taxation, short working hours, and the general submissiveness of the natives. This privileged class is a built-in lobby to perpetuate its own existence.

There's no personal income tax. This is fine for businessmen and civil servants who earn high wages or profits, but hard on everyone else hit by indirect taxes such as Customs duties, licenses, and sales taxes. In 1985 these taxes accounted for 78% of government revenue, leading to highly inflated prices which hurt the little guy most. There's also a flat 35% levy on businesses which is simply passed along to consumers. Businessmen can mark up imports as high as 47%.

Only a third of the population receives any direct benefit from French spending. The rest feel only the effects of soaring inflation, inequalities, and foreign interference. The nuclear testing program has provoked an influx of 25,000 French settlers, plus a massive infusion of capital which distorted the formerly self-supporting economy into one totally dependent on France.

In the early '60s, many Polynesians left their homes for construction jobs with the *Centre d'Experimentation du Pacifique* (CEP), the government, and hotel chains. Now that the volume of this work is decreasing, most of them subsist in precarious circumstances on Tahiti, dependent on government spending. Some 2,000 locals are presently employed by the testing program (compared to 10,000 in 1968). The CEP is headquartered at Pirae, just east of Papeete, with a major support base opposite the yacht club at Arue. Some 3,000 persons live and work for the CEP in the Tuamotus (of whom 600 are Polynesian).

Despite protests by almost every Pacific nation, the nuclear tests continue. In fact, this program has become a major incentive for the French government to hold onto their colony, since underground nuclear testing on *their* continent would never be accepted by Europeans, regardless of French assurances that it is "safe." The main objections would come from the population of France itself: any French government that moved the tests to the Massif Central would risk losing millions of votes! Polynesia is far away and the population small: it is expendable.

Business

Business is concentrated in a few hands. The Martin family (French/Polynesian) owns the electric company (EDT), Hinano brewery, and a huge commercial center called Fare Tony in Papeete. The French banker Breaud runs Total (Standard Oil of California), owns much real estate, and has an important interest in the Banque de Tahiti. The powerful Sin Tung Hing dynasty controls the local Mobil Oil of Australia, Gaz de Tahiti, the Banque de Polynesie, an insurance company, and auto imports. Aline (Chinese) dominates imports and merchandising. Virtually all shipping and docking, both local and international, is in the hands of the Cowan family (French/Polynesian). This powerful class gets the most out of French rule and is the strongest supporter of its continuation.

Tourism

Tourism only got underway with the opening of Faaa Airport in 1961. Today Tahiti-Polynesia is one of the main tourist centers of the South Pacific, with 138,400 visitors in 1988, over half of them from the U.S. Earnings from tourism cover 18% of Tahiti-Polynesia's import bill and provide 4,000 jobs. Yet 80% of the things tourists buy are also imported. Tourism is almost completely in the hands of transnational corporations, either hotel chains, tour companies, or airlines. Top management of the big hotels is invariably French or foreign. Carriers such as Air New Zealand and Qantas only promote Tahiti as a stopover on the way Down Under, limiting many tourists to a few nights in Papeete. This urban tourism has tended to create a bad impres-

the cover of an official brochure promoting tourism as a source of income for Tahiti-Polynesia

sion and the Tahiti Tourist Board is attempting to persuade more visitors to visit the less-spoiled outer islands.

Two kinds of people make it to Tahiti-Polynesia: packaged tourists on a two-week trip from the States who book all their accommodations in advance, stay at the best hotels, and travel interisland by air; and independent budget travelers (often young Europeans) who have more time, find a place to stay upon arrival, and travel by boat as much as possible. Tahiti, Moorea, Huahine, Raiatea, and Bora Bora are popular among visitors for their combination of beaches, mountain scenery, easy access, and the wealth of budget accommodations. The Society group is closely linked by sea and air, an island-hopper's playground.

Tourism is far less developed than in Hawaii. A single Waikiki hotel could have more rooms than the entire island of Tahiti; Hawaii gets more visitors in 10 days than Tahiti-Polynesia gets in a year. In Tahiti-Polynesia only one tourist is present for every 100 inhabitants at any given time, while overcrowded Hawaii has 11. Distance and reports of high prices have kept Tahiti out of the American mass market. Since 1987 when the American Hawaiian cruiseship *Liberte* withdrew from Polynesia and the Hyatt resort on Bora Bora went under, tourism to Tahiti-Polynesia has taken a nosedive. The bankruptcy of Exploration Cruise Lines in 1988 was another setback. The government has responded by reducing the tax on alcohol by 80% and persuading hotel and restaurant owners to lower their prices.

Trade

Prior to the start of nuclear testing, trade was balanced. Only 25 years later 1988 imports stood at 87.5 billion Pacific francs while exports amounted to only three billion, one of the highest disparities in the world. The "invisible export," tourism, accounted for perhaps 18 billion that year. Much of the imbalance is consumed by the French administration itself.

Half the imports come from France, which has imposed a series of self-favoring restrictions. Imports include food, fuel, building material, consumer goods, and automobiles. The main exports from the outer islands are copra and empty Hinano bottles. Copra, the main agricultural product, is crushed into coconut oil and animal feed at the Papeete mill, while cultured pearls from farms in the Tuamotus are of increasing importance. The vast distances between the islands themselves and the outside world are one reason for the slow commercial development of the territory.

Cultured Pearls

Tahiti-Polynesia's cultured-pearl industry originated in 1963 when an experimental farm was established on Hikueru atoll in the Tuamotus. Today dozens of cooperative and private pearl farms operating in Tuamotu-Gambier employ hundreds. In 1988 the value of pearls exported was 2.5 billion Pacific francs. The cooperatives sell their production at an auction in Papeete organized by the Chamber of Commerce each October. The pearls are offered to bidders in mixed lots of a hundred or more for US$10,000 and up. Local jewelers vie with Japanese buyers at these events. Private producers sell their pearls through independent dealers or plush retail outlets in Papeete.

Unlike the Japanese cultured white pearl, the Polynesian black pearl is created only by the giant blacklipped oyster (Pinctada margaritifera) which thrives in the Tuamotu lagoons. Beginning in the 19th century the oysters were collected by Polynesian divers who could dive up to 40 meters. The shell was made into mother-of-pearl buttons; finding a pearl this way was pure chance. Overharvesting had depleted the slow-growing oyster beds by the middle of this century. Today live oysters are collected only to supply cultured-pearl farms and the shell is a mere byproduct made into decorative items or exported.

It takes around three years for a pearl to form in a seeded oyster. A spherical pearl is formed when the Mississippi River mussel graft is introduced inside the coat; the oyster only creates a hemispherical half pearl if the graft goes between the coat and the shell.

Half pearls are much cheaper than real pearls and make outstanding rings and pendants.

The relative newness of this gemstone is reflected in wildly varying prices. A brilliant, perfectly round, smooth, and flawless pearl with a good depth of metalic green-gray/blue-gray color can sell for 100 times more than a similar pearl with only one or two defects. Unless you really know your pearls it's intelligent to stick to the cheaper, even "baroque" ones which, mounted in gold and platinum, still make exquisite jewelry. These pearls are now in fashion in Paris, so don't expect any bargains. Half the fun is in the shopping, so be in no hurry to decide. A reputable dealer will give you an invoice or certificate verifying the authenticity of your pearl.

Agriculture

Labor recruiting for the nuclear testing program caused local agriculture to collapse in the mid-'60s. Exports of coffee and vanilla had ceased completely by 1965 and coconut products dropped 40% despite massive subsidies. Today about 85% of all food consumed locally is imported. Tahiti-Polynesia does manage to cover three-quarters of its own fruit requirements. Most of the local pineapple and grapefruit crop is consumed by the fruit-juice factory on Moorea. In the 1880s-90s four million oranges a year were exported to Australia, New Zealand, and California. The industry was wiped out by a blight at the turn of the century and now only a few trees grow wild.

Local vegetables supply half of local needs, while Tahitian coffee only covers 20% of consumption. Considerable livestock is kept in the Marquesas. Large areas have been planted in Caribbean pine to provide for future timber needs. Aquaculture, with tanks for freshwater shrimp, prawns, live bait, and green mussels, is being developed. Most industry is related to food processing (fruit-juice factory, brewery, soft drinks, etc.) or coconut products.

The coconut tree has long been the mainstay of the outer islanders. A good tree gives nuts for 50 or 60 years (the 29-cm-wide metal bands around the trunk are for protection

Every part of the coconut tree (Cocos nucifera) can be used. The husk provides cord, mats, brushes, and fuel, the leaves thatch, baskets, and fans, and the trunk building material. Food and oil from the nuts are the greatest prize. A healthy tree will produce 50 nuts a year for over 60 years.

against rats). The green coconut provides food and drink, while the harder meat from more mature nuts is grated and squeezed to obtain coconut cream used as sauce and in cooking. The oldest nuts are cracked open and the meat dried in the sun to become copra. Schooners collect bags of copra which they carry to a mill beside the interisland wharf at Papeete. Here the copra is pressed into coconut oil used in making vegetable oil, margarine, candles, soap, cosmetics, etc. The world price for copra has been depressed for years, so the government wisely pays a subsidy (more than twice the actual price) to producers to keep them gainfully employed on their home islands.

Vanilla, a vine belonging to the orchid family, is grown on small family plantations. Brought to Tahiti from Manila in 1848, the Tahitensis type, which has a worldwide reputation, originated from a mutation of Fragrans vanilla. The plants must be hand pollinated, then harvested between April and June. The pods are then put out to dry for a couple of months—an exceptionally time-consuming process generally entrusted to the Chinese.

Between 1915 and 1933 Tahiti produced 50 to 150 tons of vanilla a year, peaking in 1949 at 200 tons. Production remained high until 1966 when a steady decline began. By 1985 production had fallen to only 25 metric tons, though the territorial government wants to get things going again.

Law Of The Sea

This law has changed the face of the Pacific. States traditionally exercised sovereignty over a three-mile belt of territorial sea along their shores; the high seas beyond these limits could be freely used by anyone. Then on 28 Sept. 1945 President Harry Truman declared U.S. sovereignty over the natural resources of the adjacent continental shelf. Other states followed with similar claims. In 1958 the United Nations convened a Conference on the Law of the Sea at Geneva which accepted national control over shelves up to 200 meters deep. Agreement could not be reached on extended territorial sea limits.

National claims multiplied so much that in 1974 another U.N. conference was convened, leading to the signing of the Law of the Sea convention at Jamaica in 1982. This complex agreement—200 pages, nine annexes, and 320 articles—extended national control over 40% of the world's oceans. The territorial sea was increased to 12 nautical miles and the continental shelf ambiguously defined as extending 200 nautical miles offshore. This 200-nautical-mile belt was declared an Exclusive Economic Zone (EEZ) with the state having full control over all resources, living or non-living. The French government passed legislation in 1976 which gave it control of this zone, not only along France's coastal waters but also around all her overseas territories and departments.

To date the EEZs have mainly affected fisheries and seabed mineral exploitation. Freedom of navigation within the zones is guaranteed. The Law of the Sea increased immensely the territory of independent oceanic states, giving them real political weight for the first time. The land area of Tahiti-Polynesia comes to only 3,265 sq km, while its EEZ totals 5,030,000 sq km! It's known that vast mineral deposits are scattered across this seabed awaiting the technology to exploit them. The National Marine Research Center and private firms have already drawn up plans to recover nickel, cobalt, manganese, and copper nodules from depths of over 4,000 meters. The French government has adamantly refused to give the Territorial Assembly any jurisdiction over this tremendous resource, an important indicator as to why they are determined to hold onto their colony at any price.

Fisheries

Tuna is the second most important fishery in the world (after shrimp and prawns), and 66% of the world's catch is taken in the Pacific. Japanese and Korean fishing boats pay annually around 100 million francs in license fees to the local government, with boat stores and provisions accounting for even greater sums. Tuna is one of the few renewable resources the islanders have and the bitter irony of local fish being sent to American Samoa to be canned, then sold back to islanders at high prices, is all too real. Most of the tuna fished from the Pacific islands region is taken by around 110 purse seiners, 65 of them affiliated with the American Tunaboat Association, and 32 of them Japanese. Longline vessels are used to supply the Japanese sashimi market. Some Pacific countries have established small pole-and-line fishing industries, but the capital-intensive, high-tech purse-seiner operations carried out by the Americans and Japanese are still beyond their means. So despite the potential, fisheries in Tahiti-Polynesia are almost totally undeveloped.

An unfortunate side effect of the purse-seiner operations is the drowning in their nets of tens of thousands of dolphins a year. Herds of dolphins tend to swim above schools of yellowfin tuna; thus unscrupulous fishermen deliberately set their nets around the marine mammals, crushing or suffocating them. As a result Greenpeace has called for a complete boycott of light-meat canned tuna. If you really must continue eating tuna, no dolphins are slaughtered to catch white-meat albacore tuna. Neither long-line nor pole-and-line tuna fishing involves killing dolphins.

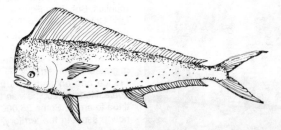

The dolphin fish (Coryphaena hippurus) or dorado is a large, fast-moving fish with a body of luminous purple, green, and gold, which fades soon after death. Mahi mahi (dolphin fish) is a favored food, but the fish has no relation to its namesake mammal dolphin.

THE PEOPLE

The criteria used for defining the racial groups making up the 1988 population of 188,814 are so unsatisfactory that only an approximate breakdown can be made: 70% Polynesian, 12% European, 10% Polynesian/European, 5% Chinese, and 3% Polynesian/Chinese. All are French citizens. The 1988 population figures for the five administrative subdivisions are Windward Islands 140,341, Leeward Islands 22,232, Austral Islands 6,500, Tuamotu/Gambier Islands 12,374, Marquesas Islands 7,358. As may be seen, about 70% of the total population lives on Tahiti. The biggest towns in 1988 were Faaa (24,048) and Papeete (23,555).

The indigenous people of Tahiti-Polynesia are the *maohi* or Eastern Polynesians (as opposed to the Western Polynesians in Samoa and Tonga). The word *colon* formerly applied to Frenchmen who arrived long before the bomb and made a living as planters or traders. Practically all of them married Polynesian women; most of these *colons*

a Polynesian woman

have already passed away. Their descendents are termed *demis* or *afa*. The present Europeans are mostly recently arrived metropolitan French *(faranis)*. Most *faranis* live in urban areas or are involved in the administration or military. Their numbers increased dramatically in the '60s and '70s.

Local Chinese *(tinito)* dominate the retail trade throughout the territory. In Papeete and Uturoa entire streets are lined with Chinese stores, and individual Chinese merchants are found on almost every island. During the American Civil War when the supply of cotton to Europe was disrupted, Scotsman William Stewart decided to set up a cotton plantation on the south side of Tahiti. Unable to convince Tahitians to accept the heavy work, Stewart brought in a contingent of 1,010 Chinese laborers from Canton in 1865-66. When the war ended the enterprise went bankrupt, but many of the Chinese managed to stay on as market gardeners or shopkeepers.

In 1964 the French government decided to assimilate the Chinese by granting them citizenship, requiring that they adopt French-sounding names, and closing all Chinese schools. Despite this the Chinese community has remained distinct. Most of the Tahiti Chinese used to be supporters of the Kuomintang regime in Taiwan and fierce anti-communists. But since France recognized mainland China in 1964 the Taiwanese consulate has been closed and many local Chinese now visit their ancestral country.

From 1976 to 1983 some 18,000 people migrated to the territory, 77% of them from France and another 13% from New Caledonia. Nearly 1,000 new settlers a year continue to arrive. Some 25,000 Europeans are now present in the territory, plus 8,000 soldiers, policemen, and transient officials. Most Tahitians would like to see this immigration restricted, as it is in virtually every other Pacific state. There's an undercurrent of anti-French sentiment; English speakers are better liked by the Tahitians. Yet inevitably the newcomers get caught up in the Polynesian openness and friendliness—even the surliest Parisian. In fact, the Gaulic charm you'll experience even in government offices is a delight. Tahiti-Polynesia really is a friendly place.

The New Class Structure

The creation of the Centre d'Experimentation du Pacifique (CEP) in the early '60s upset the economic and social equilibrium, drove up the cost of living, created artificial needs, and led to a migration toward Papeete. In 1962 46% of the labor force was engaged in fishing and agriculture. Since then there's been a massive shift to public and private services and about 80% of the working population of 58,000 are now employees. Of these, 40% work for the government, 40% in services, 11% in industry, and only 8% in agriculture.

Civil servants in Tahiti-Polynesia get 84% higher salaries than their counterparts in France and don't have to pay any income tax. There are generous expatriation benefits and six months leave is paid after three years. The minimum monthly wage in the territory is US$1500 in the public sector, but only US$675 in the private sector. Living standards in Tahiti-Polynesia may be far higher than in the surrounding insular countries due to the subsidies, yet this expansion of wealth has created inequalities; also, the number of unemployed or underemployed is increasing. The gap between an affluent foreign clique and the impoverished Tahitian mass has created an explosive situation.

In Oct. 1987 the French High Commissioner used riot police flown in from Paris to suppress a dockworkers' strike, leading to serious rioting in Papeete. The mayor of Papeete, Jean Juventin, accused French officials of deliberately provoking the violence as a way of breaking the union, which handled cargo bound for the nuclear testing facilities. Most of those eventually convicted of looting were not strikers at all but unemployed Tahitian youths who took advantage of the disturbance to grab consumer goods.

An estimated 20,000 poor, unemployed, and marginalized Tahitians live in slums on the outskirts of Papeete. In the valley shanty towns behind Papeete and Faaa 10-15 Polynesians are crammed into each neat flower-decked plywood house. Opportunities for young Tahitians with a taste for the consumer society are not adequate. Every year 3,000 young people turn 18 and begin competing for scarce jobs. The present social structure places *farani* officials at the top, followed by *demis* in the lower echelons of business and government, while *maohis* work for wages or subsist at the bottom of the shredded social fabric.

Tahitian Life

For the French lunch is the main meal of the day, followed by a siesta. Dinner may consist of leftovers from lunch. Tahitians traditionally eat their main meal of fish and native vegetables in the evening when the day's work is over. People at home often take a shower before or after a meal and put flowers in their hair. If they're in a good mood a guitar or ukulele might appear. About the only time the normally languid Tahitians go really wild is when they're dancing or behind the wheel of a car.

Tahitians often observe with amusement or disdain the efforts of individuals to rise above the group. In a society where sharing and reciprocal generosity have traditionally been important qualities the deliberate accumulation of personal wealth was always viewed as a vice. Now with the influx of government and tourist money Tahitian life is changing, quickly in Papeete, more slowly in the outer islands. To prevent the Polynesians from being made paupers in their own country, foreigners other than French are not usually permitted to purchase land here. Most land is still owned by the islanders. A new impoverished class is forming among those who have sold their ancestral lands to recent French immigrants.

The educational curriculum is entirely French. Children enter school at age three and for 12 years study the French language, literature, culture, history, and geography, but not much about Polynesia. The failure rate ranges from 40% to 60% and most of the rest of the children are behind schedule. The best students are given scholarships to continue studying, while many of the dropouts become delinquents. About half the schools are privately run by the churches, but these must teach exactly the same curriculum or lose their subsidies. The whole aim is to transform the Polynesians into "Pacific Frenchmen."

Most Tahitians live along the coast because the interior is too rugged and possibly inhabited by *tupapau* (ghosts). Some people leave a light on all night in their home for the latter reason. A traditional Tahitian residence consists of several separate buildings: the *fare tutu* (kitchen), the *fare tamaa* (dining area), the *fare taoto* (bedrooms), plus bathing and sanitary outhouses. Often several generations live together and young children are sent to live with their grandparents. Adoption is commonplace and family relationships complex. Young Tahitians generally go out as groups rather than on individual "dates."

The lifestyle may be summed up in the words *aita e peapea* (no problem) and *fiu* (fed up, bored).

a Polynesian vahine

Sex

Since the days of Wallis and Bougainville Tahitian women have had a reputation for promiscuity. Well, for better or worse, this is largely a thing of the past, if it ever existed at all. As a short-term visitor your liaisons with Tahitians are likely to remain polite. Westerners' obsession with the sexuality of Polynesians usually reflects their own frustrations. The view that Tahitian morality is loose is rather ironic considering that Polynesians have always shared whatever they have, cared for their old and young, and refrained from ostracizing unwed mothers or attaching stigma to their offspring. The good Christian Tahitians of today are highly moral and compassionate.

Polynesia's *mahus* or third sex bear little of the stigma attached to female impersonators in the West. A young boy may adopt the female role by his own choice or that of his parents, performing female tasks at home and eventually finding a job usually performed by women such as serving in a restaurant or hotel. Usually only one *mahu* exists

in each village or community, proof that this type of individual serves a certain sociological function. George Mortimer of the British ship *Mercury* recorded an encounter with a *mahu* in 1789. Though Tahitians may poke fun at a *mahu* they're fully accepted in society, seen teaching Sunday school, etc. Many, but not all, *mahus* are also homosexuals. Today with money all-important some transvestites have involved themselves in male prostitution and the term *raerae* has been coined for this category. Now there are even Miss Tane and Miss Male beauty contests! All this may be seen as the degradation of a phenomenon which has always been part of Polynesian life.

LANGUAGE

Tahitian and French are both official languages, but official documents and speeches are as a rule in French and are rarely translated. French is spoken throughout the territory and visitors will sometimes have difficulty making themselves understood in English, although everyone involved in the travel industry speaks English. The "Capsule French Vocabulary" at the end of this book will help you get along. Large Chinese stores often have someone who speaks English, though members of the Chinese community use "Hakka" among themselves.

Tahitian or *Maohi* is one of a family of Austronesian languages spoken from Madagascar through Indonesia, all the way to Easter Island and Hawaii. The related languages of Eastern Polynesia (Hawaiian, Tahitian, Marquesan, Maori) are quite different from those of Western Polynesia (Samoan, Tongan). Today as communications improve, the outer island dialects are becoming mingled with the predominant Tahitian. Among the Polynesian languages the consonants did the changing rather than the vowels. The "k" and "l" in Hawaiian are generally rendered as a "t" and "r" in Tahitian.

Instead of attempting to speak French to the Tahitians, a foreign language for you both, turn to the Tahitian vocabulary at the back of this book and give it a try. Remember to pronounce each vowel separately, "a" as the *ah* in far, "e" as the *ai* in day, "i" as the *ee* in see, "o" as the *oh* in go, and "u" as the *oo* in lulu—the same as in Latin or Spanish. Written Tahitian has only eight consonants: f, h, m, n, p, r, t, v. Two consonants never follow one another and all words end in a vowel. No silent letters exist in Tahitian, but there is a glottal stop often marked with an apostrophe. A slight variation in pronunciation or vowel length can change the meaning of a word completely, so don't be surprised if your efforts produce some unexpected results!

Some of the many English words that have entered Tahitian through contact with early seamen include: *faraipani* (frying pan), *manua* (man of war), *matete* (market), *mati* (match), *moni* (money), *oniani* (onion), *painapo* (pineapple), *pani* (pan), *pata* (butter), *pipi* (peas), *poti* (boat), *taiete* (society), *tapitana* (captain), *tauera* (towel), and *tavana* (governor).

Writer Pierre Loti was impressed by the mystical vocabulary of Tahitian: "The sad, weird, mysterious utterances of nature: the scarcely articulate stirrings of fancy....*Faafano:* the departure of the soul at death. *Aa:* happiness, earth, sky, paradise. *Mahoi:* essence or soul of God. *Tapetape:* the line where the sea grows deep. *Tutai:* red clouds on the horizon. *Ari:* depth, emptyness, a wave of the sea. *Po:* night, unknown dark world, Hell."

RELIGION

Though the old Polynesian religion died out in the early 19th century the Tahitians are still strongly religious people. Protestant missionaries arrived on Tahiti 39 years before the Catholics and 47 years before the Mormons, so about two-thirds of the Polynesians now belong to the Evangelical Church; it's strongest in the Austral and Leeward Islands. Of the 30% of the total population which is Catholic half are Polynesians from the Tuamotus and Marquesas, and the other half are Frenchmen. Another 6% are Mormons. Seventh-day Adventists, and Jehovah's Witnesses are also represented. Some Chinese are Buddhists. It's not unusual to see two or three different churches in a village of 100 people. All the main denominations operate their own schools. Local ministers and priests are powerful figures in the outer-island communities. The Evangelical Church has condemned nuclear testing.

Protestant church services are conducted mostly in Tahitian, Catholic in French. It's often worth sitting through one (one to two hours) just to hear the singing and observe the women's hats. Never wear a *pareu* to church—you'll be asked to leave. Young missionaries from the Church of Latter Day Saints (Mormons) continue to flock to Polynesia from the U.S. for two-year stays. They wear short-sleeved white shirts with ties and travel in pairs—you may spot a couple. There's also a local branch of the so-called Re-organized Church of L.D.S. whose headquarters are in Independence, Missouri, instead of Salt Lake City, Utah.

The most sinister religious development in recent years occurred on Faaite atoll in the

Tuamotus in early Sept. 1987. A pair of self-proclaimed religious crusaders from the "charismatic renewal movement" managed to instill such intense revivalist fervor in the villagers that six people were actually burned to death, some by their own children, to exorcise "devils" that threatened the island with disaster. A radio alert brought the mayor and a Catholic priest to the scene just in time to prevent another four "impure souls" to be sacrificed to the "healing" fire. The April 1988 issue of *Pacific Islands Monthly* carries the whole grisly story. Another vestige of the pre-Christian religion is a widespread belief in ghosts *(tupapau).*

ARTS AND CRAFTS

As weaving was unknown in the old days, *tapa* cloth was made by women from the bark of the paper mulberry, breadfruit, and banyan trees. The boughs were soaked in a river for several days, the outer bark then stripped off and the inner bark separated from it. The softened inner bark was placed on a block of

a contemporary tapa design from Fatu Hiva, Marquesas Is.

wood and beaten with a mallet. When the *tapa* was of a uniform thickness it was dried in the sun and dyed. Floral or geometric patterns were printed or painted on.

Early missionaries introduced the Tahitians to quilting, and two-layer patchwork *tifaifai* have now taken the place of *tapa* (bark cloth). Used as bed covers and pillows by tourists, Tahitians still use *tifaifai* to cloak newlyweds and cover coffins. To be wrapped in a *tifaifai* is the highest honor. Each woman has individual quilt patterns which are her trademarks. Bold floral designs are popular, with contrasting colors drawn from nature. A good *tifaifai* can take up to six months to complete and cost US$1000. The French artist Henri Matisse, who in 1930 spent several weeks at the now-demolished Stuart Hotel on Papeete's boulevard Pomare, was so impressed by the Tahitian *tifaifai* that he applied the same technique and adopted many designs for his "gouaches decoupees."

Spectacles

Though the missionaries banned dancing completely in the 1820s and the French colonial administration only allowed performances which didn't disturb Victorian decorum, traditional Tahitian dancing is back in a big way. During major festivals troupes of 20-50 dancers and 6-10 musicians participate in thrilling competitions. The big hotels on Tahiti and Bora Bora offer exciting dance shows several nights a week which you may attend for the price of a drink.

The Tahitian *tamure* is a fast, provocative, erotic dance done by rapidly shifting the weight from one foot to the other. The rubber-legged men are almost acrobatic, though their movements tend to follow those of the women closely. The tossing shell-decorated bast or fiber skirts *(mores),* the pandanus wands in the hands, and the tall headdresses add to the drama.

Dances such as the *aparima, ote'a,* and *hivinau* re-enacted Polynesian legends and each movement told part of a story. The *aparima* is a dance resembling the Hawaiian hula or Samoan siva executed mainly with the hands in a standing or sitting position. The hand movements tell the story which is the subject of the accompanying song. The *ote'a* is a theme dance executed to the accompaniment of drums with great precision and admirable timing by a group of men and/or women arrayed in two columns. The *ute* is a restrained dance based on ancient refrains. The *hymene* or "hymn" sung by a large choir is based on ancient chants.

Listen to the staccato beat of the *toere,* a hollow wooden drum hit with a stick. The nose flute is another traditional instrument, though today guitars and ukuleles are more often seen. The ukulele was originally the *braguinha,* brought to Hawaii by Portuguese immigrants a century ago. Homemade ukuleles with the half-shell of a coconut as a sound box emit pleasant tones, while those sporting an empty tin give a more metallic sound.

Firewalking, once a part of pagan religious rites, is still performed occasionally. A so-called "high priest" and his ti-leaf-clad assistants parade barefoot twice across a pit full of red-hot volcanic rocks. How the participants escape injury is another mystery of Polynesia! A seldom-used firewalking pit is opposite the Bali Hai Hotel on Raiatea; ask, you may be lucky.

Stone Fishing

This traditional method of fishing is now only practiced on very special occasions in the Leeward Islands. Coconut fronds are tied end to end until a line a half kilometer long is ready. Several dozen outrigger canoes form a semicircle. Advancing slowly together, men in the canoes beat the water with stones tied to ropes. The frightened fish are thus driven toward a beach. When the water is shallow enough the men leap from their canoes, push the leaf line before them, yell, and beat the water with their hands. In this way the fish are literally forced ashore.

TAHITI IN LITERATURE

Over the years the romance of legendary Tahiti has been elaborated by a succession of famous writers who came in search of Bougainville's "Nouvelle Cythere" or Rous-

seau's "noble savage." Brought to the stage or silver screen, their stories entered the popular imagination alongside Gauguin's rich images. If you can manage to read a couple of the books mentioned below before you come, your trip will be enhanced.

Herman Melville, author of the whaling classic *Moby Dick* (1851), deserted his New Bedford whaler at Nuku Hiva in 1842. *Typee* (1846) describes his experiences there. An Australian whaler carried Melville on to Tahiti where he joined a mutiny on board which landed him in the Papeete *calabooza* (prison). His second Polynesian book *Omoo* (1847) was a result. In both Melville decries the ruin of Polynesian culture by Western influence.

Pierre Loti's *The Marriage of Loti* (1880) is a sentimental tale of the love of a young French midshipman for a Polynesian girl named Rarahu. Loti's naivete is rather absurd, but his friendship with Queen Pomare IV and fine imagery make the book worth reading. Loti's writings influenced Paul Gauguin to come to Tahiti.

From 1888-90 Robert Louis Stevenson, famous author of *Treasure Island* and *Kidnapped,* cruised the Pacific in his schooner, the *Casco.* His book *In the South Seas* describes his visits to the Marquesas and Tuamotus. Stevenson and family settled at Tautira on Tahiti Iti for a time, but eventually retired at Apia in Samoa which offered the author better mail service.

Robert Louis Stevenson

TAHITIAN DANCE MOVEMENTS

anuanua
rainbow

ao
day

here
to love

maeva
welcome

mana'o
to think

marama
moon

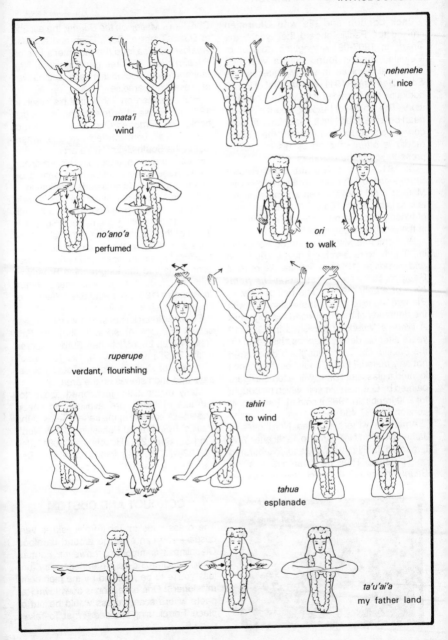

mata'i
wind

nehenehe
nice

no'ano'a
perfumed

ori
to walk

ruperupe
verdant, flourishing

tahiri
to wind

tahua
esplanade

ta'u'ai'a
my father land

Jack London and his wife Charmian cruised the Pacific aboard their yacht, the *Snark,* in 1907-09. A longtime admirer of Melville, London found only a wretched swamp at Taipivae in the Marquesas. His *South Sea Tales* (1911) was the first of the 10 books on the Pacific that he wrote. London's story "The House of Mapuhi" about a Jewish pearl buyer earned him a costly lawsuit. London was a product of his time and the modern reader is often shocked by his insensitive presentation of the islanders.

In 1913-14 the youthful poet Rupert Brooke visited Tahiti where he fell in love with Mamua, a girl from Mataiea whom he immortalized in his poem "Tiare Tahiti." Brooke died of blood poisoning on a French hospital ship in the Mediterranean in 1915.

W. Somerset Maugham toured Polynesia in 1916-17 to research his novel, *The Moon and Sixpence* (1919), a fictional life of Paul Gauguin. Of the six short stories in *The Trembling of a Leaf* (1921), "The Fall of Edward Barnard" contrasts the simple island life with the demands of the "real world." Maugham's *A Writer's Notebook* published in 1984, 19 years after his death, describes his travels in the Pacific. On Tahiti Maugham discovered not only material for his books but by chance located a glass door pane with a female figure painted by Gauguin himself, which he bought for 200 francs. In 1962 it sold at Sotheby's in London for $37,400.

American writers Charles Nordhoff and James Norman Hall came to Tahiti after WW I, married Tahitian women, and collaborated on 11 books. Their most famous was the *Bounty* trilogy (1934) which tells of Fletcher Christian's *Mutiny on the Bounty,* the escape to Dutch Timor of Capt. Bligh and his *Men Against the Sea,* and the mutineer's fate on *Pitcairn's Island.* Three generations of filmmakers have selected this saga as their way of presenting paradise.

Hall remained on Tahiti until his death in 1951; his house at Arue still stands. His last book, *The Forgotten One,* is a collection of true stories about intellectuals and writers lost in the South Seas. Hall's account of the 28-year correspondence with his American friend Robert Dean Frisbie who settled on Pukapuka in the Cook Islands is touching.

James A. Michener joined the U.S. Navy in 1942 and ended up visiting around 50 South Sea islands, among them Bora Bora. His *Tales of the South Pacific* (1947) tells of the impact of WW II on the South Pacific and the Pacific's impact on those who served. It was later made into the long-running Broadway musical, "South Pacific." Michener's *Return to Paradise* (1951) is a readable collection of essays and short stories.

Eugene Burdick is best known for his best sellers *The Ugly American* (1958) and *Fail-Safe* (1962). Like Michener, Burdick served in the Pacific during WW II. His 1961 book *The Blue of Capricorn* is a collection of essays and short stories on the area.

Many of the titles mentioned above (or extracts of them) are available in cheap paperback editions in the series "Tales of the Pacific" from Mutual Publishing, 2055 North King St., Suite 201, Honolulu, HI 96819 (tel. 808-924-7732). Write for a complete list. See also the Booklist at the end of this book.

CONDUCT AND CUSTOM

The dress code in Tahiti-Polynesia is very casual—you can even go around barefoot. Cleanliness *is* important, however. Formalwear or jacket-and-tie are unnecessary (unless you're to be received by the high commissioner!). One exception is downtown Papeete where scanty dress would be out of place. For clothing tips see "What To Take", page 67.

People usually shake hands when meeting; visitors are expected to shake hands with everyone present. If a Polynesian man's hand is dirty he'll extend his wrist or elbow. Women kiss each other on the cheeks. When entering a private residence it's polite to remove your shoes. It's okay to show interest in the possessions of a host, but don't lavish too much praise on any single object or he/she may feel obligated to give it to you. It's rude to refuse food offered by a Tahitian, but don't eat everything on your plate just to be polite as this will be a signal to your host that you want another helping. Often guests in a private home are expected to eat while the family watches.

All the beaches of Tahiti-Polynesia are public to one meter above the high-tide mark, although some bad watchdogs don't recognize this. Topless sunbathing is completely legal in Tahiti-Polynesia, though total nudity is only practiced on offshore *motus* and floating pontoons. (For information on naturism in Tahiti-Polynesia write: Marcel Arrouet, Relais Naturiste, B.P. 457, Papeete; tel. 42-90-26.)

Despite the apparent *laissez faire* attitude promoted in the travel brochures and this book, female travelers should take care: there have been sexual assaults by Polynesian men on foreign women who seemed to project an image of promiscuity by sunbathing topless on a remote beach or even by traveling alone! Women should avoid staying in isolated tourist bungalows or camping outside organized campgrounds. Rape is a less serious offense in Polynesian society than it is in ours.

a canoe race at Papeete

HOLIDAYS AND EVENTS

The big event of the year is the two-week-long *Heiva i Tahiti,* which runs from the end of June to Bastille Day (14 July). Formerly known as the Tiurai Festival or *La Fete du Juillet,* it brings contestants and participants to Tahiti from all over the territory to take part in elaborate processions, competitive dancing and singing, feasting, and partying. There are bicycle, car, horse, and outrigger canoe races, petanque, archery, and javelin-throwing contests, firewalkers from Raiatea, sidewalk bazaars, arts and crafts exhibitions, tattooing, games, and joyous carnivals. Bastille Day itself, which marks the fall of the Bastille in Paris on 14 July 1789 at the height of the French Revolution, features a military parade in the capital. Ask at the Papeete tourist office about when to see the historical reenactments at Marae Arahurahu, the canoe race along Papeete waterfront, horseracing at the Pirae track, and the traditional dance competitions at the Moorea ferry landing.

The July celebrations on Bora Bora are as good as those on Tahiti, and not as commercial. Note well that all ships, planes, and hotels are fully booked around 14 July, so be in the right place beforehand or get firm reservations, especially if you want to be on Bora Bora that day.

Chinese New Year in Jan. or Feb. is celebrated with dances and fireworks. On Nuclear Free and Independent Pacific Day (1 March), a protest march proceeds from Faaa to Papeete, to commemorate a disastrous nuclear test on Bikini atoll in Micronesia that day in 1954. This is a great opportunity to get to know some local people while showing your concern for the problems of colonialism and militarism in the Pacific. On All Saints' Day (1 Nov.) the locals illuminate the cemeteries at Papeete, Arue, Punaauia, and elsewhere with candles. On New Year's Eve the Papeete waterfront is beautifully illuminated and there's a seven-km foot race. Ask at the "Departement Fetes et Manifestations" in Papeete's Cultural Center (B.P. 1709, Papeete; tel. 42-88-50 or 42-85-69) about special events, and check the daily papers.

Public holidays in Tahiti-Polynesia include New Year's Day (1 Jan.), Gospel Day (5 March), Good Friday and Easter Monday (March/April), Labor Day (1 May), Ascension Day (May), Whitsunday and Whitmonday (May/June), Bastille Day (14 July), Assumption Day (15 Aug.), All Saints' Day (1 Nov.), Armistice Day (11 Nov.), and Christmas Day (25 Dec.). Everything will be closed these days (and maybe also the days before and after—ask).

ACCOMMODATIONS

With *Tahiti-Polynesia Handbook* in hand you're guaranteed a good, inexpensive place to stay on every island. Every hotel in the islands at press time is included herein. We don't solicit freebies from the hotel chains! Our only income is from the price you paid when you bought this book. So we don't mind telling you that, as usual, most of the luxury hotels are just not worth the exorbitant prices they charge. Many simply recreate Hawaii at three times the cost, offering far more luxury than you need. Even worse, they tend to isolate you in a French/American environment, away from the Polynesia you came to experience. We list them here for comparison and most are worth visiting as sightseeing attractions, watering holes, or sources of entertainment, but unless you're a millionaire sleep elsewhere.

One of the golden rules of independent travel is "the more you spend the less you experience." Any room you can book from the States over a toll-free number has got to be overpriced. On all the islands are middle-level hotels which charge half what the top end places ask while providing adequate comfort. These are popular weekend destinations for local French. If you really *can* afford US$200 a night and up, you'd do better chartering a skippered or bareboat yacht. For more information see pages 78 and 151.

A wise government regulation prohibiting buildings higher than a coconut tree outside Papeete means that most of the hotels are lowrise or consist of small Tahitian *fares*. When choosing a hotel keep in mind that although a thatched bungalow is cooler and infinitely more attractive than a concrete box it's also more likely to have insect problems. Hopefully there'll be a resident lizard or two to feed on the bugs. As the lagoon waters off the northwest corner of Tahiti become increasingly polluted with raw sewage, hotels like the Beachcomber and Maeva Beach fall back on their swimming pools. On all of the outer islands open to foreign tourists the water is so clear that it makes pools superfluous.

Hotel prices range from f.800 single all the way up to f.42,500 double. If your hotel can't provide running water, electricity, air conditioning, or something similar because of a hurricane or otherwise, ask for a price reduction. You'll easily get 10% off. You usually get what you pay for, so don't feel ripped off unless you're paying top dollar. A 7% room

Guynette's Lodging at Fare, Huahine, is popular among budget travelers.

tax is usually charged extra at the luxury resorts, but included in the price at the budget places. Many hotels add a surcharge to the bill unless you stay more than one night.

A room with cooking facilities can save you a lot on restaurant meals, and some moderately priced establishments have weekly rates. If you have to choose a meal plan take only breakfast and dinner (Modified American Plan) and have fruit for lunch. The cheapest hostels expect you to have your own sleeping bag and towel; linen is not usually provided. As you check into your room, note the nearest fire exits. Don't automatically take the first room offered; if you're paying good money look at several, then choose. Single women intending to stay in isolated tourist bungalows should try to find someone with whom to share.

Your best accommodations option is the well-organized homestay program, in which you get a private room or bungalow with a local family. *Logement chez l'habitant* is available on all the outer islands, and even in Papeete itself; the tourist office supplies mimeographed lists. Travel agents abroad won't book the cheaper hotels or lodgings with the inhabitants because no commissions are paid. You must make reservations directly with the owners themselves either by mail or phone. Letters are usually not answered so calling up is best; things change fast and printed listings are often out of date. Most pensions don't accept credit cards and English may not be spoken.

These private guesthouses can be hard to locate. There's usually no sign outside and they don't cater to walk-in clients who show up unexpectedly. Also, the limited number of beds in each may all be taken. Sometimes you'll get airport transfers at no additional charge if you call ahead. Don't expect a lot of privacy or hot water in the bath. Sometimes cooking facilities or meals are included (often seafood); the provision of blankets and towels may depend on the price. The family may loan you a bicycle and can be generally helpful in arranging tours, etc. It's a great way to meet the people while finding a place to stay.

In remote areas residents are often very hospitable and may offer to put you up. Try to find some tangible way to show your appreciation, such as paying for the groceries or giving a gift. It wouldn't hurt to offer cash payment if a stranger helps you when you're in a jam. Once you get home, don't forget to mail prints of any photos you've taken. If you do make friends on one island, ask them to write you a letter of introduction to their relatives on another.

A tent saves the budget traveler a lot of money and proves very convenient to fall back on. The Polynesians don't usually mind if you camp, and quite a few French locals also have tents. As yet the only regular campgrounds are on Tahiti, Moorea, and Bora Bora catering to the growing number of camper-tourists. On the outer islands there should be no problem but ask permission of the landowner, or camp well out of sight of the road. Ensure this same hospitality for the next traveler by not leaving a mess. Make sure your tent is water- and mosquito-proof. Never pitch a tent directly below coconuts hanging from a tree or a precariously leaning trunk.

FOOD AND DRINK

The restaurants are expensive but you can bring the price way down by ordering only a single main dish. Fresh bread and cold water come with the meal. Avoid appetizers, alcohol, and desserts. No taxes or service charges are tacked on and tipping is unnecessary. So it's really not as expensive as it looks! US$10 will get you through an excellent no-frills lunch of fried fish at a small French restaurant. The same thing in a five-star hotel dining room will be only a few dollars more. Even the finest places are affordable if you order this way.

Most restaurants post their menu in the window. If not, have a look at it before sitting down. Check the entrees as that's all you'll need to take. If the price is right, the *ambiance* congenial, and local French are at the tables, sit right down. In Tahiti-Polynesia it's actually hard to get a bad meal! Sure, food at a snack bar would be half as much, but your Coke will be extra. In the end it's smart to pay a little more to enjoy the excellent cuisine once in a while. Steer clear of restaurants where you see a big plastic bottle of mineral water on every table as this will add a couple of hundred francs to your bill. Also beware of set meals designed for tourists: if you can't order a la carte walk back out the door.

Local restaurants offer French, Chinese, Vietnamese, Italian, and, of course, Tahitian dishes. The *nouvelle cuisine Tahitienne* is a combination of European and Oriental recipes with local seafoods and vegetables, plus the classic *maa Tahiti*. The French are famous for their sauces, so try something exotic. Lunch is the main meal of the day in Tahiti-Polynesia and many restaurants offer a *plat du jour* designed for regular customers. This is often displayed on a blackboard near the entrance and is usually good value. Most restaurants stop serving lunch at 1400, dinner at 2200. The prices of alcoholic drinks dropped recently as taxation was eased to encourage tourism. Don't expect snappy service: what's the rush, anyway?

If it's all too expensive groceries are a good alternative. There are lots of nice places to picnic and at f.30 a loaf, that crisp French white bread is incredibly cheap and good. Cheap red wines like Selection Faragui (f.400 a liter) are imported from France in bulk and bottled locally in plastic bottles. Add a nice piece of French cheese to the above and you're ready for a budget travelers' banquet. There's also Martinique rum, and Hinano beer brewed locally by Heineken. Remember the f.60 deposit on Hinano beer bottles, which makes beer cheap to buy cold and carry out. Coconut patties (f.100) are a local treat to watch for on grocery-store check-out counters. *Casse croutes,* big healthy sandwiches made with those long French *baguettes,* are f.150.

If you're going to the outer islands, take as many edibles with you as possible; it's always more expensive there. Keep in mind that virtually every food plant you see growing on the islands is cultivated by someone. Even fishing floats or sea shells washed up on a

beach, or fish in the lagoon near someone's home, may be considered private property.

Tahitian Food

If you can spare the cash attend a Tahitian *tamaaraa* (feast) and try some Polynesian dishes roasted in an *ahimaa* (underground oven). Basalt stones are preheated with a wood fire in a meter-deep pit, then covered with leaves. Each type of food is wrapped separately in banana leaves to retain its own flavor and lowered in. The oven is covered with more banana leaves, wet sacking, and sand, and left one to three hours to bake: suckling pig, mahimahi, taro, *umara* (sweet potato), *uru* (breadfruit), and *fafa,* a spinach-like cooked vegetable made from taro tops. Also sample the gamey flavor of *fei,* the red cooking banana that grows wild in Tahiti's uninhabited interior. *Miti hue* is a coconut-milk sauce fermented with the juice of river shrimp. Traditionally *maa Tahiti* is eaten with the fingers.

Poisson cru (ia ota), small pieces of raw bonito (skipjack) or yellowfin marinated with lime juice and soaked in coconut milk, is enjoyable, as is *fafaru* ("smelly fish"), prepared by marinating pieces of fish in sea-water in an airtight coconut-shell container. Like the durian, although the smell is repugnant, the first bite can be addicting. Other typical Tahitian plates are chicken *fafa* and kid cooked in ginger.

Poe is a sweet pudding made of starch flour flavored with banana, vanilla, papaya, taro, or pumpkin, and topped with salted coconut-milk sauce. Many varieties of this treat are made throughout Polynesia. *Faraoa ipo* is Tuamotu coconut bread. The local coffee is flavored with vanilla bean, and served with sugar and coconut cream.

Taro is an elephant-eared plant cultivated in freshwater swamps. The sweet potato *(umara)* is a vegetable of South American origin—how it reached Oceania is still a mystery. Papaya (pawpaw) is nourishing: a third of a cup contains as much vitamin C as 18 apples. To ripen a green papaya overnight, puncture it a few times with a knife. Don't overeat papaya—unless you *need* an effec-

breadfruit (Artocarpus altilis)

tive laxative. Atoll dwellers especially rely on the coconut for food. The tree reaches maturity in eight years, then produces about 50 nuts a year for 60 years. Many islanders eat raw shellfish and fish, but know what you're doing before you join them—their stomachs may be stronger than yours. It's safer to eat well-cooked food, and to peel your own fruit.

Breadfruit

The breadfruit *(uru)* is the plant most often associated with Tahiti. The theme of a man turning himself into such a tree to save his family during famine often recurs in Polynesian legends. Ancient voyagers brought breadfruit shoots or seeds from Southeast Asia. When baked in an underground oven or roasted over flames, the now seedless Polynesian variety resembles bread. Joseph Banks, botanist on Capt. Cook's first voyage, wrote: "If a man should in the course of his lifetime plant 10 trees, which if well done might take the labor of an hour or thereabouts, he would completely fulfill his duty to his own as well as future generations."

The French naturalist Sonnerat transplanted breadfruit to Reunion in the Indian Ocean as early as 1772, but it's Capt. William Bligh who shall always be remembered when the plant is mentioned. In 1787 Bligh set out to collect young shoots in Tahiti for transfer to the West Indies where they were to be planted to feed black slaves. On the way back his crew mutinied in Tongan waters and cast off both breadfruit and Bligh. The indominable captain managed to reach Dutch Timor in a rowboat and in 1792 returned to Tahiti with another ship to complete his task.

The breadfruit *(Artocarpus altilis),* a tall tree with large green leaves, provides shade as well as food. A well-watered tree can produce as many as 1,000 pale green breadfruits a year. Robert Lee Eskridge described it thus: "Its outer rind or skin, very hard, is covered with a golf-ball-like surface of small irregular pits or tiny hollows. An inner rind about a half-inch thick surrounds the fruit itself, which when baked tastes not unlike a doughy potato. Perhaps fresh bread, rolled up until it becomes a semi-firm mass, best describes the breadfruit when cooked." The starchy, easily digested fruit is rich in vitamin B. When consumed with a protein such as fish or meat it serves as an energy food. The Polynesians learned to preserve breadfruit by pounding it into a paste which was kept in leaf-lined pits to ferment into *mahi.* Like the coconut, the breadfruit tree itself had many uses, including the provision of wood for outrigger canoes.

Entertainment
The Tahitian dance shows put on at the hotels are invariably free (no cover charge)—you only pay for the food and drink you consume. Most of the big hotels have a Tahitian show several nights a week, usually accompanied by a barbecue or traditional feast. If the price asked for the meal is too steep, settle for a drink at the bar and enjoy the show. Many of the regular performances are listed in this book, but be sure to call the hotel to confirm the time and date as these do change to accommodate tour groups. The drinking age in Tahiti-Polynesia is officially 18, but it's not strictly enforced.

SHOPPING

Most local souvenir shops sell Marquesas-style wooden "tikis" carved from wood or stone. The original Tiki was a god of fertility, and really old tikis are still shrouded in superstition. Today they're mainly viewed as good-luck charms and often come decorated with mother of pearl. Other items carved from wood include mallets (to beat *tapa* cloth), *umete* bowls, and slit *toere* drums. Carefully woven pandanus hats and mats come from the Australs. Other curios to buy include vanilla for use in flavoring coffee, hand-carved mother-of-pearl shell, bamboo fishhooks, and Tahitian music cassettes.

As this is a French colony it's not surprising that many of the best buys are related to fashion. A tropical shirt, sundress, or T-shirt is a purchase of immediate use. The *pareu* is a typically Tahitian leisure garment consisting of a brightly colored hand-blocked or painted local fabric about two meters long and a meter wide. There are dozens of ways both men and women can wear a *pareu*. Local

cosmetics like Monoi Tiare Tahiti, a fragrant coconut-oil skin moisturizer, and coconut-oil soap will put you in form. Jasmine shampoo, cologne, and perfume are also made locally from the tiare Tahiti flower. Imported perfumes from France are sold, too.

Black-pearl jewelry is non-traditional but widely available throughout Tahiti-Polynesia. The color, shape, weight, and size of the pearl are important. The darkest pearls are the most valuable. Prices vary considerably, so shop around before purchasing pearls. For more information on Polynesia's fabulous black pearls, see "Economy" above. Sharks'-tooth pendants also make fine jewelry.

If you buy any commercial travel videotapes keep in mind that three incompatible video systems are loose in the world: NTSC (used in North America), PAL (used in Britain, West Germany, Japan, and Australia), and SECAM (used in France and the USSR). Don't get the wrong one.

Hustling and bargaining are not customs in

Monoi Tiare Tahiti is a scented coconut oil used to replenish natural skin oils lost to the effects of the tropical sun and seas.

Tahiti- Polynesia: it's expensive for everyone. Haggling may even by considered insulting, so just pay the price asked or keep looking. Many local food prices are fixed by the government. Avoid whopping mark-ups and taxes; instead purchase food and handicrafts from the producers themselves at markets or roadside stalls.

When making purchases, beware of objects made from turtle shell/leather or marine mammal ivory. These are prohibited entry into the U.S. and many other countries with endangered species acts (fine of US$20,000 and five years imprisonment). Also resist the temptation to purchase jewelry or other items made from seashells and corals, the collection of which damages the reefs. When you return home Customs may wish to see receipts to judge whether you're within your tax exemption limits ($400 for Americans).

VISAS

Everyone needs a passport. French citizens are admitted freely for an unlimited stay, and citizens of the European Economic Community (EEC) countries and the Swiss get three months without a visa. Citizens of the United States, Canada, and Japan can obtain a three-month "visa" free upon arrival at Papeete (no different than any other passport stamp). Most others (Australians and New Zealanders included) must apply to a French diplomatic mission for a three-month visa, but it's usually issued without delay. Extensions of stay up to three months are possible after you arrive, but it's better to ask for enough time upon arrival. Visa regulations for Tahiti have a way of changing according to the political climate in France, but your airline will know the current requirements.

Tahiti-Polynesia requires a ticket to leave of everyone (even French!). If you arrive without one, you'll be refused entry or required to post a cash bond equivalent to the value of a ticket back to your home country. If you're on an open-ended holiday, you can easily get around this requirement by purchasing a refundable ticket back to the U.S. from Air New Zealand before leaving home. If you catch a boat headed to Fiji (for example), simply have the airline re-issue the ticket so it's a ticket to leave your next destination—and on you go. You may also be required to prove that you have "sufficient funds."

Here are a few **French consulates general:**

Australia: St. Martin's Tower, 31 Martin St., Sydney, NSW 2000 (tel. 612- 261-5779); 492 St. Kilda Rd., Melbourne, Victoria 3004 (tel. 613-266-2591)

Canada: French consulates general are found in Edmonton, Moncton, Montreal, Ottawa, Quebec, Toronto, and Vancouver.

Chile: Calle Condell 65, C.C. 38-D, Santiago de Chile (tel. 562-225-1030)

Fiji: Dominion House, Thomson St., Private Mail Bag, Suva (tel. 679-300991)

Hawaii: 2 Waterfront Plaza, 500 Ala Moana Blvd., Honolulu, HI 96813 (tel. 808-599-4458)

Japan: 1-1-44, 4 Chome, Minami Azabu, Minato-Ku, Tokyo 106 (tel. 813-473- 0171); Ohbayashi Bldg., 37 Kyobashi 3, Chome Higashi-Ku, Osaka (tel. 8106- 946-6181)

Hong Kong: Admiralty Center Tower 2, 26th Floor, 18 Harcourt Rd., G.P.O. Box 13, Hong Kong (tel. 852-5-294351)

New Zealand: 1 Willeston St., Box 1695, Wellington (tel. 644-720200)

Singapore: 5 Gallop Rd., Box 42, Singapore 1025 (tel. 65-466-4861)

U.S.A.: French consulates general exist in Boston, Chicago, Detroit, Houston, Los Angeles, Miami, New Orleans, New York, San Francisco, and Washington. Get the address of the one nearest you by dialing the toll-free number of UTA French Airlines or Air France.

Yacht Entry

The main port of entry for cruising yachts is Papeete. Upon application to the local gendarme, entry may also be allowed at Moorea, Huahine, Raiatea, Bora Bora, Rurutu, Tubuai, Raivavae, Rangiroa, Nuku Hiva, Hiva Oa, or Ua Pou. The gendarmes are usually friendly and courteous. Boats arriving from Tonga, Fiji, and the Samoas must be fumigated.

Anyone arriving by yacht without an onward ticket must post a bond equivalent to the airfare back to the country of origin at a local bank. In Taiohae the bond is US$1200 pp, in Papeete it's only US$600 (for Americans). This is refundable upon departure at any branch of the same bank, less a 1% fee. Make sure the receipt shows the original currency in which the deposit was made. If the individual doesn't have the money, the captain is responsible. Once the bond is posted a "temporary" three-month visa (US$30) is issued, which means you have three months to get to Papeete where an additional three months (another US$30) may be granted. Actually, the rules are not hard and fast, and everyone has a different experience.

Yachts staying longer than one year are charged full Customs duty on the vessel. After clearing Customs in Papeete, outbound yachts may spend the duration of their period of stay cruising the outer islands. Make sure

every island where you *might* stop is listed on your clearance. The officials want all transient boats out of the country by 31 Oct., the onset of the hurricane season. Crew changes should be made at Papeete.

TAHITI - POLYNÉSIE FRANÇAISE
CARTE DÉBARQUEMENT - EMBARQUEMENT/*Disembarkation - Embarkation card*

IMPORTANT
Veuillez remplir ce document avec soin.
Toutes les copies doivent être lisibles.
Please print clearly.
All copies must be legible.

Nom/*Surname* (En caractères d'imprimerie/*Block letters*)

Nom de jeune fille/*Maiden name*

Prénom/*Given name*

Sexe/*Sex*: ☐ Masculin/*Male* ☐ Féminin/*Female*
(Cochez/*Tick*)

Date de naissance
Date of birth Quantième/*Day* Mois/*Month* Année/*Year*

Lieu de naissance
Place of birth

Nationalité
Nationality

Profession
Occupation

Domicile permanent
Permanent address Rue/*Street*

Ville/*City* Département/*State* Pays/*Country*

Port d'embarquement Vol n°
Port of embarkation *Flight*

Port de débarquement après la Polynésie Frse
Port of disembarkation after French Polynesia

Adresse ou hôtel(s) en Polynésie Frse
Address or hotel(s) in French Polynesia

Durée de séjour en Polynésie Frse .... jours ☐ Transit (moins de 24 h)
Length of stay in French Polynesia .... days *(less than 24 h)*

Je suis ☐ Visiteur ☐ Résident temporaire de P.F. ☐ Résident permanent de P.F
I am ☐ *Visitor* ☐ *Temporary resident of F.P* ☐ *Permanent resident of F P*

Passeport N°
Passport N°

N° 144196

MONEY AND MEASUREMENTS

The French Pacific franc or *Cour de Franc Pacifique* (CFP) is legal tender in both Tahiti-Polynesia and New Caledonia. The origin of this currency is interesting. During WW II the French franc (FF) had been devalued to less than a third its prewar value, while prices remained stable in the Pacific. When the French colonies re-established contact with metropolitan France after wartime separation, a new currency was needed to avoid economic chaos. Thus the CFP was created in 1945 at the rate of 2.4 FF to one CFP. Over the next few years the French franc was further devalued three times and each time

the CFP was revalued against it, lowering the French franc to 5.50 to one CFP by 1949. At the same time 100 old FF became one new FF, thus 5.5 new FF equaled 100 old CFP, a relationship which has been maintained ever since. Until 1967 the Banque de l'Indochine was responsible for issuing and circulating the Pacific franc, a function now carried out by the French government.

The CFP is fixed at one French franc to 18.18 Pacific francs, so you can determine how many CFP you'll get for your dollar or pound by finding out how many FF you get, then multiplying by 18.18. Or to put it another way, 5.5 FF equals f.100, so divide the number of FF you get by 5.5 and multiply by 100. A rough way to convert CFP into U.S. dollars is simply to divide by 100, so f.1000 is US$10, etc. There are beautifully colored big banknotes of 500, 1000, 5000, and 10,000 francs, coins of 1, 2, 5, 10, 20, 50, and 100 francs.

Banking hours are variable, either 0800-1530 or 0800-1100/1400-1700 weekdays. A few open Sat. mornings (ask). Many banks levy a ripoff commission of f.300 on each transaction. Instead, patronize the **Banque Socredo** (B.P. 130, Papeete; tel. 41-51-23) which charges no commission and has branches everywhere. Travelers cheques bring a higher rate of exchange than cash. You'll probably do better waiting to change money upon arrival rather than trying to purchase CFP from your home bank which may give you a poor rate, if they accomplish it at all.

If your American Express travelers cheques are stolen call Australia tel. 61-886-0688 collect to report the loss and find out about a refund. BankAmerica's lost travelers cheque number is San Francisco tel. 415-624-5400 collect (24 hours). They'll also cancel lost credit cards if stolen with the cheques. Of course, they'll need to know the numbers! Many BankAmerica branches in the U.S. sell travelers cheques without the usual 1% commission (ask).

Credit cards are accepted at the large hotels, but cash is easier at restaurants, shops, etc. To avoid wasting time hassling at banks for cash advances it's best to bring enough travelers cheques to cover all your out-of-pocket expenses and then some. If you do wish to use a credit card at a restaurant, ask first. VISA credit cards are universally accepted but MasterCard is not. Bargaining is not common in Tahiti-Polynesia and no one

will try to cheat you. There's **no tipping** and they *mean* it.

Post

The 34 regular post offices and 58 authorized agencies throughout Tahiti-Polynesia are open weekdays from 0700-1500. Main branches sell ready-made padded envelopes and boxes. Parcels with an aggregate length, width, and height of over 90 cm or weighing more than 20 kg cannot be mailed. Rolls (posters, calendars, etc.) longer than 90 cm are also not accepted. Letters cannot weigh over two kilograms. Registration *(recommandation)* and insurance *(envois avec valeur declaree)* are possible. Always use airmail *(poste aerienne)* when posting a letter; surface mail takes months to arrive.

To pick up *poste restante* (general delivery) mail you must show your passport and pay f.40 apiece. If you're going to an outer island and are worried about your letters being returned to sender after 15 days, pay f.600 for a *garde de courrier* which obliges the post office to hold all letters for at least a month. For a flat fee of f.800 you can have your mail forwarded by surface mail for one year, f.1600 by airmail. Ask for an *"Ordre de Reexpedition Temporaire."*

In this book all post office box numbers are rendered B.P. *(Boite Postale)*. Always include the B.P. when writing to a local address as there are usually no street addresses. The postal authorities recognize "French Polynesia" as the official name of this country and it's best to add "South Pacific Ocean" to that for good measure. Tahiti-Polynesia issues its own colorful postage stamps—available at local post offices. They're good investments and make excellent souvenirs. On Tahiti the postal information number is tel. 41-43-00.

Telephone

Local telephone calls are f.50 and the pay phones usually work! All calls within a single island are considered local calls, except on Tahiti which is divided into two zones. Long-distance calls are placed at post offices, which also handle fax *(posteclair)* services.

Calls made from hotel rooms are charged double. Collect calls overseas are possible. Dial 19 and say you want a *conversation payable a l'arrive*. To get the operator dial 12.

It's *much* cheaper to call Tahiti from the U.S. than the other way around, so if you want to talk to someone periodically leave your hotel telephone numbers (provided in this book) and travel dates with them so they can try to get ahold of you. If you need to consult the local phone book ask for the *annuaire*. To call Tahiti-Polynesia direct from California dial 011-689 and the six-digit telephone number. International access codes do vary, so check in the front of your telephone book.

Throughout this book we've tried to supply the local telephone numbers you'll need. Any tourist-oriented business is sure to have someone handy who speaks English, so don't hesitate to call ahead. You'll get current information, be able to check prices and perhaps make a reservation, and often save yourself a lot of time and worry.

Electricity

The electric voltage is 220 volts AC, 60 cycles. If you're taking along an American 110-AC razor or other appliance you'll need a converter. Some hotels with their own generators operate on 110 volts, 60 cycles, however, so be sure to ask before plugging in. Most electrical outlets have two round holes, so an adaptor may also be necessary. Also keep this situation in mind if you buy any duty-free appliances.

Time

Tahiti-Polynesia operates on the same time as Hawaii, 10 hours behind Greenwich Mean Time or two hours behind California (except May to Sept. when it's three hours). The Marquesas are 30 minutes behind the rest of Tahiti-Polynesia. Tahiti-Polynesia is east of the International Dateline so the day is the same as that of the Cook Islands, Hawaii, and the U.S., but a day behind Fiji, New Zealand, and Australia.

In this book all clock times are rendered according to the 24-hour airline timetable

1. Marae Arahurahu, Tahiti (Tahiti Tourist Board photo by Tini Colombel);
2. Ahu O Mahine, Moorea (D. Stanley)

1.vanilla stalk (D. Stanley); 2. black noddy (Tahiti Tourist Board); 3. frangipani (Richard Eastwood);
4. dipladenia (Robert K. Yarnell); 5. tiare Tahiti (D. Stanley); 6. Afareaitu Falls, Moorea (Don Pitcher)

system, i.e. 0100 is 1:00 a.m., 1300 is 1:00 p.m., 2330 is 11:30 p.m. Normal shopping hours in Papeete are weekdays 0730-1130/ 1400-1730, Sat. 0800-1100. Islanders operate on coconut time: the nut will fall when it is ripe.

HEALTH

For a tropical location, Tahiti-Polynesia has very few pest or insect problems. Malaria is non-existent. Yellow-fever vaccinations are required if you've been in an infected area (such as the Amazon basin) within the previous six days (infants under the age of one are excused). Cholera vaccinations are not really effective but may be required if there was an outbreak in your last destination. Tetanus-diphtheria, polio, and typhoid boosters are not required, but always a good idea if you're going to out-of-the-way places. Filariais (elephantiasis), leprosy, and dengue fever are the endemic diseases of Polynesia, but there's little chance of visitors contacting these. By mid-1987 eight cases of AIDS had been reported in Tahiti-Polynesia, not to mention hepatitis B and the others.

Cuts and scratches infect easily and take a long time to heal. Prevent infection from coral cuts by washing with soap and fresh water, then rubbing vinegar or alcohol (whisky will do) into the wounds—painful but effective. Tahitians usually dab coral cuts with lime juice. For bites, burns, and cuts, an antiseptic spray such as Solarcaine speeds healing and helps prevent infection. Bites by nono flies itch for days and can become infected.

Prickly heat, an intensely irritating rash, is caused by wearing heavy, inappropriate clothing. When the glands are blocked and the sweat is unable to evaporate, the skin becomes soggy and small red blisters appear. Synthetic fabrics like nylon are especially bad in this regard. Take a cold shower, apply calamine lotion, dust with talcum powder, and take off those clothes! Until things improve avoid alcohol, tea, coffee, and any physical activity which makes you sweat. If you're sweating profusely increase your intake of salt slightly to avoid fatigue, but not without concurrently drinking more water.

Frequently the feeling of thirst is false and only due to mucous membrane dryness. Gargling or taking two or three gulps of warm water should be enough. Other means to keep moisture in the body is to have a hot drink like tea or black coffee, or any kind of slightly salted or sour drink in small quantities. Salt in fresh lime juice is remarkably refreshing. For diarrhea take egg yolk mixed with nutmeg or have a rice and tea day. For constipation eat pineapple or any fruit you

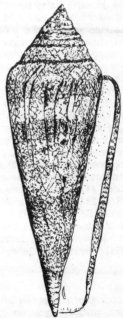

Less than 200 specimens of the rare glory-of-the-sea cone (Conus gloriamaris) are known. Some species of cone shells have a deadly stinging dart which can reach anywhere on the shell's outer surface, so never pick one up.

have peeled. The tap water is safe to drink in Papeete, but ask first elsewhere. The local bottled mineral water is called Eau Royale.

Most of the products in local pharmacies are imported from France, although some U.S. brands are available at twice U.S. prices. If you're not particular about the kind of medicine you take go to any large Chinese general store and ask the owner to recommend a good Chinese patent medicine for what ails you. The price will be a third what the European medicines or herbs cost and they're often just as effective or better.

Don't go from winter weather into the steaming tropics without a rest before and after. Turn in early the day before you leave to allow for the two-hour time difference (from California). Airplane cabins have low humidity, so drink lots of juice or water instead of carbonated drinks. It's also best to forego coffee as it will only keep you awake. Alcohol helps dehydrate you. Avoid overeating inflight. Don't scuba dive on your departure day as you're risking a severe case of the bends.

To buy travel insurance covering emergency medical and legal assistance plus trip cancellation/interruption insurance write: WorldCare, 2000 Pennsylvania Ave. N.W., Suite 7600, Washington, DC 20006 (tel. 202-293-0335). For a token donation of US$10 the International Association for Medical Assistance to Travellers will provide a membership card guaranteeing medical attention at controlled prices in Papeete. Here are a few IAMAT offices: 417 Center St., Lewiston, NY 14092, USA; 1287 St. Clair Ave. West, Toronto, ON M6E 1B8, Canada; 575 Bourke St., 12th floor, Melbourne 3000, Australia; Box 5049, Christchurch 5, New Zealand; 57 Voirets, 1212 Grand-Lancy-Geneva, Switzerland.

Toxic Fish

Over 400 species of tropical reef fish, including wrasses, snappers, groupers, barracudas, jacks, moray eels, surgeonfish, and shellfish, are known to cause seafood poisoning *ciguatera*. There's no way to tell if a fish will cause *ciguatera:* a species can be

poisonous on one side of the island but not on the other.

Several years ago scientists on Tahiti determined that a micro-algae called *dinoflagellate* was the cause. Normally these algae are found only in the ocean depths, but when a reef is disturbed by natural or human causes they can multiply dramatically in a lagoon, and enter the food chain through the fish which feed on them. Tahiti-Polynesia's 700-800 cases of *ciguatera* a year are more than the rest of the South Pacific combined, leading to the suspicion that the French nuclear testing program may be connected. *Ciguatera* didn't exist on Hao atoll in the Tuamotus until military dredging begin in 1965. Soon 43% of the population had been affected. Mangareva had suffered a similar outbreak.

There's no treatment except to relieve the symptoms (tingling, prickling, itching, vomiting, joint and muscle pains), which usually subside in a few days. Avoid biointoxication by cleaning fish as soon as they're caught, discarding the head and organs, and taking special care with oversized fish. Whether the fish is consumed cooked or raw has no bearing on this problem. Local residents often know from experience which species may be eaten.

Sunburn

The Tahitian name for Europeans, *papaa,* means literally "red lobster." Though you may think a tan will make you *look* healthier and more attractive, it's very damaging to the skin, which becomes dry, rigid, and prematurely old and wrinkled, especially on the face. And a burn from the sun greatly increases your risk of getting skin cancer. Begin with short exposures to the sun, perhaps half an hour, followed by an equal time in the shade. Drink plenty of liquids to keep your pores open. Avoid the sun from 1000 to 1400. Clouds and beach umbrellas will not protect you fully. Wear a T-shirt while snorkeling to protect your back. Beware of reflected sunlight. Sunbathing is the main cause of cataracts to the eyes, so wear sunglasses and a wide-brimmed hat.

Use a sunscreen lotion containing PABA rather than oil (don't forget your nose, lips, forehead, neck, hands, and feet). Sunscreens protect you from ultraviolet rays (a leading cause of cancer), while oils magnify the sun's effect. Apply the lotion *before* going to the beach to avoid being burned on the way, and re-apply periodically to replace sunscreen washed away by perspiration. After sunbathing take a tepid shower rather than a hot one which would wash away your natural skin oils. Stay moist and use a vitamin E evening cream to preserve the youth of your skin. Calamine ointment soothes skin already burned, as does coconut oil. A local remedy for sunburn is Wing Wah's Soothing Lotion (Lotion Magic), available at Chinese general stores. Pharmacists recommend Solarcaine (more expensive) to soothe burned skin. A vinegar solution reduces peeling. Take aspirin if your skin itches. Vitamin A and calcium counteract overdoses of vitamin D received from the sun. The fairer your skin the more essential it is to take care.

Just Testing

Although cancer is on the upswing among Polynesians, short-term visitors are still unlikely to be affected by contamination from the nuclear testing program. Fallout from the atmospheric French tests in the '60s is still ticking away in the tissues of local residents, and the bitter harvest may not be reaped until the mid-'90s onward. Unofficial reports of increasing cases of leukemia and thyroid tumors are confirmed by the refusal of the French military authorities to release complete public health statistics for the territory. French officials have attempted to hush up certain nuclear accidents (see page 188) and keep tourists away from the sensitive areas. However, no checks are made to determine whether the fish sold at Papeete market are radioactive. Jean Rostard, a biologist at the French Academy, has warned: "Every increase of the radioactive dose, however slight it may be, enhances the possibility of a mutation."

Elephantiasis and leprosy are endemic to the Pacific.

INFORMATION

Tourism to Tahiti-Polynesia is organized by the "Office de Promotion et d'Animation Touristique de Tahiti et ses Iles" (OPATTI), or simply the Tahiti Tourist Promotion Board. They can provide free brochures and answer questions, but are not a travel agency. Below is a list of their offices around the world.

There are two French-owned morning papers, *La Depeche de Tahiti* (B.P. 50, Papeete; tel. 42-43-43) and *Les Nouvelles de Tahiti* (B.P. 629, Papeete; tel. 43-44-45), each f.100 a copy. *La Depeche* is the larger with more international news, but both papers provide the daily exchange rate. The weekly *Tahiti Sun Press* (B.P. 887, Papeete; tel. 42-68-50), edited by Al Prince, is well worth perusing (free). The best by far of the free advertising brochures is the *Tahiti Clever Guide* with very extensive listings of hotels, restaurants, shops, etc. Ask for it at hotel receptions.

The French government attempts to control what happens in the territory through the state-owned TV and radio. Television was introduced to Tahiti in the mid-1960s and two government-operated stations broadcast in French and Tahitian. Nine private radio stations also operate. For a recorded weather report (in French) call tel. 42-27-27; for the time dial tel. 41-84-00.

The best local guidebook is *Tahiti, Circle Island Tour Guide* by Bengt Danielsson (Singapore, Les Editions du Pacifique, 1986). Bengt and his wife, Marie-Therese, have also written a superb account of the French nuclear testing program entitled *Poisoned Reign* (Australia, Penguin Books, 1986). Other books on Tahiti-Polynesia are described in the Booklist at the back of this volume.

TAHITI TOURIST BOARD OFFICES

Tahiti Tourist Board,
  B.P. 65, Papeete,
  Tahiti-Polynesia
  (tel. 42-96-26)

Tahiti Tourist Board,
  12233 West Olympic Blvd.,
  Suite 110,
  Los Angeles, CA 90064, USA
  (tel. 213-207-1919)

French Government Tourist Office,
  645 North Michigan Ave.,
  Chicago, IL 60611, USA
  (tel. 312-337-6301)

French Government Tourist Office,
  610 Fifth Ave.,
  New York, NY 10020, USA
  (tel. 212-757-1125)

Tahiti Tourist Board,
  12 Castlereagh St.,
  Sydney, NSW 2000,
  Australia
  (tel. 612-221-5811)

Tahiti Tourist Board,
  Box 37237,
  Auckland, New Zealand
  (tel. 34-243)

Pacific Leisure Group,
  1401 Tung Ming Bldg.,
  40 Des Voeux Road,
  Central, Hong Kong
  (tel. 524-1361)

New Tahiti Promotion Inc.,
  Roppongi Kowa Bldg.,
  3-1-1 Roppongi, Minato-ku,
  Tokyo 106, Japan
  (tel. 03-586-6599)

Delegacion de Tahiti,
  Casilla 14002,
  Santiago 21, Chile
  (tel. 562-696-1008)

Office du Tourisme de Tahiti,
  28 Blvd. Saint Germain,
  75005 Paris, France
  (tel. 46-34-5070)

WHAT TO TAKE

Packing

Assemble everything you simply must take and cannot live without—then cut the pile in half. If you're still left with more than will fit into a medium-size backpack, continue eliminating. Now put it all into your pack. If the total (pack and contents) weighs over 16 kg, you'll sacrifice much of your mobility. If you can keep it down to 10 kg, you're traveling *light*. Categorize, separate, and pack all your things into plastic bags or stuff sacks for convenience and protection from moisture. In addition to your backpack you'll want a day-pack or flight bag. When checking in for flights carry anything which can't be replaced in your hand luggage.

Your Pack

A medium-size backpack with an internal frame is best. Big external-frame packs are fine for mountain climbing, but don't fit into public lockers and are very inconvenient on public transport. Some packs have a zippered compartment in back where you can tuck in the straps and hip belt before turning your pack over to an airline or bus. Jansport's "Framesack," among others, is of this type.

Look for a pack with double, two-way zipper compartments and pockets, which you can lock with miniature padlocks. It might not *stop* a thief, but it could be deterrent enough to make him look for another mark. A 60-cm length of lightweight chain and another padlock will allow you to fasten your pack to something. Keep valuables locked in your bag, out of sight.

Camping Equipment And Clothing

A small nylon tent guarantees you a place to sleep every night. It *must* be mosquito- and waterproof. Get one with a tent fly, then waterproof both tent and fly with a can of waterproofing spray such as Thompson's Water Seal (available at any U.S. hardware or outdoors store). You'll seldom need a sleeping bag in the tropics. A youth hostel sleeping sheet is ideal—all YHA handbooks give instructions on how to make your own.

For clothes take loose-fitting cotton washables, light in color and weight. Synthetic fabrics are hot and sticky in the tropics. The dress is casual with slacks and a sports shirt okay for men even at dinner parties. Local women wear long colorful dresses in the evening, but shorts are okay in daytime. If you're in doubt pack clothes which can be discarded and buy tropical garb here. Stick to clothes you can rinse in your room sink. The *pareu* (pronounced "par-RAY-o") is a bright two-meter piece of cloth both men and women wrap about themselves as an all-purpose garment. Any Tahitian can show you how to wear it.

Neutral gray eyeglasses protect your eyes from the sun and give the least color distortion. Take comfortable shoes that have been broken in. Rubber thongs (zories) are very handy. Scuba divers' rubber booties are lightweight and perfect for both crossing rivers and reefwalking, though an old pair of sneak-

Go native in a Tahitian pareu. Throw one corner over your right shoulder, then pass the other under your left arm and pull tight. Tie the ends and you're dressed.

ers may be just as good. Below we've provided a few checklists to help you assemble your gear. All the listed items weigh well over 16 kg, so eliminate what doesn't suit you:

> pack with internal frame
> day pack or airline bag
> nylon tent and fly
> tent patching tape
> mosquito net
> synthetic sleeping bag
> YH sleeping sheet
> sun hat
> essential clothing only
> bathing suit
> hiking boots
> rubber thongs
> rubber booties
> mask and snorkel

Accessories

Look in the ads in photographic magazines for the best deals on mail-order cameras and film, or buy at a discount shop in any large city. Run a roll of film through it to be sure it's in good working order. Register valuable cameras or electronic equipment with Customs before you leave home so there won't be any argument about where you bought the items when you return, or at least carry the original bill of sale.

The type of camera you choose could depend on the way you travel. If you'll be mostly staying in one place a heavy SLR with spare lenses and other equipment won't trouble you. If you'll be moving around a lot for a considerable length of time a 35mm compact camera may be better. The compacts are mostly useful for close-up shots; landscapes will seem spread out and far away. A wide-angle lens gives excellent depth of field but hold the camera upright to avoid converging verticals. A polarizing filter prevents reflections from glass windows. Avoid over-exposure at midday by reducing the exposure half a stop. Ask permission before photographing people.

Keep your camera in a plastic bag during rain and while traveling in motorized canoes, etc. Silica-gel crystals in the bag will protect film from humidity and mold growth. Protect camera and film from direct sunlight and load film in the shade. Never leave camera or film in a hot place like a car floor or glove compartment. When packing protect your camera against vibration. Checked baggage is scanned by powerful airport x-ray monitors, so carry both camera and film aboard in a clear plastic bag and ask for a visual inspection. Otherwise use a lead-laminated pouch. On Tahiti camera film costs over double what you'd pay in the U.S., so bring along the 10 rolls you're allowed to import duty free. Whenever purchasing film in the islands take care to check the expiry date. Don't plan on having any slides developed locally: it can cost over US$50 to develop a roll of 36!

> camera and five rolls of film
> compass
> pocket flashlight
> extra batteries
> candle
> pocket/alarm calculator
> pocket watch
> sunglasses
> padlock and lightweight chain
> collapsible umbrella
> twine for a clothes line
> powdered laundry soap
> sink plug (one that fits all)
> mini-towel
> sewing kit
> mini-scissors
> nail clippers
> fishing line for sewing gear
> plastic cup
> can and bottle opener
> cork screw
> pen knife
> spoon
> water-bottle
> matches
> tea bags
> dried fruits
> nuts
> crackers
> plastic bags
> gifts

soap in plastic container
soft toothbrush
toothpaste
stick deodorant
shampoo
comb and brush
skin creams
makeup
tampons or napkins
white toilet paper
multiple vitamins and minerals
Cutter's insect repellent
PABA sunscreen
ChapStick
a motion sickness remedy
contraceptives
iodine
water purification pills
delousing powder
a diarrhea remedy
Tiger Balm
a cold remedy
Alka Seltzer
aspirin
antihistamine
antifungal
Calmitol ointment
antibiotic ointment
painkiller
antiseptic spray
disinfectant
simple dressings
Band-Aids

Bring some reading material as English-language books are expensive or hard to find. A clip-on book light and extra batteries allows campers to read at night. A mask and snorkel are essential equipment—you'll be missing half of Polynesia's beauty without them. Serious scuba divers bring their own regulator and buoyancy-control device.

Toiletries And Medical Kit
Since everyone has his/her own medical requirements and brand names vary from country to country, there's no point going into detail here. Note, however, that even the basics (such as aspirin) are unavailable on some outer islands, so be prepared. Bring medicated powder for prickly heat rash. Charcoal tablets are useful for diarrhea and poisoning (absorbs the irritants). Bring an adequate supply of any personal medications, plus your prescriptions (in generic terminology).

Women should know that high humidity causes curly hair to swell and bush, straight hair to droop. If it's curly have it cut short or keep it long in a ponytail or bun. A good cut is essential with straight hair. Water-based makeup is best as the heat and humidity cause oil glands to work overtime. See "Health" above for more ideas.

Money And Documents
All post offices have passport applications. Carry your valuables in a money belt worn around your waist or neck under your clothing; most camping goods stores have these. Leave unneeded credit cards and jewelry at home. Bring along a small supply of US$1 and US$5 bills to use if you don't manage to change money immediately upon arrival or if you run out of CFP and can't get to a bank. If you have a car at home, bring along the insurance receipt so you don't have to pay insurance every time you rent a car. Ask your agent about this.

passport
vaccination certificates
airline tickets
scuba certification card
drivers license
travelers cheques
some U.S. cash
photocopies of documents
money belt
address book
notebook
envelopes
extra ballpoints

Make several photocopies of the information page of your passport, personal identification, driver's license, scuba certification card, credit cards, airline tickets, receipts for purchase of travelers cheques, etc.—you should be able to get them all on one page. A brief medical history with your blood type, allergies, chronic or special health problems, eyeglass and medical prescriptions, etc. might also come in handy. Put these inside plastic bags to protect them from moisture. Carry the lists in different places, and leave one home.

How much money you'll need depends on your lifestyle, but time is also a factor. The longer you stay, the cheaper it gets. Suppose you have to lay out US$1000 on airfare, and have (for example) US$35 a day left over for expenses. If you stay 15 days, you'll average US$102 a day ($35 times 15 plus $1000, divided by 15). If you stay 30 days, you'll average US$68 a day ($35 times 30 plus $1000, divided by 30). If you stay 90 days, the per-day cost drops to US$46 ($35 times 90 plus $1000, divided by 90). If you stay a year it'll cost only US$38 a day.

GETTING THERE

Your plane ticket will be your biggest single expense, so spend some time considering the possibilities. Start by calling the airlines directly at their toll-free 800 numbers to get current information on fares. The ones to call are Air France, Air New Zealand, Continental Airlines, Hawaiian Airlines, LAN Chile, Qantas, and UTA French Airlines. In North America, to get the airline's toll free number call tel. 1-800-555-1212 (all 800 numbers are free). Call them all and say you want the *lowest possible fare*. Ask about restrictions. If you're not happy with the answers you get, call back later and try again. Many different agents take calls on these lines and some are more knowledgeable than others. The numbers are busy during business hours, so call at night or on the weekend. *Be persistent*.

Also try your local travel agent, though any agent worth his/her commission will want to sell you a package tour. Even if you decide to take advantage of the convenience of an agent, do call the airlines yourself beforehand so you'll know if you're getting a good deal. Often vacation packages cost less than regular roundtrip airfare. If they'll let you extend your stay to allow the time you want to yourself this could be a good deal, especially with the hotel thrown in for "free." But check the restrictions. Airline tickets are often refundable only in the place of purchase, so ask about this before you invest in a ticket you may not use.

Check the Sunday travel section in a newspaper like the *San Francisco Chronicle* or a major entertainment weekly. They often carry ads for "bucket shops," agencies which sell seats for less than airline offices will. Most airlines have more seats than they can market through normal channels, so they sell their unused long-haul capacity on this "gray" market at discounts of 40-50% off the official IATA tariffs. There are well-known centers around the world where globetrotters regularly pick up onward tickets (Amsterdam, Athens, Bangkok, Hong Kong, London, San Francisco, and Singapore are only a few). Rates are competitive so check a few agencies before deciding. Despite the shady appearance, most of the bucket shops are perfectly legitimate and your ticket will probably be issued by the airline itself. Don't hand over the full price until you see it, though. Most discounted tickets look and are exactly the same as regular full fare tickets. They're usually non-refundable.

UTA French Airlines (Union de Transports Aeriens) is *the* international carrier to the French colonies in the South Pacific. Their schedules are more convenient than those of some of the others, since they're built around Tahiti rather than mere stopovers on the way to somewhere else. Their inflight meals and service are excellent, but you pay for it. UTA has a policy of keeping their ticket prices high in France, North America, Tahiti, Australia, and New Zealand. You can buy exactly the same UTA tickets for much less at bucket shops in Amsterdam, London, and Singapore. It's actually cheaper to fly from the U.S. to Rarotonga or Fiji than to fly to Tahiti! Fortunately, there are alternatives to UTA.

PACIFIC AIR ROUTES

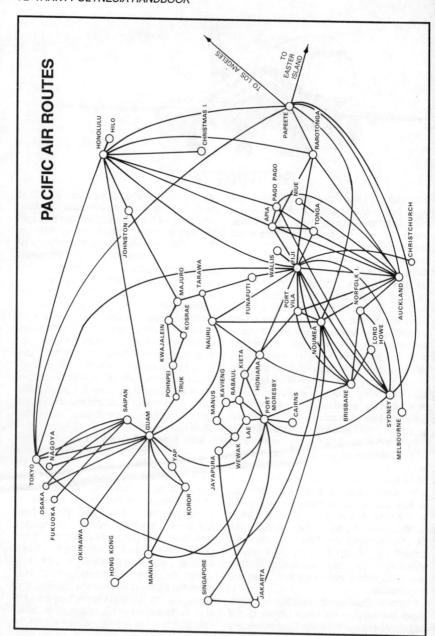

AIR SERVICES

From North America

UTA French Airlines has the most flights to Papeete, with two nonstop overnight services a week from Los Angeles and three from San Francisco. Air France, Air New Zealand, Continental, and Qantas also arrive from Los Angeles. All these companies have toll-free 800 numbers you can use to compare fares. Canadian passengers are routed through San Francisco or Los Angeles.

Flight times to Tahiti are 7.5 hours from Los Angeles, 5.5 hours from Honolulu. Most flights arrive at Papeete in the middle of the night. The Air New Zealand schedules are especially inconvenient as Tahiti is but a stopover and flight times are planned so the aircraft arrive in Auckland in the morning. Air New Zealand flights back to Los Angeles also depart at 0405 or 0525, costing you another night's sleep. At last report **Continental Airlines** had the most convenient services of the lot with three weekly overnight flights from Los Angeles to Papeete, departing in the evening and arriving in the morning at both ends.

UTA's roundtrip advance purchase excursion (APEX) fare from San Francisco or Los Angeles to Papeete is US$1081 from 9 Dec. to 23 Dec., US$976 the rest of the year. The date of outbound travel from the U.S. determines the roundtrip airfare. Tickets must be paid 14 days in advance, and there's a 35% cancelation penalty. The maximum stay on an APEX ticket is 45 days. Reduced add-on fares to the West Coast gateways are available from cities all across the U.S.

Hawaiian Airlines offers nonstop service to Papeete from Honolulu with excellent connections from Anchorage, Guam, Las Vegas, Los Angeles, Portland, Seattle, and San Francisco. Their fares are very competitive with those of the other carriers and Hawaii is thrown in as a bonus. For example, their roundtrip 14-day advance purchase excursion fares to Papeete are US$678 from Honolulu, US$849 for California/Nevada,

and US$899 from Portland, Seattle, or Anchorage. You're allowed to stay up to a year but must provide dates when booking. For only a few dollars more they'll throw in seven nights at Papeete's Hotel Tahiti or Moorea's Kaveka Beach Club with transfers—ask your travel agent to check on this. Hawaiian's Papeete-Rarotonga flight allows you to include the Cook Islands in your trip. Hawaiian also offers the best connections to Papeete from Seoul, Taipei, and Tokyo through Honolulu.

Overseas Tours (475 El Camino Real #206, Millbrae, CA 94030; tel. 415-692-4892) offers circle Pacific fares on Air New Zealand and Malaysian Airlines routed Los Angeles-Tahiti-Rarotonga-Fiji-Auckland-Sydney- Melbourne-Singapore-Kuala Lumpur-Hong Kong-Tokyo-Los Angeles, all for US$1138 (Oct. and Nov.), US$1185 (April to Sept.), or US$1299 (Dec. to March). Other variations of this ticket throw in Honolulu, Perth, Bangkok, and Taipei. This is great if you want Tahiti to be the first stop on a *big* trip.

Charter Flights

Nouvelles Frontieres Inc. handles charter flights to Papeete on **Minerve,** the largest independent French charter company. The weekly flight from San Francisco to Papeete is $599 RT. Once ticketed there's a $50 penalty to change your flight dates. In Papeete changes of date must be made 15 days in advance. Refunds (minus a $75 penalty) are only possible if the agency manages to resell your ticket, but you're forbidden to sell your own ticket to a third party. Minerve reserves the right to alter flight times up to 48 hours without compensation, but if you miss your flight you lose your money. Still, if you're sure when you'll be traveling, these prices are a couple of hundred dollars lower than anything offered by the scheduled airlines.

A few Nouvelles Frontieres offices selling these tickets include: 12 East 33rd St., 11th Floor, New York, NY 10016, tel. 212-779-0600; 209 Post St., Suite 1121, San Francisco, CA 94108, tel. 415-781-4480; 6363 Wilshire Blvd., Suite 200, Los Angeles, CA 90048, tel. 213-658-8955; 800 boulevard de

Maisonneuve Est, Montreal, PQ H2L 4M7, Canada, tel. 514-842-1450; and 1-2 Hannover St., London W1, England, tel. 01-629-7772.

From The South Pacific

Most flights from the insular South Pacific countries connect through Rarotonga in the Cook Islands. Air New Zealand has a weekly flight from Fiji to Papeete via Rarotonga. Hawaiian Airlines also flies to Papeete from the Cook Islands.

In Rarotonga you're able to link up with Polynesian Airline's **Polypass** which allows 30 days unlimited travel in the South Pacific for US$799. For an extra US$100 Papeete can be added to the Polypass, with its validity extended seven days. Restrictions are that your itinerary must be worked out in advance and can only be changed once. Travel cannot begin in Dec. or Jan. and these tickets are not sold in Papeete. Polynesian Airlines is represented around the world by Ansett Airlines of Australia. Their U.S. office is at 9841 Airport Blvd., Suite 418, Los Angeles, CA 90045 (tel. 213-642- 7487).

Virtually all UTA flights across the South Pacific from Singapore to Los Angeles call at Noumea and Papeete. This is an excellent way to combine Melanesia with Polynesia, especially if you're using a cheap ticket purchased in Singapore. Minerve also operates one Papeete-Noumea flight every two weeks (f.39,900 RT).

From Australia And New Zealand

Tahiti can usually be included as a stopover on tickets to the U.S. from Down Under. Roundtrip fares are high but check for low-season rates. Air New Zealand, Continental, and UTA all have nonstop flights between Auckland and Papeete. If you have a choice of airlines, compare flight times. Air New Zealand and Continental schedule their aircraft to land at Tahiti at night, while UTA arrives in the very early morning saving you a hotel bill.

Continental, Qantas, and UTA all have direct flights from Sydney, but only Qantas has nonstops. Qantas also offers direct service from Melbourne. The overnight UTA flights call at Noumea, but they have the big advantage of arriving at Papeete in the morning. Continental and Qantas fly by day, costing you a day in Sydney and an extra night at a hotel in Papeete.

One Australian travel agent who's no stranger in paradise is Val Gavriloff of **Hideaway Holidays,** 994 Victoria Rd., West Ryde, NSW 2114 (tel. 807-4222). Val specializes in off-the-beaten-track locations and he's often able to book hotel accommodations as part of a specially packaged program at greatly reduced rates.

From Singapore And Bangkok

The bucket shops of Southeast Asia are famous for selling air tickets at enormous discounts. The budget travelers' standby is the cheap UTA ticket from Singapore to Los Angeles with stops in Jakarta, Sydney, Noumea, Auckland, and Papeete (about US$800). To get the cheapest ticket you must shop around. These are open tickets and you can fly any flight. Often the planes are full, so book and reconfirm your next leg well ahead.

One recommended agency is **German Asian Travels Ltd.** (9 Battery Road, #14-03 Straits Trading Building, Singapore 0104; tel. 533-5466). They have the ticket mentioned above, plus a routing Singapore-Jakarta-Sydney-Noumea-Papeete-Easter Island-Santiago-Lima-Miami, all for US$1650. An extra $50 will carry you on to New York. Among the many variations available at German Asian are Singapore-Auckland-Nandi-Rarotonga-Papeete-Los Angeles (US$835) and Singapore-Sydney-Papeete-Los Angeles (US$645).

Similar tickets are available from **MAS Travel Center Ltd.** (19 Tanglin Road, #05-50 Tanglin Shopping Center, Singapore 1024; tel. 737-8877) and **K. Travel Service** (21/33 Soi Ngarmdupli, near Malaysia Hotel, Bangkok 10120, Thailand; tel. 286-1468). All of these companies have been operating for many years.

From South America

LAN Chile Airlines runs their Boeing 707 service from Santiago to Tahiti via Easter Island twice a week. The regular oneway fare Santiago-Easter-Papeete is US$950 in economy. Their 30-day roundtrip excursion fare between these points is US$1050 with a stopover on Easter Island, available year-round. The seven-day advance purchase excursion (APEX) fare for the same trip is US$899 return, plus another US$50 to stop on Easter Island. The APEX fare is only valid on certain flights (ask). If you only want to visit Easter Island, excursion tickets Papeete-Easter-Papeete are available in Papeete for around US$1000. Flights through Easter Island and Tahiti can also be included in cheap tickets from South America to Southeast Asia purchased in Europe or Singapore (but not available in Santiago or Tahiti).

From Europe

Air New Zealand offers direct weekly flights London-Papeete (via Los Angeles). Both UTA and Air France have direct flights to Papeete from Paris, (UTA via) San Francisco, and (Air France via) Los Angeles. UTA flies around the world several times a week on a routing San Francisco-Papeete-Auckland-Noumea-Sydney- Jakarta-Singapore-Bahrein-Paris- San Francisco.

The French charter company **Minerve** (4 rue Cambon, 75001 Paris) has a weekly flight Paris-San Francisco-Papeete. Although the fare is much lower than those asked by UTA or Air France, the various restrictions must be carefully considered before you put down your money. Flight dates can only be changed 15 days in advance and then with a f.5,000/500 FF penalty. A substantial administration fee is deducted to refund a Minerve

ticket. Full information is available at **Nouvelles Frontieres** offices throughout Europe.

Flights from London to Australia via the U.S. and the Pacific used to be more expensive than eastern hemisphere flights. Things have changed. Now **Trailfinders** (42-48 Earls Court Road, Kensington, London W8 6EJ; tel. 01-938-3366) includes Tahiti in their discount flights to Auckland and Sydney (561 pounds oneway). A return flight from London to Auckland with a stop in Tahiti is 825 pounds. Around the world via Tahiti is 937 pounds from London.

In Amsterdam **Malibu Travel** (Damrak 30, 1012 LJ Amsterdam; tel. 020-234912) has low round-the-world fares which include Tahiti and Easter Island. Their ticket Amsterdam-Singapore-Perth-Sydney-Tahiti-Los Angeles is 2095 Dutch guilders. The same thing but from Tahiti to Easter Island and Santiago is 3250 Dutch guilders.

In Switzerland try **Globetrotter Travel Service** (Rennweg 35, 8001 Zurich; tel. 01-211-7780) with offices in Zurich, Bern, Basel, Luzern, St. Gallen, and Winterthur. Their newsletter *Ticket-Info* lists hundreds of cheap flights, including many through Tahiti.

Student Fares

If you're a student or recent graduate you can benefit from lower student fares by booking through a student travel office. There are two rival organizations of this kind. In the U.S. **Council Travel Services** (312 Sutter St., San Francisco, CA 94108; tel. 415-421-3473) has offices in college towns right across the country. Their roundtrip student fare from California to Auckland with a stop in Papeete is US$748. Sydney and Noumea can be added for only US$20 extra. To go all the way from California to Singapore via Tahiti is

US$799. All fares quoted are low season (April to Sept.). There are no restrictions on these tickets but you do have to prove that you're really a student. In Canada try **Travel Cuts** (171 College St., Toronto, Ont. M5T 1P7; tel. 416-977-3703) with offices in all large Canadian cities.

The other such company is **Student Travel Australia** (220 Faraday St., Carlton, Melbourne, Victoria 3053; tel. 03-347-6911). In the U.S. they're called the **Student Travel Network** (7204-1/2 Melrose Ave., Los Angeles, CA 90046; tel. 213-380-2184). Both STA and STN have many branch offices in their home countries—call for the nearest.

PROBLEMS

If your flight is cancelled due to mechanical problems with the aircraft, the airline will cover your hotel bill and meals. If they reschedule the flight on short notice for reasons of their own or you're bumped off an overbooked flight, they should also pay. They may not feel obligated to pay, however, if the delay is due to weather conditions, a strike by another company, national emergencies, etc., although the best airlines still pick up the tab in these cases. But don't expect much from small commuter companies.

To compensate for "no shows," most airlines overbook their flights. To avoid being "bumped," check in early and go to the departure area well before flight time. Overbooked airlines often offer meals, rooms, and even cash to volunteers willing to relinquish their seats. In some airports flights are not called over the public address system, so keep your eyes open. Whenever you break your journey for more than 72 hours, always reconfirm your onward reservations. Failure to do so could result in the cancellation of your complete remaining itinerary. When planning your trip allow a minimum two-hour stopover between connecting flights, although with airport delays on the increase even this might not be enough. Whenever traveling always have a paperback or two, some toiletries, and a change of underwear in your hand luggage.

Baggage

Hawaiian Airlines allows two pieces of checked baggage plus a carry-on on their big jets. Surfboards and bicycles are carried for US$50 extra. If you'll be changing aircraft at a gateway city don't check your baggage straight through or it could be left behind. Collect it at the transfer point and check in again. Stow anything which could conceivably be considered a weapon (scissors, pen knife, toy gun, mace, etc.) in your checked luggage.

Tag your bag with name, address, and phone number inside and out. Get into the habit of removing used baggage tags, unless you want your luggage to travel in the opposite direction. As you're checking in, look to see if the three-letter city code on your baggage tag and the one on your boarding pass are the same. If your baggage is damaged or doesn't come out on arrival at your destination, future claims for compensation will be compromised unless you inform the airline officials *immediately* and have them fill out a written report.

Airlines usually reimburse out-of-pocket expenses if your baggage is lost or delayed over 24 hours—the amount varies from US$25-50. Your chances of getting the cash are better if you're polite but firm. Keep receipts for any money you're forced to spend to replace missing articles. Claims for lost luggage can take weeks to process. Keep in touch with the airline to show your concern; also, hang onto your baggage tag until the matter is resolved. If you feel you did not receive the attention you deserved, write the airline an objective letter outlining the case. Get the names of the employees you're dealing with so you can mention them in the letter.

ORGANIZED TOURS

Inclusive Tours

Continental Newmans Vacations with offices in Los Angeles, Toronto, Sydney, and Auckland offers six-day package tours to Moorea starting at US$799 pp (double occupancy), including airfare from Los Angeles, transportation from Tahiti to Moorea, and four nights accommodations on the island. Meals are extra. This is cheaper than a regular roundtrip plane ticket and extensions of stay are possible, combining packaged with independent travel. You must book 45 days in advance and there are penalties if you cancel. Newmans and some of the other mass-market tour operators mentioned in this section don't accept consumer inquiries, so you must work through a travel agent. **Bali Hai Holidays** (3636 4th Ave., San Diego, CA 92103) offers similar tours at similar prices.

Ted Cook's Islands in the Sun (760 West 16th St., Suite L, Costa Mesa, CA 92627; tel. 714-645-8300), founded in 1965, was the first American travel company to specialize exclusively in the South Pacific (no connection with James or Thomas). Ted offers the same cheap packages as Newmans, but with a much better selection of options. Other companies specializing in packaged holidays to Tahiti-Polynesia include **Tahiti Nui** (1750 Bridgeway, Suite 101B, Sausalito, CA 94965; tel. 415-331-8300) and **Antipodes Tours.** Any travel agent can book these trips.

If you want a quality "grand tour" of Tahiti-Polynesia and the price isn't important, consider the 16-day escorted "Polynesia Explored" package offered six times a year by **Hemphill/Harris Travel Corporation** (16000 Ventura Blvd., Encino, CA 91436). The price is US$3260 double occupancy plus US$742 airfare from Los Angeles plus US$365 interisland airfare in Tahiti, but you get the finest hotels, all meals, sightseeing tours, tour escort, transfers, and six islands on a well-planned itinerary.

Club Mediterranee offers one-week packages to their Moorea resort for US$1350-1550 from Los Angeles or San Francisco. The price includes room (double occupancy), food, watersports, airfare, and transfers. Rental bicycles are charged extra. Ask if you're allowed to extend your stay on the group ticket, allowing yourself time to see Tahiti and the other islands. Book a couple of months in advance, especially if you want to travel in July, Aug., or December. For more information on **le Club** see the Moorea chapter in this book.

In Canada check with **WestCan Treks Adventure Travel** (tel. 800-661-7265) in Calgary, Edmonton, Toronto, and Vancouver for packages and plane tickets to Tahiti-Polynesia.

Tours For Children
About the only package to Tahiti-Polynesia designed specifically for families traveling with children is the "Rascals in Paradise" program offered by **Adventure Express** (185 Berry St., Suite 5503, San Francisco, CA 94107; tel. 415-442-0799). Their groups of three to five families are met by a credentialed teacher who organizes activities for the kids, provides babysitters, children's menus and mealtimes, etc. The nine-day tour to Rangiroa operates three times a year and is US$1775 per adult, US$275 for children under 11 (US$100 for infants three and under). This includes accommodations at the Kia Ora Village and meals, but airfare is extra. Keep in mind too that these prices are based on two adults with at least one child. A single parent with child would have to pay two adult fares.

Tours For Naturalists
Perhaps the most rewarding way to visit Tahiti-Polynesia is with **Earthwatch** (Box 403, Watertown, Massachusetts 02272; tel. 617-926-8200), a nonprofit organization founded in 1971 to serve as a bridge between the public and the scientific community. Earthwatch sends teams to Moorea for two weeks each month to assist marine biologist Michael Poole in his efforts to save dolphins from the depredations of tuna fishermen. These are not study tours but an opportunity for amateurs to help out with Poole's survey of groups of spinner dolphins, kind of like a short-term scientific Peace Corps. As a research volunteer, a team member's US$1595 share of project costs is tax-deductible in the U.S. For more information contact Earthwatch at the address above, or Eve Doyle, 39 Lower Fort St., Sydney, NSW 2000, Australia (tel. 02-251-2928), or Louise Henson, 29 Coniston Ave., Headington, Oxford OX3 OAN, England.

Cruises Out Of Papeete

Windstar Sail Cruises (7205 N.W. 19th St., Suite 410, Miami, FL 33126; tel. 305-592-8008) offers cruises around the Society Islands year-round in their gigantic, four-masted *Wind Song*. Participants join the boat at Papeete. The pp price for one of 74 double, classless cabins for a seven-day cruise varies according to season: US$1895 (low), US$2195 (base), US$2495 (peak), plus US$42 port charges. Single occupancy is 50% more. Airfare to Tahiti is extra. Although this 134-meter-long, 62-meter-high Norwegian-registered ship could hardly be classed as a yacht, it is a step up from the impersonal pretention of a love boat. One of three identical high-tech vessels which also ply the Mediterranean and Caribbean, the *Wind Song's* sails are fully computer-controlled saving on both fuel and crew! Though the ship can heel up to six degrees, balast tanks and stabilizers ensure a smooth ride. The Windstar fleet, commissioned at Le Havre, France, from 1986-88, deserves credit for experimenting with an alternative energy (the wind!).

Five times a year **Sitmar Cruises** (39 Martin Place, Sydney, NSW 2000, Australia; tel. 239-9000) includes five days in Tahiti-Polynesia in the 14-night South Pacific voyages of the cruiseship *Fairsea* out of Sydney. The A$3030-4960 pp double-occupancy price includes the flight back to Sydney or out to Papeete to meet this huge vessel carrying hundreds of passengers.

Society Expeditions Inc. (3131 Elliott Ave., Suite 700, Seattle, WA 98121, USA; tel. 206-285-9400) offers luxury cruises from Tahiti to Easter I. twice a year. Their *Society Explorer* uses zodiacs to ferry the 100 passengers ashore at remote islands like Raivavae, Rapa, Mangareva, and Pitcairn. The double-occupancy cabins begin at US$4650, plus another US$1200 roundtrip airfare from the States. Also check with **Victor Emanuel Nature Tours** (Box 33008, Austin, Texas 78764, USA; tel. 512-328-5221) which sometimes offers birdwatching tours based on the same cruise at slightly lower prices.

For information on cruises to the Marquesas Islands aboard the freighter *Aranui*, see "Getting Around" below.

Yacht Tours

Ocean Voyages Inc. (1709 Bridgeway, Sausalito CA 94965-1994; tel. 415-332-4681) arranges yacht cruises throughout Tahiti-Polynesia. They have eight boats based in the islands which take groups of two to eight on one- or two-week trips. For example the *Epicurien II*, a luxurious 19-meter sloop with three double cabins, is US$8980 a week for four persons or US$9800 a week for six. The *Epicurien* is based at Raiatea and available for use among the Leeward Islands. The 14-meter ketch *Roscop* is also based at Raiatea (US$5040 a week for four, US$7680 a week for six), but will tour as far as the Marquesas upon request. The *Esope*, a smaller 13.5-meter boat costing US$3750 a week for two, US$4200 a week for three, US$4950 a week for four, is designed for custom charters to the outer islands of Polynesia. Scuba diving is possible at extra cost on some boats (ask).

If there's only one or two of you and these prices seem high, Ocean Voyages also offers yacht cruises on fixed one-week (US$1095 pp) and two-week (US$1795 pp) itineraries, usually between Huahine and Bora Bora. Individuals are welcome and there are about 10 departures a year from April to November. Trips should be booked and paid for at least 60 days in advance. All prices above are inclusive of meals, but not drinks or airfare to Tahiti. Ocean Voyages is a reliable, experienced company which takes all the worry out of chartering. A similar operation in Australia is **Charter World** (1285 Dandenong Road, Chadstone 3148; tel. 03-568-4220).

Bareboat yacht charters in the Leeward Islands are offered by **The Moorings Ltd.** (1305 US 19 South, Ste. 402, Clearwater, FL 34624; tel. 813-535-1446). Prices begin at US$1785 a week for a small yacht accommodating four and go up to US$3248 weekly for a large eight-person sailing boat. "Sail-away gourmet" provisioning is US$26 pp a day

INTRODUCTION 79

(plus US$38 a day for a cook, if required). If you're new to sailing a skipper can be hired at US$58 a day. The charterer is responsible for the skipper/cook's provisions. Security insurance is US$10 a day and local tax 3%. All charters are from noon to noon. Compared to the luxury hotels this is still good value! More information is provided in the Raiatea chapter of this book.

BY SAILING YACHT

Papeete is one of the prime yachting centers of the South Pacific. If you don't have your own boat and can't afford a charter, signing on as crew is an alternative. After a month at sea some of the original crew may have flown home or onward, opening a place for you at Tahiti. Cruising yachts are recognizable by their foreign flags, wind-vane steering gear, sturdy appearance, and laundry hung out to dry. Ask around. It's also quite possible to arrive this way. The **Seven Seas Cruising Association** (Box 1256, Stuart, FL 34995, USA; tel. 407-287-5615) is in touch with yachties all around the Pacific.

Most yachts sail from California to Tahiti via the Marquesas or Hawaii, then on to Rarotonga, Vava'u, Suva, and New Zealand. In the other direction, you'll sail on the westerlies from New Zealand to a point south of the Australs, then north on the trades to Tahiti. Some 300 yachts leave the U.S. West Coast

for Tahiti every year, almost always crewed by couples or men only. Most stay in the South Seas about a year before returning to North America. Cruising yachts average about 150 km a day. When calculating time allow a month to get from the West Coast to Hawaii, then another month from Hawaii to Papeete. Be aware of the hurricane season Nov. to March as few yachts will be cruising at this time.

If you've never crewed before it's better to try for a short passage the first time. Once at sea there's no way they'll turn around to accommodate a seasick crew member. Good captains evaluate crew on personality and attitude more than experience, so don't lie. Be honest and open when interviewing with a skipper—a deception will soon become apparent.

To crew on a yacht you must be willing to wash and iron clothes, cook, steer, keep watch at night, and help with engine work. Other jobs might include changing and resetting sails, cleaning the boat, scraping the bottom, pulling up the anchor, climbing the main mast to watch for reefs, etc. Expense-sharing crew members pay US$50 or more a week per person. Crew members are very much under the control of the captain who's entitled to hold their passports and onward plane tickets. If there's any chance you'll want to do something like this read up on sailing before you leave home.

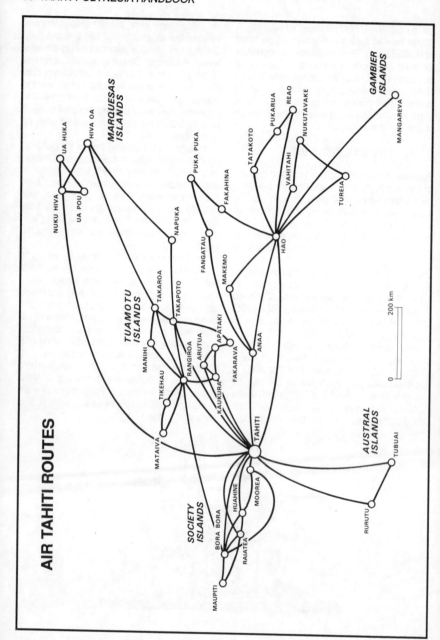

AIR TAHITI ROUTES

GETTING AROUND

BY AIR

The domestic carrier, **Air Tahiti** (B.P. 314, Papeete; tel. 42-63-11), flies to 35 airstrips in every corner of Tahiti-Polynesia. They don't allow stopovers on their tickets, so if you're flying RT from Tahiti to Bora Bora and want to stop at Raiatea on the way out and Huahine on the way back, you'll have to purchase four separate tickets (total US$250). No student discounts are available.

A better deal than point-to-point fares are the Air Tahiti "Air Passes." These are valid 28 days and one stopover can be made on each island included in the package. For f.38,000, for example, you can go Papeete-Moorea-Huahine-Raiatea-Bora Bora-Rangiroa-Manihi-Papeete. Otherwise pay f.42,000 to visit the main Society and Austral islands. Tahiti Tourist Board offices around the world act as Air Tahiti agents, so inquire at any of them about Air Passes.

Air Tahiti tickets are refundable at the place of purchase, but you must cancel your reservations at least two hours before flight time to avoid a 25% penalty. Do this in person and have your flight coupon amended. "No shows" are charged f.2000 to make a new reservation. Always reconfirm your onward flight from an outer island and beware of planes leaving 20 minutes early.

The main Air Tahiti office in Papeete is upstairs in Fare Tony, the commercial center off boulevard Pomare just west of rue Georges Lagarde. They're closed on weekends. Check carefully to make sure all the flights listed in their published timetable are actually operating! Any travel agency in Papeete can also book Air Tahiti flights for the same price and the service tends to be better than at the Air Tahiti office itself.

If you buy your ticket locally the baggage allowance on domestic flights is 10 kg. If your flight tickets were purchased prior to your arrival in Tahiti-Polynesia, however, the allowance is 20 kg. Exceptions are flights to Hiva Oa, Ua Huka, and Ua Pou where the small size of the aircraft makes the 10-kg limit mandatory for everyone. Fresh fruit and vegetables cannot be carried from Tahiti to the Austral, Tuamotu, Gambier, or Marquesas islands.

Air Tahiti uses 46-seat ATR 42 aircraft and 19-seat Twin-Otter 300s. Smoking aboard the aircraft is prohibited. On Bora Bora, Maupiti, and Nuku Hiva passengers are transfered from the airport to town by boat. This ride is included in the airfare at Bora Bora, but costs extra at Maupiti (f.400) and Nuku Hiva (f.800).

Air Moorea (B.P. 6019, Papeete; tel. 42-44-29 or 56-10-34) has hourly flights between Tahiti and Moorea (f.2500 OW). Reservations are not necessary on this commuter service. Just show up 15 minutes before the flight you wish to take. The Air Moorea terminal is in a separate building at the east end of Faaa Airport. You can also charter an Air Moorea plane.

Air Tahiti Services

Air Tahiti flies from Papeete to Hauhine (f.7645), Raiatea (f.8795), and Bora Bora (f.10,405) several times a day. Twice a week there's a direct connection from Moorea to Huahine (f.8095), as well as a flight from Raiatea to Maupiti (f.4865). The twice weekly transversal flight between Bora Bora and Rangiroa (f.15,600) avoids backtracking to Papeete.

Flights between Papeete and Rangiroa (f.12,000) operate daily, continuing on from Rangiroa to Manihi (f.7400) three times a week. Air Tahiti has numerous flights to the East Tuamotu atolls and Mangareva, but these are usually closed to tourists due to French military activity in the area. Check with Air Tahiti or the Tahiti Tourist Board for the current situation.

Flights bound for the Marquesas are the longest, most expensive, and most heavily booked of Air Tahiti's services. Try to get confirmed reservations before arriving in Tahiti-Polynesia if you'll be heading this way. A weekly Twin-Otter flight links Rangiroa to Hiva Oa (f.28,700). More commonly used is the direct ATR 42 service from Papeete to Nuku Hiva (f.36,700), operating twice a week. This connects with weekly services from Nuku Hiva to Ua Pou (f.4500), Hiva Oa (f.7800), and Ua Huka (f.4500). If you know you'll be going on to Ua Pou or Ua Huka, get a through ticket there from Papeete; the fare is the same as a ticket only as far as Nuku Hiva.

The Austral Group is better connected to Papeete with flights to Rurutu (f.16,000) and Tubuai (f.17,900) twice a week. These operate Papeete-Rurutu-Tubuai-Papeete one day, Papeete-Tubuai-Rurutu-Papeete the other, with the leg Tubuai-Rurutu costing f.7300. Rurutu gets a third weekly flight.

Air Tahiti is fairly reliable. Still, you should never schedule a flight back to Papeete on the same day that your international flight leaves Tahiti. It's always best to allow a couple of days leeway in case there's a problem with the air service. Maybe save your travels to Moorea or around Tahiti till the end.

BY SEA

The best way to really get the feel of Tahiti-Polynesia is to take a field trip by ship. And there's a certain romance and adventure to taking an interisland freighter. You can go anywhere by copra boat, including islands without airstrips and popular resorts like Moorea, Bora Bora, and Rangiroa. Ships leave Papeete several times a day for the different island groups. You'll meet local people and fellow travelers, and receive a gentle introduction to the island of your choice. Problems about overweight baggage, tight reservations, and airport transport are eliminated, and travel by ferry or passenger-carrying freighter is four times cheaper than the plane. Sea sickness, cockroaches, diesel fumes, and the heavy scent of copra are all part of the experience.

Below you'll find specific information on the main interisland boats. The tourist office in Papeete also has lists. Prices and schedules have been fairly stable over the past few years and new services are being added all the time. Lots of visitors travel this way to Moorea and Bora Bora, so don't feel intimidated if you've never done it before.

For the cheapest ride and the most local color, travel deck class. There's usually an awning in case of rain and you'll be surrounded by Tahitians, but don't count on getting a lot of sleep if you go this way—probably no problem for one night, right? Otherwise take a cabin which you'll share with three or four other passengers, still a lot cheaper than an airplane seat. Food is usually not included (ask), but may be sold on board. On a long trip you're better off taking all your own food than buying a meal plan.

For any boat trip farther than Moorea check the schedule and pick up tickets the day before at the company office listed below. If you're headed for a remote island outside the Societies or want cabin class, visit the office as far in advance as possible. Except on the *Aranui* it's not possible (nor recommended) to book your passage before arriving on

Tahiti. If you really want to go there'll be something leaving around the date you want. On an outer island be wary when someone, even one of the crew, tells you the departure time of a ship: they're as apt to leave early as late.

Boat trips are always smoother westbound than eastbound because you go with the prevailing winds. Take this into consideration if you plan to come back by air or vice versa. *Bon voyage.*

Ferry To Moorea

Two large car ferries named *Tamarii Moorea* (B.P. 9012, Papeete; tel. 43-76-50) shuttle five times a day between Papeete and Vaiare on Moorea (f.700 OW, bicycle f.200). Departure times are posted at the ferry landing on the Papeete waterfront. Reservations are not required: buy your ticket just before you board. Stroll around the open upper deck and enjoy the scenic 1.5-hour crossing. Coffee is available at the snack bar below. *Le truck* meets all ferries on the Moorea side and will take you anywhere on that island for f.200.

Ships To The Leeward Islands

You have lots of choices if you're headed for the Leeward Islands. Two ships, *Taporo IV* and *Temehani*, depart Papeete every Mon. afternoon around 1700. *Taporo IV* calls at Huahine (at 0200) and Raiatea (at 0600), reaching Bora Bora at 1100 Tuesday. It departs for Papeete once again Tues. at 1300, calling at Raiatea (at 1600) and Huahine (at 1930), reaching Papeete early Wed. morning (you can stay on board till dawn). *Temehani* follows a similar route, but turns around at Tahaa.

Wednesday at 1700 *Taporo IV* makes the shorter trip to Huahine, Raiatea, and Tahaa only, while *Temehani* goes on to Bora Bora.

LEEWARD ISLAND FERRY SCHEDULES

MV *Taporo IV* 1030 tons (160 passengers)
MV *Raromatai Ferry* (550 passengers, 50 cars)

	Northbound					Ports of Call		Southbound				
A	C	E	G	I				B	D	F	H	J
1700	1700	1700	2030	2030	dep.	Papeete	arr.	0500	0300	0330	0530	0530
0200	0200	0200	0600	0600	arr.	Huahine	dep. 2030		1600	1700	2000	2000
0400	0400	0400	0700	0700	dep.	Huahine	arr. 1930		1500	1600	1900	1900
0600	0600	0600	0900	0900	arr.	Raiatea	dep. 1700		1200	1400	1630	1630
0800	0800	0800	1000	1000	dep.	Raiatea	arr. 1600		1100	1300	1500	1530
	0900	0900	1100		arr.	Tahaa	dep.	1000	1200			1430
		1000	1130		dep.	Tahaa	arr.		1100			1400
1100		1200	1330	1300	arr.	Bora Bora	dep. 1300			0800	1200	1200

A— *Taporo IV* departs Papeete Monday
B— *Taporo IV* departs Bora Bora Tuesday
C— *Taporo IV* departs Papeete Wednesday
D— *Taporo IV* departs Tahaa Thursday
E— *Taporo IV* departs Papeete Friday
F— *Taporo IV* departs Bora Bora Sunday
G— *Raromatai Ferry* departs Papeete Tuesday
H— *Raromatai Ferry* departs Bora Bora Thursday
I— *Raromatai Ferry* departs Papeete Friday
J— *Raromatai Ferry* departs Bora Bora Sunday
Schedules can be modified during holidays or otherwise.

Taporo IV undertakes a third weekly voyage from Papeete Fri. at 1700 to all four Leeward Islands. Although they do make an effort to stick to their timetables these times are approximate—ask at the company offices. Beware of voyages marked "carburant" on the schedules: they don't take passengers.

Temehani is slightly larger than *Taporo IV* and has a good covered sleeping area for deck passengers. They'll open the hold for you if there's not too much cargo. You won't get much sleep, however, due to noise and commotion during the early-morning stops. No mattresses or bedding are provided for deck passengers. *Taporo IV* has a huge inside dormitory with 50 beds.

Fares on the *Taporo IV* to Huahine are f.1100 deck, f.1540 dorm; to Raiatea f.1300 deck, f.1820 dorm; to Bora Bora f.1500 deck, f.2100 dorm. *Temehani* charges the same deck fare, but also has small four-bed cabins which are twice the deck fare. If you're only traveling between the islands of Huahine, Raiatea, and Bora Bora the interisland deck fare is f.550 each. A bicycle is about f.600 extra, but if you say nothing and load/unload it yourself you may not be charged. (Don't tell anyone you read that here!) No meals are included, although *Taporo IV* has a snack bar. Take food with you.

The **Bureau Temehani** (B.P. 9015, Papeete; tel. 42-98-83) is near the interisland wharf at Motu Uta and *Taporo IV* has an office in the next room. The main *Taporo IV* ticket agency is the **Compagnie Francaise Maritime de Tahiti** (B.P. 368, Papeete; tel. 42-63-93) in Fare Ute. This company also runs the *Taporo V* from Papeete to Maiao monthly. (The CFMT itself has a place in local history, having been founded around 1890 by Sir James Donald who had the contract to supply limes to the British Pacific fleet. At the turn of the century Douglas' schooner, the *Tiare Taporo*, was the fastest in Polynesia. The CFMT is still the Lloyd's of London agent.)

Cabin or dormitory space on the ships is recommended—try to reserve at least a week ahead. Deck passage is usually available right up to departure day (except holidays), but buy your ticket in advance as there can

be problems for non-Tahitians trying to pay once the ship is underway. In the Leeward Is. buy a ticket from the agent on the wharf as soon as the boat arrives. If you've got some time to kill before your ship leaves Papeete, have a look around the coconut-oil mill beside the wharf.

The **Compagnie Maritime des Iles Sous-Le-Vent** ,(85 rue des Remparts prolongee, Fare Ute, Papeete; tel. 43-90-42); (open weekdays 0730-1145/1330-1630), handles the car-carrying, 550-passenger *Raromatai Ferry*. This ship departs from the landing behind the tourist office downtown for Huahine, Raiatea, Tahaa, and Bora Bora Tues. and Fri. at 2030. Tickets for walk-on passengers are usually available just prior to departure. Prices from Papeete to Bora Bora are f.3600 for a seat in the salon, f.5500 in a four-berth cabin, f.500 for a bicycle. A double "cruise cabin" is f.16,000 for two people.

The *Raromatai* salon is a spacious sitting room with aircraft-style pullman seats, but French TV shows blast at you non-stop and the over-powerful air conditioning means you freeze at night unless you have a sleeping bag. The *Raromatai* rolls a lot in rough weather. Between the Leeward Is. the *Raromatai* is a good deal (f.1000 salon interisland) for these daylight crossings with an excellent open promenade deck on top, but on the overnight run between Papeete and Huahine *Taporo IV* and *Temehani* are better value.

Ships To The Austral Islands

The *Tuhaa Pae II* leaves twice a month for the Austral Is.: f.22,750 cabin for the 10-day RT (no meals included). Food is f.2300 pp a day extra. Their office (Societe Anonyme d'Economie Mixte de Navigacion des Australes, B.P. 1890, Papeete; tel. 43-15-88) is at the interisland wharf on the west side of the copra sheds. Some of the cabins are below the waterline and very hot. The rear deck has a diesely romantic feel, for a day or two. For sanitary reasons the seats have been removed from the ship's toilets (squat). The *Tuhaa Pae II* calls at Rimatara, Rurutu, Tubuai, Raivavae, and very occasionally Rapa Iti. Maria Atoll is visited annually. Another ship, the *Manava III,* occasionally goes to Tubuai and Raivavae only.

Ships To The Tuamotus And Gambiers

Many smaller copra boats such as the *Auura Nui II, Manava II, Manava III, Maina Nui, Matariva, Rairoa Nui, Rauhatu, Saint-Corentin, Saint-Xavier Marie-Stella,* and *Vaihere* service the Tuamotu and Gambier groups. Ask around the large workshops west of the interisland wharf. Some of the ships serving the forbidden military zone in the Tuamotus won't accept tourists as passengers (see page 182).

The *Manava II* (tel. 43-76-17) runs to the northern Tuamotus (Rangiroa, Tikehau, Mataiva, Ahe, Manihi, Takaroa, Takapoto, Aratika, Kauehi, Fakarava, Toau, Apataki, Arutua, and Kaukura) once or twice a month. There are no cabins: the deck passage to Rangiroa is f.2400. Due to the vessel's routing it can take only 22 hours to go from Papeete to Rangiroa but 72 hours to return. The *Manava III* (tel. 43-32-65) departs Papeete for Rangiroa every Monday.

The *Ruahatu* (tel. 43-86-82) runs to the southern Tuamotu and Gambier islands monthly. The deck fare to Rikitea is f.5500 OW for the nine-day trip, plus f.1700 a day for food. A roundtrip on the *Ruahatu* is f.60,000 deck, food included. The *Vaihere* (tel. 43-76-58) plies to the southern Tuamotus (Anaa, Faaite, Katiu, Hikueru, Marokau, Hao, Amanu, and Anaa) twice a month. Deck passage to Anaa or Faaite is f.2000 (no cabins) with f.1700 a day extra for food.

The *Kauaroa Nui* (office opposite the Bureau Temehani at the interisland wharf) has three departures a month for the middle Tuamotus (Fakarava, Faaite, Raraka, Katiu, and Makemo), leaving Thurs. afternoons. Roundtrip fares are f.8000 deck, f.14,000 in a basic double cabin, f.20,000 in a a/c single cabin, no meals included. For information on travel restrictions within the Tuamotu Is. see page 182.

The motor vessel *Dory* leaves every Mon. at 1600 from the Moorea ferry wharf for Tikehau (Tues. 1100), Rangiroa (Tues. 1500), Ahe, Manihi, Arutua, and Apataki, arriving back in Papeete Fri. at 1100 (f.6000 RT). The OW fare to Ahe is about US$30 and there are no cabins. The *Dory* delivers frozen bread, chicken, and ice cream to the islands, picking up fish.

Ships To The Marquesas

The *Taporo V* departs Papeete Thurs. at 1400 every two weeks for Tahuata, Hiva Oa, Nuku Hiva, and Ua Pou. Three to eight hours are spent at each port. The RT fare is f.30,000 deck, f.45,000 cabin, or f.14,000 deck and f.20,625 cabin OW to Hiva Oa. Food is included but it's marginal, so take extras like grapefruit and nuts. Bring your own bowl. Meals are served at 0600, 1100, and 1800. No pillows or towels are supplied in the cabins. The shower is open three hours a day. The agent is Compagnie Francaise Maritime (B.P. 368, Papeete; tel. 42-63-93) at Fare Ute. If you can avoid taking the meals you should be able to cut the fare in half.

The *Tamarii Tuamotu II* departs every five weeks to the Marquesas, f.5500 OW deck (no cabins), plus f.1750 a day for basic meals. This ship runs from Papeete direct to the Marquesas, but visits several of the Tuamotu atolls on the way back. It calls at every inhabited bay in the Marquesas (this alone takes 12 days). Check at their city office (Vonken et Cie., B.P. 2606, Papeete; tel. 42-95-07), corner of rue des Remparts and Ave. du Prince Hinoi.

The *Aranui,* a luxury passenger-carrying freighter, cruises monthly between Papeete and the Marquesas. The ship calls at most of the inhabited Marquesas islands, plus a couple of the Tuamotus. The routing might be Papeete-Takapoto-Ua Pou-Nuku Hiva-Hiva Oa-Fatu Hiva-Hiva Oa-Ua Huka-Nuku Hiva-Ua Pou-Manihi-Papeete. There's a vigorous daily program with fairly strenuous hikes (included in the tour price). The only docks in the Marquesas are at Taiohae, Hakahau, and Atuona; elsewhere everyone must get in and out of whale boats and wade ashore, a problem for elderly passengers. Still, the *Aranui* is fine for the adventuresome visitor who wants to see a lot in a short time. The cabins aboard the *Aranui* are a little cramped, but the food's good and the largely French roster of passengers is congenial. There's a large covered area on deck where deck passengers can sleep.

This 80-meter, German-built freighter has been refurbished for tourists. It's clean and pleasant compared to the other schooners, but more expensive, far more than *Taporo V.* Forty passengers are accommodated in a/c cabins and another 40 are given mattresses on the bridge deck. Deck passage for a 16-day, eight-island cruise to the Tuamotus and Marquesas costs US$1130 roundtrip; the cheapest cabin is US$1920 roundtrip, all meals included. One-way deck fares on the *Aranui* are more affordable. Their office (Compagnie Polynesienne de Transport Maritime, B.P. 220, Papeete; tel. 42-62-40) is at the interisland wharf adjacent to Bureau Temehani. In the U.S. contact Jules C. Wong, 114 Sansome St., Suite 1102, San Francisco, CA 94104 (tel. 415-421-6066). Schedules are regular and unlike *Tamarii Tuamotu II*, no permit from the harbormaster is required for travel on the *Aranui*.

LOCAL TRANSPORT

By Road

Polynesia's entertaining *le truck* provides an unscheduled passenger service on Tahiti and some outer islands. Passengers sit on long wooden benches in back and there's no problem with luggage. Fares are fairly low and often posted on the side of the vehicle. You pay through the window on the right side of the cab. Drivers are generally friendly and will stop to pick you up anywhere if you wave—they're all privately owned so no way they'd miss a fare! On Tahiti the larger *trucks* leave Papeete for the outlying districts periodically throughout the day until 1700; they continue running to Faaa Airport and the Maeva Beach Hotel until around 2200. On Huahine and Raiatea service is usually limited to a trip into the main town in the morning and a return to the villages in the afternoon. On Moorea and Bora Bora they meet the boats from Papeete.

Car rentals are available at most of the airports served by Air Tahiti, but they ain't cheap. On the big islands of Tahiti and Raiatea there's often a mileage charge, whereas all rentals on Moorea and Bora Bora come with unlimited mileage. Public liability insurance is included by law, but gas and collision damage waver (CDW) insurance are extra. If you can get a small group together consider renting a minibus for a do-it-yourself island tour. Unless you have a major credit card you'll have to put down a cash deposit on the car. Your home driver's license will be accepted, although visitors under the age of 25 are usually refused service unless they show a major credit card. Those under 21 cannot rent a car and you must have had your driver's license for at least a year. Rental scooters are not available on Tahiti but you can usually get them elsewhere. A strictly enforced local regulation requires you to wear a helmet *(casque)* at all times (f.5000 fine).

Two traffic signs to know: a white line across a red background indicates a one-way street, while a slanting blue line on a white background means no parking. At unmarked intersections in Papeete the driver on the right has priority. As in France and the U.S., driving is on the righthand side of the road. The speed limit is 40 kph in Papeete, 60 kph around the island. Drive with extreme care in congested areas—traffic accidents are frequent.

Taxis are a ripoff in Papeete, but may be usable elsewhere. Always verify the fare before getting in. The hitching is still fairly good in Polynesia, although local residents along the north side of Moorea are getting tired of it. Hitching around Tahiti is only a matter of time.

By Ocean Kayak

Ocean kayaking is experiencing a boom in Hawaii, but Polynesia is still virgin territory. Many islands have a sheltered lagoon readymade for the excitement of kayak touring, but this new transportation mode hasn't yet arrived. So you can be a real independent 20th century explorer! Many airlines accept folding kayaks as checked baggage at no charge.

Companies like **Long Beach Water Sports** (730 E. 4th St., Long Beach, CA

a pirogue *Tahiti*

90802; tel. 213-432-0187) sell inflatable one-person Tradewind sea kayaks for US$1,395 (US$1,545 for the two-person variety), fully equipped. LBWS runs four-hour sea kayaking classes ($40) every Sat. morning and all-day advanced classes ($70) about once a month. Part of the tuition is deductible from the price of any kayak you purchase from them. They also rent kayaks by the day or week.

Adventure Kayaking International (Box 61609, Honolulu, HI 96822; tel. 808-988-5515) also sells the Tradewind. Better yet, they offer five-day kayak tours to Molokai and Na Pali (US$625 from Honolulu), allowing you to experience ocean kayaking while seeing Hawaii. Five-hour kayak trips to Kahana Bay (US$39) depart Waikiki every morning. AKI has other expeditions around Hawaii and to the South Pacific, so write for their brochure. They also sell low-cost air tickets from the U.S. mainland to Hawaii in conjuction with their tours.

For a better introduction to ocean kayaking than is possible here check at your local public library for *Sea Kayaking, A Manual for Long-Distance Touring* by John Dowd (Seattle: University of Washington Press, 1981) or *Derek C. Hutchinson's Guide to Sea Kayaking* (Seattle: Basic Search Press, 1985).

By Canoe
Never attempt to take a dugout canoe through even light surf: you'll be swamped. Don't try to pull or lift a canoe by its outrigger: it will break. Drag the canoe by holding the solid main body. A bailer is *essential* equipment. If you get off the beaten track, more than likely a local friend will offer to take you out in his canoe.

By Bicycle
Cycling in Polynesia? Sure, why not? You'll be able to go where and when you please, stop easily and often to meet people and take photos, save money on taxi fares—really *see* the islands. It's great fun, but it's best to have bicycle-touring experience beforehand. Most roads are flat along the coast but be careful on coral roads, especially inclines: if you slip and fall you could hurt yourself badly.

A sturdy, single-speed mountain bike with wide wheels, safety chain, and good brakes might be best. Thick tires and a plastic liner between tube and tire will reduce punctures. Know how to fix your own bike. Take along a good repair kit (pump, puncture kit, freewheel tool, spare spokes, cables, chain links, assorted nuts and bolts, etc.) and a repair manual; bicycle shops are poor to non-existent in the islands. Don't try riding with a backpack: sturdy, waterproof panniers (bike bags) are required. You'll also want a good lock, and refuse to lend your bike to *anyone*.

Many international airlines will carry a bicycle free as checked luggage. Take off the pedals and panniers, turn the handlebars sideways, and clean off the dirt before checking in (or use a special bike-carrying bag). Air Tahiti won't usually accept bikes on their small planes. Boats sometimes charge a token amount to carry a bike; other times it's free. Bicycling on the island of Tahiti is risky due to wild devil-may-care motorists, but most of the outer islands (Moorea included) have excellent uncrowded roads. It's best to use *le truck* on Tahiti, though a bike will come in real handy on the other islands where *le truck* is rare. The distances are just made for cycling!

INTERNATIONAL AIRPORT

Faaa Airport (PPT) is 5.5 km southwest of Papeete. A taxi into town is f.1000 (f.1200 on Sun.), double that after 2200. *Le truck* up on the main highway will take you to the same place for only f.95 (f.150 at night) and they start running around 0530. There's a self-serve tourist information counter at the airport. The airport information numbers are tel. 42-60-61 and 42-95-71. The Banque Indosuez (f.300 commission) opens weekdays 0730-1600, and one hour before and after the arrival and departure of all international flights. The airport Banque Socredo branch (no commission fee) is up the stairs beside the snack bar on the left, open during banking hours only. If you don't change at these you can use cash U.S. dollars to pay for your *truck* into town.

The airport luggage storage counter is open from 0700-1700 and two hours prior to international departures (you hope). They charge f.120 per piece per day (f.300 for surfboards, etc.). A bookstore in the terminal and duty free shops in the departure lounge can help you spend those leftover Pacific francs. The Fare Hei just outside the terminal sells shell and flower leis for presentation to arriving or departing passengers.

Many flights to Tahiti arrive in the middle of the night, but if you go up the stairs to the terrace, turn left, and stretch out on the clean floor the security guard will wake you gently at dawn. All passengers arriving from Samoa or Fiji must have their baggage fumigated upon arrival, a process which takes about two hours (don't laugh if you're told this is to prevent the introduction of the "rhinoceros" into Polynesia—they mean the rhinoceros *beetle*). Fresh fruits, vegetables, and flowers are prohibited entry. There's no airport tax.

One nice touch is the welcoming committee the Tahiti Tourist Board sends out to meet every incoming international flight. As *pareu*-clad musicians strum their guitars or ukuleles, a smiling *vahine* puts a white *tiare Tahiti* blossom behind your ear. There's no catch, it's only their way of saying *maeva*.

SOCIETY ISLANDS

The Windward Islands

Tahiti, Moorea, Tetiaroa

*King Pomare II of Tahiti
(reigned 1803-1821)*

Parau na te Varua ino (Words of the Devil); *Paul Gauguin; National Gallery of Art, Washington;
gift of the W. Averell Harriman Foundation in memory of Marie N. Harriman*

TAHITI

Tahiti, largest of the Societies, is an island of legend and song lying in the eye of Polynesia. Though only one of 118, this lush island of 131,309 inhabitants (1988) is paradise itself to most people. Here you'll find an exciting city, big hotels, restaurants, nightclubs, things to see and do, valleys, mountains, reefs, trails, and history, plus transportation to everywhere. Since the days of Wallis, Bougainville, Cook, and Bligh, Tahiti has been the eastern gateway to the South Pacific.

In 1891 Paul Gauguin (goh-GANN) arrived at Papeete after a 63-day sea voyage from France. He immediately felt that Papeete "was Europe—the Europe which I had thought to shake off...it was the Tahiti of former times which I loved. That of the present filled me with horror." So Gauguin left the town and rented a native-style bamboo hut in Mataiea on the south coast, where he found happiness in the company of a 14-year-old Tahitian *vahine*, whose "face flooded the in-terior of our hut and the landscape round about with joy and light." Somerset Maugham's *The Moon and Sixpence* is a fictional tale of Gauguin's life on the island.

Legends created by the early explorers, amplified in Jean-Jacques Rousseau's "noble savage" and taken up by the travel industry, make it difficult to write objectively about Tahiti. Though the Lafayette Nightclub is gone from Arue and Quinn's Tahitian Hut no longer graces Papeete's waterfront, Tahiti remains a delightful, enchanting place. In the late afternoon, as Tahitian crews practice canoe racing in the lagoon and Moorea gains a pink hue, the romance surfaces. If you steer clear of the traffic jams and congestion in commercial Papeete and avoid the tourist ghettos west of the city, you can get a taste of the magic Gauguin encountered. In fact, it's only on the outer islands of Polynesia, away from the tourists and military complexes, that the full flavor lingers.

Orientation

Almost everyone arrives at Faaa International Airport five km west of Papeete, the capital and main tourist center of Tahiti-Polynesia. East of Papeete are Arue and Mahina with a smattering of hotels and things to see, while south of Faaa lie the commuter communities Punaauia, Paea, and Papara. On the narrow neck of hour-glass Tahiti is Taravao, a refueling stop on your 117-km way around Tahiti Nui. Tahiti Iti is a backwater, with dead-end roads on both sides. Boulevard Pomare curves around Papeete's harbor to the tourist office near the market—that's where to begin. Moorea is clearly visible to the northwest and the mornings are softly, radiantly calm.

THE LAND

The island of Tahiti accounts for almost a quarter of the land area of Tahiti-Polynesia. Like Hawaii's Maui, Tahiti was formed by two ancient volcanoes joined at the isthmus of Taravao. The rounded, verdant summits of Orohena (2,241 meters) and Aorai (2,066 meters) rise in the center of Tahiti Nui and deep valleys radiate in all directions from these central peaks. Steep slopes drop abruptly from the high plateaus to coastal plains. The northeast coast is rugged and rocky without a barrier reef and thus exposed to intense, pounding surf; villages lie on a narrow strip between mountains and ocean. The south coast is broad and gentle with large gardens and coconut groves; a barrier reef shields it from the sea's fury.

Tahiti Iti (also called Taiarapu) is a peninsula with no road around it. Mount Rooniu (1,323 meters) is its heart. The populations of big *(nui)* and small *(iti)* Tahiti are concentrated in Papeete and along the coast; the interior of both Tahitis is almost uninhabited. Contrary to the popular stereotype, mostly brown/black beaches of volcanic sand fringe this turtle-shaped island. To find the white/golden sands of the travel brochures you must cross over to Moorea.

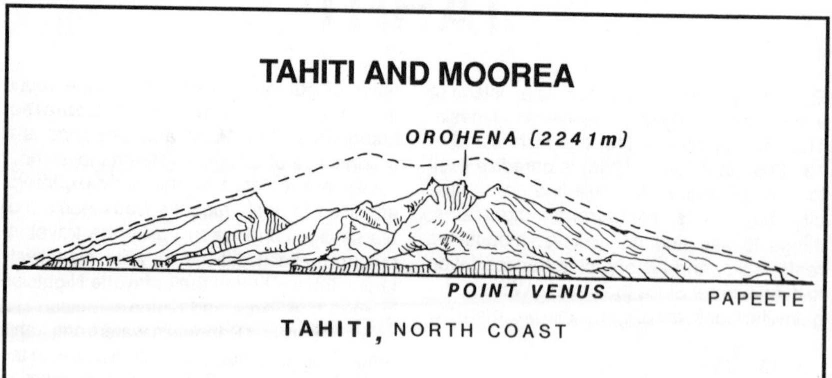

TAHITI AND MOOREA

OROHENA (2241m)

POINT VENUS   PAPEETE

TAHITI, NORTH COAST

TOHIVEA (1212m)

MOOREA, EAST COAST

Papeete as it looked around the turn of the century

PAPEETE

Papeete (pa-pay-EH-tay) means "Water Basket." The most likely explanation for this name is that in the old days islanders used to fetch water at a spring behind the present Territorial Assembly in calabashes enclosed in baskets. In the 1820s whalers began frequenting its port, which offered better shelter than Matavai Bay. It became the seat of government when young Queen Pomare settled here in 1827. The French governors who "protected" the island from 1842 also used Papeete as their headquarters.

Today Papeete is the political, cultural, economic, and communications hub of Tahiti-Polynesia. Some 68,701 (1988) persons live in this cosmopolitan city and its satellite towns, Faaa, Pirae, and Arue—over half the people on the island. "Greater Papeete" extends for 32 km from Paea to Mahina. In addition, some 4,000 French soldiers are stationed here, mostly hardened foreign legionnaires and policemen. The French Navy maintains facilities in the harbor area to support its nuclear testing program in the Tuamotus. If you don't see any ships it means there's about to be another test and they're down there patrolling the site.

Since the opening of Faaa Airport in 1961 Papeete has blossomed with new hotels, expensive restaurants, bars with wild dancing, radio towers, skyscrapers, and electric rock bands pulsing their jet-age beat. Where a nail or red feather may once have satisfied a Tahitian, VCRs and Renaults are now in demand. Over 70,000 registered vehicles jam Tahiti's 200 km of roads. Noisy automobiles and motorbikes clog Papeete's downtown and roar along the boulevards buffeting pedestrians with pollution and noise. Crossing the street you can literally take your life in your hands.

Yet along the waterfront the yachts of many countries rock luxuriously in their Mediterranean moorings (anchor out and stern lines ashore). Many of the boats are permanent homes for expatriate French working in the city. "Bonitiers" moored opposite the Vaima Center fish for *auhopu* (bonito). One should not really "tour" Papeete, just wander about without any set goal. Visit the highly specialized French boutiques, Chinese stores trying to sell everything, and Tahitians clustered in the market. Avoid the capital on weekends when life washes out into the countryside; on Sunday afternoons it's a ghost town. Explore Papeete, but make it only your starting point and not a final destination.

Orientation

Thanks to airline schedules you'll probably arrive at the crack of dawn. Change a travelers cheque at the airport bank or use a US$1 bill to take a *truck* to Papeete market. The helpful tourist office on the waterfront nearby opens early, as does the Banque Socredo branch nearby. You'll probably want a hotel in town for the first couple of nights to attend to "business." Reconfirm your flights, check out the boats or planes, then kick back.

A trip around the island will occupy a day if you're waiting for connections and Papeete itself can be fun. Fare Ute, north of French naval headquarters, was reclaimed with material dredged from the harbor in 1963. West across a bridge, past more military muscle, is Motu Uta where you may catch your boat. For a day at the beach take a *truck* to Point Venus (see below).

SIGHTS

Papeete

Begin your visit at teeming Papeete **market**, a sensual delight. You'll see Tahitians selling fish, fruit, root crops, and breadfruit, Chinese gardeners with their tomatoes, lettuce, and other vegetables, and Frenchmen or Chinese offering meat and bakery products. The colorful throng is especially picturesque from 1600-1700 when the fishmongers spring to

life. The biggest market of the week begins around 0500 Sun. morning and is over by 0730. You can catch a *truck* to anywhere from here.

The streets to the north of the market are lined with two-story Chinese stores built after the great fire of 1884. **Notre Dame Catholic Cathedral** (1875) is on rue du General de Gaulle 1.5 blocks southwest of the market. Notice the Polynesian faces and the melange of Tahitian and Roman dress on the striking series of paintings of the crucifixion inside.

Farther down on rue de Gaulle is Place Tarahoi. The **Territorial Assembly** on the left occupies the site of the former royal palace demolished in 1966. The adjacent residence of the French high commissioner is private, but the assembly and its lovely gardens are worth a brief visit. In front of the entrance gate is a monument to **Pouvanaa a Oopa** (1895-1977), a Tahitian WW I hero who struggled all his life for the independence of his country. The plaque on the monument says nothing about Pouvanaa's fight for independence and against the bomb!

Beside the post office across the busy avenue from Place Tarahoi is **Bougainville Park**. A monument to Bougainville himself, who sailed around the world in 1766-69, is flanked by two old naval guns. One, stamped "Fried Krupp 1899," is from the German raider *Seeadler* which ended up on the Maupihaa reef in 1917; the other is off the French gunboat *Zelee* sunk in Papeete harbor by German cruisers in 1914.

Much of the bureaucracy works along Ave. Bruat just west, a gracious tree-lined French provincial avenue. You may observe French justice in action at the **courthouse** (weekdays 0800-1100/1400-1600). The public gallery is up the stairway and straight ahead. Farther up Ave. Bruat, beyond the War Memorial, are the colonial-style French army barracks, **Quartier Broche**.

Back on the waterfront just before the Protestant church is the **Tahiti Perles Center** (B.P. 850, Papeete; tel. 43-85-58). A black-pearl museum (weekdays 0800-1730, Sat. 0900-1200; admission free) and aquarium are the main attractions, but look around the

1. the beach near Club Med, Moorea (Don Pitcher); 2. a peak on Moorea (Tahiti Tourist Board)

1. Mouaroa or "Shark's Tooth," Moorea (Paul Bohler); 2. Papeete, Tahiti (Tahiti Tourist Board)

Matavai Bay, Tahiti, as it appeared in the early 19th century

showroom where the famous Gambier black pearls are sold. A 20-minute video presentation shown on request explains how cultured black pearls are "farmed" in the Gambier Islands.

Next to the pearl museum is Paofai, the headquarters of the Evangelical Church in Tahiti-Polynesia with a church (rebuilt 1980), public cafeteria, girl's hostel, and health clinic. The British consulate occupied the hostel site from 1837 to 1958 and George Pritchard had his office here. Continue west along the bay past the outrigger racing canoes to the "neo-Polynesian" **OTAC Cultural Center** (1973) which houses a library, snack bar, notice boards, and auditoriums set among pleasant grounds. The municipal swimming pool is beyond.

Back east of the downtown is the Catholic **Archbishop's Palace** (1869), a lonely remnant of the Papeete that Gauguin saw. To get there take the road behind the Catholic Cathedral, keep straight, and ask for the *archeveche catholique*. Without doubt, this is the finest extant piece of colonial architecture in a territory where historic buildings are fast disappearing. The park grounds planted in citrus and the modern open-air church nearby also merit a look.

Bain Loti

If you'd like to make a short trip out of the city, go to the corner of rue Paul Gauguin and rue Albert Leboucher near the market and take a MAMAO-TITIORO *truck* to the **Bain Loti**, three km up the Fautaua Valley from the Mormon Temple. A bust of writer Pierre Loti marks the spot where he had the love affair described in *The Marriage of Loti,* but the area has been spoiled by tasteless construction. Since the valley is part of a water catchment you're not permitted to walk farther up, the most beautiful part.

Back on Ave. Georges Clemenceau near the Mormon Temple is the impressive **Kanti Chinese Temple,** built in 1986. On the fourth floor at **Mamao Hospital** (1967) nearby you can peep at newborn babies through the windows!

East of Papeete

Point Venus and the tomb of Pomare V at Arue (pronounced a-roo-AY) can be easily done as a half-day sidetrip from Papeete by *truck* (12 km each way). Begin by taking a MAHINA *truck* from the market to the **Hotel Taharaa** (PK 8.1) on One Tree Hill. There's a superb view of Point Venus, Tahiti, and Moorea from the "Governor's Bench" on the knoll just beyond the hotel entrance. In Matavai Bay below the Tahara'a, Capt. Samuel Wallis anchored in 1767 after having "discovered" Tahiti.

Go into the hotel itself (part of the Hyatt Regency chain) to see the Polynesian artifacts and historical displays tastefully arrayed

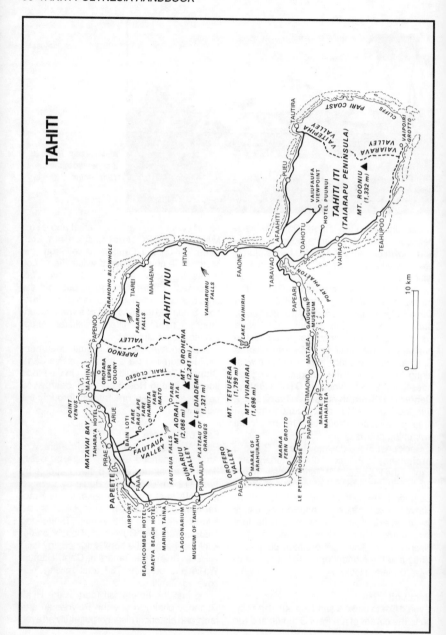

in showcases around the lobby. Outside the gift shop downstairs is a free cold water fountain. The Mahana Bar by the pool nearby offers two drinks for the price of one during happy hour 1700-1800. This hotel was built in 1968 on a spectacular series of terraces down the hillside to conform to a local regulation that no building should be more than two-thirds the height of a coconut tree.

Capt. James Cook (1728-1779) as painted at the Cape of Good Hope by John Webber, 1776

Catch another *truck* or walk on to **Point Venus** (PK 10). Captain Cook camped on this point between the river and the lagoon during his visit to observe the transit of the planet Venus across the Sun on 3 June 1769. Captain Bligh also occupied Point Venus for two months in 1788 while collecting breadfruit shoots for transportation to the West Indies. Bligh moved his ship over to Arue, where the Yacht Club now is, at Christmas 1788. On 5 March 1797, the first members of the London Missionary Society landed here, as a monument recalls. From Tahiti Protestantism spread throughout Polynesia and as far as Vanuatu.

Today there's a beautiful park on the point with a 25-meter-high lighthouse (1867) among the palms and ironwood trees. A great trunk of wood inscribed "Wallis 1767," "Bougainville 1768," and "Cook 1769" was placed

there for the bicentenary of the observation of the transit of Venus in 1969, even though Bougainville never came near Point Venus. The view of Tahiti across Matavai Bay is superb and twin-humped Orohena, highest peak on the island, is in view (you can't see it from Papeete itself). Topless sunbathing is common on the wide dark sands along the bay. Weekdays, Point Venus is a peaceful place, the perfect choice if you'd like to get away from the rat race in Papeete and spend some time at the beach (weekends it gets crowded).

To get in a little **hiking** take the road inland by the bridge just east of the Point Venus turnoff. You can drive a car 3.5 km along the Tuauru River past several ugly garbage dumps, then bushwhack up the valley through a forest of wild orchids. There are many river crossings along the way, so wear rubber booties or immersible tennis shoes. In his *Journal of Researches* Charles Darwin described a hike he made up this way in Nov., 1835.

As you're returning to Papeete stop to visit the **tomb of King Pomare V** at PK 4.7 Arue, five km outside the city. The mausoleum was built in 1879 for Queen Pomare IV, but her remains were subsequently removed to make room for her son, Pomare V, who died of drink in 1891. Paul Gauguin witnessed the funeral. A century earlier on 13 Feb. 1791 his grandfather, Pomare II, then nine, was made first king of Tahiti on the great *marae* (Polynesian temple) which once stood on this spot. Pomare II, the first Christian convert, built a 215-meter-long version of King Solomon's Temple here. Nothing remains of either temple.

AROUND THE ISLAND

A 117-km Route de Ceinture (Belt Road) runs right around Tahiti Nui, the larger part of this hourglass-shaped island. Construction began in the 1820s as a form of punishment. For orientation you'll see red-and-white kilometer stones, called PK *(point kilometrique),* along the inland side of the road. These are numbered in each direction from

Papeete cathedral, meeting at Taravao. Go clockwise to get over the most difficult stretch first; also, you'll be riding on the inside lane of traffic and less likely to go off a cliff in case of an accident (an average of 55 people a year are killed and 700 injured in accidents on the island). If you need a friend to take along pick up Bengt Danielsson's *Tahiti, Circle Island Tour Guide* at a Papeete bookstore before you set out. Southern Tahiti is much quieter than the northwest, whereas from Paea to Mahina it's even hard to slow down as tailgating motorists roar behind you.

The Northeast Coast
The coast is very rugged all along the northeast side of the island. The **leper colony** at Orofara (PK 13.2) was founded in 1914. Previously the colony was on Reao atoll in the Tuamotus, but this proved too remote to service. Some 50 patients are housed at Orofara today.

the "buffoon" of the leper colony, Tahiti

Surfers ride the waves at Chinaman's Bay, Papenoo (PK 16). The bridge over the broad **Papenoo River** (PK 17.1) allows a view up the largest valley on Tahiti.

At the **Arahoho Blowhole** (PK 22) jets of water shoot up through holes in the lava rock beside the highway. Just a little beyond it a road to the right leads to the three **Faarumai Waterfalls**. Vaimahuta Falls is accessible on foot in five minutes along the easy path to the right across the bridge. The trail to the left leads to two more waterfalls, but it's more difficult and even impassible if the river is high. The farthest falls has a pool deep enough for swimming. Bring insect repellent. Beware of theft if you park a rental car at these falls.

At **Mahaena** (PK 32.5) is the battleground where 441 well-armed French troops defeated a dug-in Tahitian force twice their size on 17 April 1844 in the last fixed confrontation in the French-Tahitian War. The Tahitians carried on a guerrilla campaign another two years until the French captured their main mountain stronghold.

The French ships *La Boudeuse* and *L'Etoile* carrying explorer Louis-Antoine de Bougainville anchored by the southernmost of two islets off **Hitiaa** (PK 37.6) on 6 April 1768. Unaware that an Englishman had visited Tahiti a year before, Bougainville christened the island "New Cythera" after the Greek isle where love goddess Aphrodite rose from the sea. A plaque near the bridge recalls the event. The clever Tahitians recognized a member of Bougainville's crew as a woman disguised as a man. An embarrassed Jeanne Baret entered history as the first woman to sail around the world.

From the bridge over the Faatautia River at PK 41.8 **Vaiharuru Falls** are visible in the distance. The American filmmaker John Huston intended to make a movie of Herman Melville's *Typee* here in 1957. When Huston's other Melville film *Moby Dick* became a box office flop the idea was dropped.

Tahiti Iti
At Taravao (PK 53), on the strategic isthmus joining the two Tahitis where the PKs meet,

Capt. Louis-Antoine de Bougainville

is an **old fort** built by the French in 1844 to cut off the Tahitians who had retreated to Tahiti Iti after the battle mentioned above. Germans were interned here during WW II and the fort is still in use today.

The small assortment of grocery stores, banks, gasoline stations, and restaurants at Taravao make it a good place to break your trip around the island, but accommodations in this area are inadequate. If you have your own transportation three roads are explorable on rugged Tahiti Iti. If you're hitching or traveling by *truck* choose the Tautira route.

A paved nine-km road runs straight up the Taravao Plateau from just before the hospital in Taravao. If you have a car and only time to take one of Tahiti Iti's three roads, this one should be your choice. At the 600-meter level on top is the **Vaiufaufa Viewpoint** with a breathtaking view of both Tahitis. No one lives up here: in good weather it would be possible to pitch a tent on the grassy hill above the reservoir at the end of the road (or sleep in your car if it's raining). The herds of cows grazing peacefully among the grassy meadows give this upland an almost Swiss air. A paved sideroad near the viewpoint cuts down to join the Tautira road.

An excellent 18-km highway runs east from Taravao to **Tautira,** where Spaniards from Peru attempted to establish a Catholic mission in 1774; it lasted for only one year. Scottish author Robert Louis Stevenson stayed at Tautira for two months in 1888 and called it "the most beautiful spot, and its people the most amiable, I have ever found."

The road peters out a few km beyond Tautira. Obstructions by landowners and high cliffs make it impractical to try hiking right around the Pari Coast to Teahupoo. Intrepid sea kayakers have been known to paddle the 30 km around, although a wild four-km stretch is not protected by reefs.

The unoccupied beach at the mouth of the **Vaitepiha River** near Tautira is a perfect campsite. A dirt road runs two km up the right bank of the river, where you could find more secluded places to camp. Hike beyond the end of the road for a look at this majestic, unoccupied valley and a swim in the river. In the dry season rugged backpackers could hike south across the peninsula to the Vaiarava Valley and Teahupoo in two days (guide necessary). The ruins of at least three old *maraes* are at the junction of the Vaitia and Vaitepiha rivers a couple of hours inland, and it's reported *tikis* are hidden in there.

The third road on Tahiti Iti runs 18 km along the south coast to Teahupoo. At the bottom of the hill below Hotel Puunui is a **marina** with an artificial white-sand beach (admission f.300) where outrigger canoes may be rented for f.500 an hour. The marina restaurant offers a salad bar (f.1000) at lunchtime weekends. American pulp Western writer Zane Grey had his fishing camp near here in the '30s. Just east of the marina is a natural white-sand beach. **Restaurant Anne de Bretagne** (tel. 57-14-07) faces this beach (crepes from f.250 all day on weekends, fish and chips for f.900). Tahiti's best surfing is possible out there in the pass, but you'll need a boat.

The **Teahupoo** road ends abruptly at a river crossed by a narrow footbridge. There's an excellent mountain view from this bridge, but walk east along the beach to capture one of the only remaining glimpses of outer-island Polynesian lifestyle remaining on Tahiti. After a couple of km the going becomes difficult due to yelping dogs, seawalls built into the lagoon, fences, fallen trees, and *tapu* signs. Beyond is the onetime domain of "nature men" who tried to escape civilization by living alone with nature in there over half a century ago.

Three hours on foot from the end of the road is **Vaipoiri Grotto**, a large water-filled cave best reached by boat. Try hiring a motorized canoe or hitch a ride with someone at the end of the road. Beyond this the high cliffs of Te Pari terminate all foot traffic along the shore; the only way to pass is by boat. All the land east of Teahupoo is well fenced off, so finding a campsite would involve getting someone's permission.

Gauguin Museum

Port Phaeton on the southwest side of the Taravao Isthmus is an excellent harbor. Timeless oral traditions tell that the first Polynesians to reach Tahiti settled at Papeari (PK 52—measured now from the west). In precontact times the chiefly family of this district was among the most prestigious on the island.

The **Gauguin Museum** (B.P. 7029, Taravao; tel. 57-10-58; open daily 0900-1700,

Teha'amana, who lived with Gauguin at Mataiea from 1892-93, was Gauguin's great love and is mentioned often in Noa Noa.

f.350) is at PK 51.2 in Papeari District. The museum, opened in 1965, tells the painter's tormented life story and shows the present location of his works throughout the world. A couple of his minor woodcarvings and prints are exhibited.

Ex-Paris stockbroker Paul Gauguin arrived at Papeete in 1891 at age 43 in search of the roots of "primitive" art. He lived at Mataiea with his 14-year-old mistress Teha'amana for a year and a half, joyfully painting. In 1893 he returned to France with 66 paintings and about a dozen woodcarvings which were to establish his reputation. Unfortunately, his exhibition flopped and Gauguin returned to Tahiti a second time, infected with V.D. and poor, settling at Punaauia. After a failed suicide he recovered somewhat and obtained a minor post in the colonial administration. In 1901 an art dealer in Paris commissioned Gauguin to do a series of works. His financial problems alleviated, the painter left for Hiva Oa, Marquesas Is., to find an environment uncontaminated by Western influences. During the last two years of his life at Atuona Gauguin's eccentricities put him on the wrong side of the ecclesiastical and official hierarchies. He died in 1903 at age 53, a near outcast among his countrymen in the islands, yet today a Papeete street and school are named after him!

The two-meterish, two-ton stone *tiki* on the museum grounds is said to be imbued with a sacred *tapu* spell. Tahitians believe this *tiki*, carved on the island of Raivavae hundreds of years ago, still lives. When it was to be moved from Papeete in 1965, no Tahitian would handle it. Finally four Marquesans were made a deal they couldn't refuse. A curse is said to befall all who touch the *tiki*.

A **botanical gardens** rich in exotic species is part of the Gauguin Museum complex. If you're on foot visit the gardens first, before going into the museum; the grounds are open to the left as soon as you pass the gate. If you see the gardens second, you'll be charged f.200 extra admission. (Motorists can't escape as the ticket office faces the parking lot.) The park along the beach behind the museum snack bar is free to everyone. This garden was created in 1919-21 by the American botanist Harrison Smith (1872-1947) who introduced over 200 new species to the island, among them the sweet grapefruit (pomelo), mangosteen, rambuntan, and durian. The gardens would be a lot more interesting if the plants were labeled.

Lake Vaihiria

From PK 47.6 a rough track leads 12 km up to **Lake Vaihiria**, Tahiti's only lake. The route follows the Vaihiria River, which has been harnessed for hydroelectricity. Two km up the road you'll encounter a white hydro substation and the first of a series of PISTE PRIVEE signs advising motorists that the road is closed to non-residents, though open to pedestrians. This regulation is not always enforced and in dry weather a rental car could continue another five km to a dam and the lower power station.

A km beyond is an archaeological site with restored *marae*. Three km beyond this (11 km from the main road) is a second dam and an upper (larger) power station. Beyond this point only a four-wheel drive jeep could proceed, passing prominent DANGER signs, another km up a steep concrete track to Lake Vaihiria itself.

Sheer cliffs and spectacular waterfalls squeeze in around the spring-fed lake, and the shore would make a fine campsite (overrun by mosquitos). Native floppy-eared eels known as *puhi taria* up to 1.8 meters long live in these cold waters. With its luxuriant vegetation this rain-drenched 473-meter-high spot is one of the most evocative on the island. The track proceeds up and over to the Papenoo Valley, a four-hour trip by four-wheel-drive jeep.

The South Coast

The **International Golf Course Olivier Breaud** (B.P. 4202, Papara; tel. 57-40-32) at PK 41, Atimaono, stretches up to the mountainside on the site of "Terre Eugenie," a cotton and sugar plantation established by Scotsman William Stewart at the time of the U.S. Civil War (1863). Many of today's Tahitian Chinese are descended from Chinese laborers imported to do the work. A novel by A. T'Serstevens, *The Great Plantation,* is set here. The present 6,355-meter, 18-hole course (run by the Tahiti Tourist Board) was laid out in 1970 with a par 72 for men, par 73 for women. If you'd like to do a round the green fees are f.2000 and clubs rent for another f.2300 (daily 0800-1700). The Tahiti Open in June attracts professionals from around the Pacific.

The **Marae of Mahaiatea** (PK 39.2) at Papara was once the most hallowed temple on Tahiti. Captain Cook's botanist Joseph Banks wrote: "It is almost beyond belief that Indians could raise so large a structure without the assistance of iron tools." Less than a century later planter William Stewart raided the *marae* for building materials and storms did the rest. Today it's only a rough heap of stones, but still worth visiting for its aura and setting. The unmarked turnoff is a hundred meters west of Chez Mahaiatea Restaurant, then straight down to the beach.

Surfers take the waves at Papara Beach (PK 38), one of the best sites on Tahiti. By the church at **Papara** (PK 36) is the grave of Dorence Atwater (1845-1910), U.S. consul to Tahiti from 1871-1888. Atwater's claim to fame dates back to the American Civil War when he recorded the names of 13,000 dead Union prisoners at Andersonville Prison, Georgia, from lists the Confederates had been withholding. Himself a Union prisoner, Atwater escaped with his list in March 1865. When you consider the concern the U.S. government still shows about troops allegedly missing in Vietnam, the importance to them of Atwater's contribution is clear. Atwater's tombstone provides details.

At PK 31 stop for some "Eau de Roche, Pape Mato"—fill your water bottle with the fresh mineral water! **Maraa Fern Grotto** (PK 28.5) is also by the road just across the Paea border. An optical illusion, the grotto at first appears small but is quite deep. Some Tahitians believe *varua ino* (evil spirits) lurk in the shadowy depths. Others say that if you follow an underground river back from the grotto you'll emerge at a wonderful valley in the spirit world. Paul Gauguin wrote of a swim he

Tahiti's Mahaiatea Marae as illustrated in James Wilson's A Missionary Voyage (London, 1799): This 11-step pyramid was once the largest pagan temple on the island.

took across the small lake in the cave; you're also welcome to jump in the ice-cold black water.

The Southwest Coast

The **Marae Arahurahu** at PK 22.5, Paea, is up the road from Magasin Laut—take care, the sign faces Papeete, not visible if you're traveling clockwise. This temple, lying in a tranquil verdant spot under high cliffs, is perhaps Tahiti's only remaining pagan mystery. The ancient open altars built from thousands of cut stones were completely restored in 1954 (open daily). Historical pageants recreating pagan rites are performed here during the July festivities.

For some hiking Paea's **Orofero Valley** is recommended; camping might be possible up beyond the end of the road (six km). From the main highway take the first road inland south of the large Catholic church by the Vaiatu River at PK 20. You can drive a car three km up. When you get to the *tapu* sign, park, cross the river, and continue up the other side on foot. A jeep track runs another three km up the valley (half-hour walk) through half a dozen river crossings (wear rubber booties or zorries). At the end of the road a tall waterfall is to the left and the trail continues ahead. Orofero is one of the few Tahitian valleys free of trash!

At PK 20 by the mouth of the Vaiatu River **handicrafts** are sold in a pavilion beside the tiny post office. Three long rectangular compounds comprise **Marae Taata,** just off the road inland from PK 19.

The West Coast

On Fishermen's Point, Punaauia, is the **Museum of Tahiti and the Islands** (B.P. 6272, Faaa; tel. 58-34-76; open Tues. to Sun. 0930-1615; admission f.300). Located in a large, modern complex on the lagoon about a km down a narrow road from PK 15.1, this worthwhile museum has four halls devoted to the natural environment, the origins of the Polynesians, Polynesian culture, and the history of Polynesia. Outside is a huge double-hulled canoe and Capt. Cook's anchor from Tautira. Most of the captions are in French, Tahitian, and English (photography allowed).

When the waves are right you can sit on the seawall behind the museum and watch the Tahitian surfers bob and ride, with the outline of Moorea behind. On your way back to the main highway from the museum, look up to the top of the hill at an **old fort** used by the French to subjugate the Tahitians in the 1840s. The crown-shaped pinnacles of **Le Diademe** (1,321 meters) are also visible from this road.

If you want to see pollution on a massive

scale follow the route up the once-beautiful **Punaruu Valley** behind the Punaauia industrial zone (PK 14.8). You can drive a normal car five km up a valley incredibly trashed out with garbage dumps all the way. At the end of the valley is a water catchment and, although the way leads on to the fantastic **Plateau of Oranges,** entry is forbidden. Tahitian enterprises dump their refuse in valleys all around the island, but this has got to be the ugliest!

Gauguin had his studio at PK 12.6 Punaauia from 1896-1901, but nothing remains of it; his *Two Tahitian Women* was painted here. The **Lagoonarium** (B.P. 2381, Papeete; tel. 43-62-90) below the lagoon behind Captain Bligh Restaurant at PK 11.4, Punaauia, provides a vision of the underwater marinelife of Polynesia safely behind glass. The big tank full of black-tip sharks is a feature. Entry is f.500 pp, open Tues. to Sat., half price for restaurant customers. The shark feeding takes place around noon.

Punaauia and Paea are Tahiti's "Gold Coast," with old colonial homes along the lagoonside and *nouveau riche* villas dotting the hillside above. At PK 8 is the turnoff for the RDO bypass to Papeete, Tahiti's only superhighway!

On the old airport road just north are Tahiti's biggest hotels: the **Sofitel Maeva Beach** (PK 7.5) and **Beachcomber** (PK 7), both worth a stop—though their beaches are polluted. From the point where the Beachcomber is today the souls of deceased Tahitians once lept onto their journey to the spirit world. A sunset behind Moorea's jagged peaks across the Sea of the Moon from either of these hotels is a spectacular finale to a circle-island tour. If you're there by 1730 you'll also coincide with happy hour at the bar.

If you've been living rough on your way around the island and could use a wash, patronize the public toilets at Faaa Airport (PK 5.5). The runway here was created in 1959-61, using material dredged from the lagoon or trucked in from the Punaruu Valley. The municipality of Faaa has declared itself a nuclear-free zone; a monument at a Faaa intersection recalls Tahitian resistance to French colonialism. As you re-enter Papeete, **Uranie Cemetery** (PK 1.5) is on your right.

The west coast of Tahiti can also be visited as a daytrip from Papeete; start by taking a *truck* to Paea and work your way back. *Trucks* back to Papeete from the vicinity of the Maeva Beach Hotel run late into the night, but the last one from the Museum of Tahiti is around 1630.

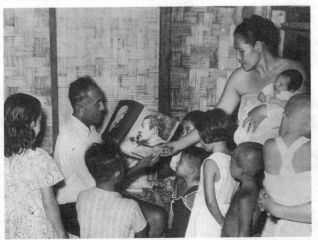

This photo, taken by Bengt Danielsson in the 1950s and published in his book Gauguin in the South Seas, *shows Emile Marae a Tai, son of Gauguin and his vahine, Pau'ura a Tai. The resemblance is striking.*

You'll get this unobstructed view of Le Diademe from the Mt. Aorai Trail.

MOUNTAIN CLIMBING

Tahiti's finest climb is to the **summit of Aorai** (2,066 meters), second highest peak on the island. A beaten track all the way to the top makes a guide optional. Food, water, flashlight, and long pants *are* required, plus a sleeping bag and sweater if you plan to spend the night up there. Some maps show "chalets" and "refuges" along the trail, but don't count on it. At last report they'd all been blown away by hurricanes. There are places to pitch a tent at Hamuta (750 meters), Fare Mato (1,403 meters), Fare Ata (1,836 meters), and on the summit itself, but try to keep your weight down as this climb is tough.

Le Belvedere (B.P. 5588, Pirae; tel. 42-73-44), an expensive restaurant near the trailhead at Far Rau Ape (600 meters), offers a free *truck* from Papeete at 1100 and 1700 for clients (f.3500 a meal), the easiest way to get there. Taxis want f.3000 for the eight-km trip to the restaurant. Few people live up there, so hitching would be a matter of finding some tourists headed for the restaurant. Weekends are best for this.

Just above the restaurant is the French Army's Centre d'Instruction de Montagne,

where you must sign the register. From Fare Rau Ape to the summit takes seven hours: 1.5 hours to Hamuta, another two to Fare Mato (good view of Le Diademe, not visible from Papeete), then 2.5 to Fare Ata, where most hikers spend the first night in order to cover the last 40 minutes to the summit the following morning.

The view from Aorai is magnificent, with Papeete and many of the empty interior valleys in full view. To the north is Tetiaroa atoll, while Moorea's jagged outline fills the west. Even on a cloudy day the massive green hulk of neighboring **Orohena** (2,241 meters) often towers above the clouds like Mt. Olympus. A bonus is the chance to see some of the original native vegetation of Tahiti, which survives better at high altitudes and in isolated gulleys. In good weather Aorai is exhausting but superb; in the rain it's a disaster.

When the author of this book climbed Aorai in 1984 the trip could be done by anyone in reasonable physical shape. Since then the route seems to have deteriorated. In mid-1988 we received this from Rolf Reinstrom, a reader from Altenmoor, Germany: "It's now very, very dangerous with sheer slopes and slippery, crumbly ridges. The shelters have disppeared. There are long ridges with nothing to hold onto. I lost my backpack and almost my life when a whole part of the trail broke off. Very few people do the trail and most of the few are French soldiers. I didn't reach the top and I don't mind. Otherwise it's beautiful scenery up there." Let us know what you find if you're crazy enough to venture up that way!

Orohena is seldom climbed since the way involves even more of the risks Rolf encountered. For the record the route up Orohena begins at the townhall *(mairie)* of Mahina opposite the military laboratories. You can drive about six km to the 500-meter level, where the road deadends at PRIVATE PROPERTY signs and warnings about dogs.

These and other hikes on Tahiti are led on weekends and holidays by Pierre Florentin (B.P. 5323, Pirae; tel. 43-72-01), a professional mountain guide with years of experience. His rates are high but worth considering by small groups of serious climbers concerned about both safety and success. Otherwise write: Alpine Club of Tahiti, B.P. 2435, Papeete (tel. 48-10-59).

OTHER WINDWARD ISLANDS

Mehetia is an uninhabited high island (435 meters) about 100 km east of Tahiti. It's less than two km across with no lagoon and landing is difficult. Fishermen from the south coast of Tahiti visit occasionally.

Maiao or Tapuaemanu, 70 km southwest of Moorea, is a low coral island with an elongated 154-meter-high hill at the center. On each side of this hill is a large greenish-blue lake. Around Maiao is a barrier reef with a pass on the south side accessible only to small boats. In 1988, 231 people lived on 8.3-sq-km Maiao, all Polynesians. Europeans and Chinese are not allowed to reside on the island as a result of problems with an Englishman, Eric Trower, who attempted to gain control of Maiao for phosphate mining in the 1930s.

There are no tourist accommodations; an invitation from a resident is required to stay. There's no airstrip. For information on the monthly supply ship from Papeete contact the **Compagnie Francaise Maritime de Tahiti** (B.P. 368, Papeete; tel. 42-63-93) at Fare Ute. A roundtrip voyage on this ship would at least give you a glimpse of Maiao.

TETIAROA

Tetiaroa, 42 km north of Tahiti, is a low coral atoll with a turquoise lagoon and 13 deep green coconut-covered islets totaling 490 hectares. Only small boats can enter the lagoon. Tahuna Iti has been designated a seabird refuge, the lagoon a marine reserve. On three-km-long Rimatuu islet may be seen the remains of Polynesian *maraes* and giant *tuu* trees.

Once a Tahitian royal retreat, in 1904 the Pomare family gave it to the British dentist Walter Williams to pay their bills. Dr. Williams, who was also the British consul from 1923 to 1935, had a daughter who sold Tetiaroa to actor **Marlon Brando** in 1962. Brando came to Tahiti in 1960 to play Fletcher Christian in the MGM film *Mutiny on the Bounty.* He ended up marrying his leading lady, Tarita;

MAIAO

TEPUATAU POINT

LAKE ROTO ITI

(154 m)

VAVATUNU POINT

PAPAROA POINT

LAKE ROTO RAHI

LAGOON

AUPARIRUA POINT

0   1 km

APOOTOO PASS

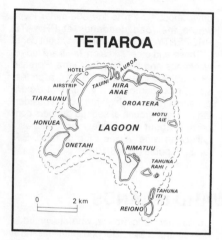

she and her family still run the small tourist resort on Tetiaroa. Marlon visits every year on his daughter's birthday.

Getting There

A reservation office (B.P. 2418, Papeete; tel. 42-63-03) in the Air Moorea terminal at Faaa Airport arranges flying visits to Tetiaroa. A seven-hour daytrip including airfare, bird island tour, and lunch is f.25,000 pp. If you arrange this trip through your hotel their com-

mission will boot the price up to f.29,000 pp. To spend the night at the **Tetiaroa Village Hotel** in a rustic bungalow with private bath and all meals add f.15,000 s, f.24,000 d, f.27,000 t, to the per-person tour price. An attempt has been made to keep things as natural as possible, so—though the price may suggest it—don't expect a luxury resort. The hotel is often closed for extended periods.

Less expensive visits to Tetiaroa Can be arranged at **Tahiti Mer et Loisirs** (B.P. 3488, Papeete; tel. 43-97- 99), in a houseboat on the Papeete waterfront opposite the post office. Their yacht cruises to the atoll are f.12,000 pp for one day, f.21,000 pp for two days (f.19,000 pp on weekends), including snorkeling gear, trips ashore, and all meals. Longer stays are possible, for example, f.41,500 pp a week all inclusive. Scuba diving is available at f.2500.

The powerboat *Revatua* (B.P. 3734, Papeete; tel. 43-28-21) also offers cruises to Tetiaroa, departing the Papeete waterfront at 0600, returning at 1800 (f.13,000 pp including bird island visit, snorkeling, and picnic lunch). A weekend trip to Tetiaroa on the *Revatua* is f.22,000 pp all inclusive; for f.34,000 pp you can spend two days at Maiao.

PRACTICALITIES

ACCOMMODATIONS

Almost all of the places to stay are in the congested Mahina to Punaauia strip engulfing Papeete and Faaa Airport. Representatives of the various hotels often meet incoming flights and most provide free transport to their establishments. If they're not there, call them up and ask. The hotels are listed below clockwise in each category, beginning in Punaauia.

Cheaper Hotels Around Papeete

The only inexpensive place in Punaauia is **Chez Solange** (Solange Vandeputte, B.P. 4230, Papeete; tel. 58-21-07) at PK 13, Socredo Residence #123 up in the subdivision from Coco's Restaurant. This informal guesthouse (with cooking facilities) has a double room with shared bath (f.3000 d) and a four-bed dorm (f.1500 pp), Continental breakfast included. Solange goes out of her way to help female travelers, but call first as all the beds may be taken (three-night minimum stay).

Coco's Hostel (Coco Dexter, B.P. 8039, Tahiti; tel. 42-83-60), Lot 39, Puurai, Faaa, provides the closest budget accommodations to the airport: bunks in the dorm at f.1500 pp and four individual rooms for f.4000 d. You can camp on the grass beside the house for f.500. Two-nights' lodging must be paid in advance upon arrival, and check-out time is 1100. It's a little cramped but there's a swimming pool, washing machine (f.500 a load), kitchen, and store nearby. From the airport go one km along the highway toward Papeete, then another km up steep Puurai Road. Ask for directions at the second store past the autoroute underpass. Otherwise watch for the PUURAI OREMU *truck* at Papeete market (no service after 1700). Coco is a local taxi driver so also look for his red Mercedes at the airport for a free ride. He offers a tour around the island in this vehicle for f.3000 pp.

The **Hotel Shogun** (Bruno Gato, B.P. 2880, Papeete; tel. 43-13-93), 10 rue de Commandant Destremeau, Papeete, has a comfortable, quiet dormitory with bunkbeds for f.1900 pp. The 11 a/c rooms are f.5500 s, f.6000 d. Check in at the Boutique Keiko below the hotel. If they're closed when you arrive call tel. 48-08-75 and someone will come to let you in.

The **Hotel Mahina Tea** (B.P. 17, Papeete; tel. 42-00-97), up rue Sainte-Amelie from Ave. Bruat, is about the only regular budget hotel in the city. The 16 rooms with private bath are f.3800 s or d (f.3300 for twin beds), discounted if you stay three or more nights. There are also six small studios with cooking facilities at f.60,000 a month double. Dishes are not provided, electricity is extra, and the hot water is irregular. The Mahina Tea could be cleaner and friendlier. And quieter—at night, the rooster noise here can be annoying.

To meet interesting people stay at **Hostel Teamo** (Kay and Gerald, B.P. 2407, Papeete; tel. 42-00-35), 8 rue du Pont Neuf, Quartier Mission, a characterful century-old house in an attractive neighborhood just a short walk east of downtown near the Archbishop's Palace. To get there from the market walk straight inland on rue Cardella. It's a little hard to find the first time, but very convenient once you know it. Shared accommodations with satisfactory cooking facilities are f.1500 pp. Teamo is run by the retired Tahitian couple who live in the house at #3 across the street, so check there if no one's around. If you arrive in the middle of the night there's a couch on the verandah where you can stretch out. The place is clean, has a nice verandah with French TV, English is spoken, but beware of mosquitos. The owner, Mr. Tiger, does seven-hour tours around the island for f.1200 pp if enough people sign up. He also provides free airport transfers upon request.

A step down from these is the **Lagon Hotel "Le Point"** (B.P. 634, Papeete; tel. 42-98-46)

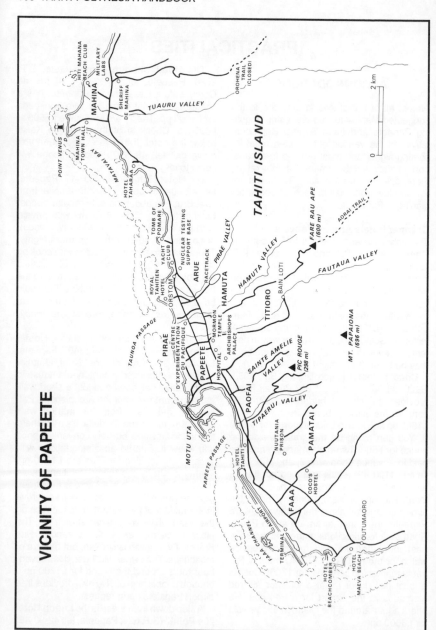

VICINITY OF PAPEETE

windsurfers at Hiti Mahana Beach Club, Tahiti

on Chemin Val de Patutoa. Rooms with private bath (only double beds and no hot water) are f.3000 s or d, shared bath f.2000 s or d. There's no sign outside but you may know this place by the nasty dogs. It's also popular with cockroaches, tars, and tarts. There are reduced rates for short times, if that's what you're after.

Chez Bennett (Frederic Bennett, B.P. 4279, Papeete; tel. 48-20-65) is a bungalow on the inland side of the road just east of the Tahara'a Hotel turnoff (look for the sign "Cite Jay"). The one double room and two singles are f.3000 s, f.5000 d, f.6000 t, and you can cook. Call or write in advance.

Youth Hostels

The **Papeete Youth Hostel** (Centre d'Accueil Territorial, B.P. 1709, Papeete; tel. 42-68-02) on boulevard Pomare opposite the Cultural Center offers accommodations in 18 three-bed dorms to those with a current Youth Hostel Association or student card only. There always used to be a line of people waiting to get in here; to reduce demand they doubled their prices to f.2200 for one night, f.1600 a night for two nights or more. Now you should have no problem getting a bed. You can check in weekdays 0800-1200/1400-1800, Sat. 0800-1200/1500-1800, Sun. 1000-1200. The rooms are accessible all day (midnight curfew), but there are no cooking facilities or hot water. The management does not allow visitors or alcohol in the rooms, nor is it permitted to store luggage for friends not staying there.

In July and Aug. women can stay at the **Foyer de Jeunes Filles de Paofai** (B.P. 1719, Papeete; tel. 42-87-80) near the Protestant church on boulevard Pomare. Bed and breakfast at this Evangelical Church-operated girls' residence is f.1400 a day, f.10,400 a month.

Camping

The nicest (and as yet only) regular campsite on Tahiti is **Hiti Mahana Beach Club** (Pat and Coco Pautu, B.P. 11580, Mahina; tel. 48-16-13) near Point Venus, 12 km east of Papeete. It's f.700 pp to camp under the fruit trees on the spacious fenced grounds; if you don't have your own tent they're for rent (f.500 a day extra). Otherwise pay f.1500 to stay in the dorm, "Fare Au," a Tahitian-style longhouse complete with four beds to a room, communal kitchen, toilet, showers, and dining/lounge area. If you don't have a sleeping bag sheets are available for f.200, towels f.100. Private bungalows run f.3000-4000 per night. A special "Blue Room" with king-size bed is f.4500 s, f.6000 d. Reduced weekly and monthly rates are available for dormitory and private room accommodations (but not camping).

Cooking facilities and a shared fridge come with the above. Campers have simpler facilities of their own and there's a lighted area for reading in the evening. Only cold showers are available at Hiti Mahana, except in the Blue Room which has hot water. Other facilities include a beach barbecue with firewood provided, washing machine, and luggage storage. Princess The Horse grazes nearby. She loves old bread, but don't get behind her: she's not always friendly!

The best thing about Hiti Mahana is its location right on a black-sand beach. Sporting equipment is for rent and the resort has a tiny off-shore island of its own within swimming distance where you could sunbathe nude or surf off the *motu's* east end. There's good snorkeling and plenty of fish. Windsurfers churn the waters. Cold beer and rum punch are on tap daily and happy hour runs from 1600-1900. Video films are shown on rainy days at 2030. The resort snack bar is only open weekends, but back on the main road are a few restaurants such as **Snack Tamarii Mahina** (steak and frites for f.650). The resort offers excursions to Faarumai Falls in the back of a pickup truck. Hiti Mahana is also the perfect place to get an early start on a circle-island tour (clockwise).

To get to Hiti Mahana at PK 10.5 Mahina take the MAHINA *truck* (f.130, no service after 1715) from rue Colette near Papeete market. You pass the Point Venus turnoff, cross a bridge, then turn left at a school and follow the road straight to the beach (one km). The Hiti Mahana *truck* is often at the airport in search of arriving clients, so ask. The office closes from 1200-1400. Resort owner Pat Pautu is a world of information, if you catch her. Picnickers pay f.300 for day use of the beach and facilities at Hiti Mahana (no charge to residents). Highly recommended.

Expensive Hotels Around Papeete
The French-owned **Sofitel Maeva Beach** (B.P. 6008, Faaa; tel. 42-80-42) at PK 7.5, Punaauia, is the oldest of the three big international hotels on Tahiti (the others are the Beachcomber and Tahara'a). The 230 a/c rooms in this pyramidal highrise begin at

f.18,000 s, f.20,000 d, f.23,500 t (children under 12 free). Breakfast and dinner are f.2900 pp extra. Decorated with Melanesian artifacts, the seven-story Maeva Beach faces a man-made white beach. With pollution on the increase in the adjacent lagoon most swimmers stick to the hotel pool. The Tahitian dancing and feasting here are attractions.

The **Hotel Belair** (B.P. 6634, Faaa; tel. 42-09-00) at PK 7.2, Punaauia, is one of the few large hotels owned and operated by a Tahitian family. Rates are f.8000 s, f.9000 d, f.11,500 t for a garden bungalow or standard room. The beach is poor. Scuba divers should contact Tahiti Plongee (B.P. 2192, Papeete) prior to arrival for concessional divers' rates at the Belair.

The **Tahiti Country Club** (B.P. 13019, Punaauia; tel. 42-60-40), the former Ibis "Belle-Fleur" and Climat Punaauia, is up on the hillside above the Belair. The 40 a/c rooms with fridge in a neat two-story building are officially f.5600 s, 8000 d (children under 12 free), plus f.2600 pp extra for breakfast and dinner (if desired). You should be able to wangle a reduction here, but only if you deal direct and not through a travel agency which adds on their commission. Swimming pool, volleyball, and tennis courts are on the premises (free). This is a good middle-price choice.

The **Tahiti Beachcomber** (B.P. 6014, Faaa; tel. 42-51-10), PK 7 Faaa, formerly the TraveLodge, is the first hotel west of the airport and one of the most expensive. The 185 rooms in the main building begin at f.18,900 s, f.22,500 d, f.25,500 t; for one of the 17 overwater bungalows add 50% again. Children and teens sharing the room with their parents are free. A breakfast and dinner meal plan is f.3950 pp extra. Tahitian dancing and craft demonstrations are regular features. The hotel pool is reserved for guests and the beach is artificial, but the attendants in the watersports kiosk on the beach will gladly ferry you out to the nudist pontoons anchored in mid-lagoon for f.500 RT. Every afternoon at 1630 there's a 1.5-hour sunset cruise along the coast from the Beachcomber (f.900 including one drink).

the black volcanic sands of Tahiti

The traditional **Hotel Tahiti** (B.P. 416, Papeete; tel. 42-95-50) at PK 2.6 between Papeete and the airport is the most charming of the higher-priced hotels, with a gracious South-Seas atmosphere. There are 110 units beginning at f.6500 s, f.7500 d, f.8550 t, or lagoon-front bungalows at f.10,000 s or d—good value for Tahiti. Some of the rooms near the highway are prone to traffic noise, however. This colonial-style hotel opened in 1960 with a pool, bar, restaurant, etc., plus a lovely lagoonside setting on the grounds of what was the residence of Princess Pomare, daughter of the last king of Tahiti. Recommended.

The 146-room **Hotel Matavai** (B.P. 32, Papeete; tel. 42-67-67) has little going for it except price: f.8800 s, f.11,700 d, f.14,600 t. You can almost tell this four-floor concrete ediface was once a Holiday Inn—strippers in an upstairs lounge are its biggest attraction today.

If you want to be right in the center of town consider highrise **Ibis Papeete** (B.P. 4545, Papeete; tel. 42-32-77), Ave. du Prince Hinoi at boulevard Pomare. Businessmen often stay here. The 72 small a/c rooms are f.10,500 s or d, plus f.2200 for breakfast and dinner (if desired).

A quieter choice might be **Hotel Le Mandarin** (B.P. 302, Papeete; tel. 42-16-33), 51 rue Colette, a modern hotel with an Oriental flair. The 37 rooms begin at f.9800 s, f.10,500 d, f.12,000 t (children under 12 free). The Mandarin's attractive Cantonese restaurant is closed Sunday.

The elegant old **Hotel Royal Papeete** (B.P. 919, Papeete; tel. 42-01-29), downtown on boulevard Pomare opposite the Moorea ferry landing, would be nice if it weren't for the noisy electric generating plant adjacent. Papeete's nightlife also throbs in and around this hotel (perhaps an attraction!). The 83 "soundproofed" rooms begin at f.6300 s, f.6600 d, f.8100 t. Ask for one on the quieter south side of the building. The management is friendly and helpful.

Hotel Pacific (B.P. 111, Papeete; tel. 43-72-82), formerly Hotel Kon Tiki, is the cheapest highrise hotel in the city center. The 44 big rooms begin at f.6000 s, f.6500 d, f.8500 t. Be aware, though, that the Pacific is on the opposite side of the same generating plant which buffets the Royal Papeete and is just as noisy. This hotel is popular with military personnel and French secret agents in transit. Immerse yourself in the intrigue (and get an eyeful of Papeete) by having a drink in the

PAPEETE

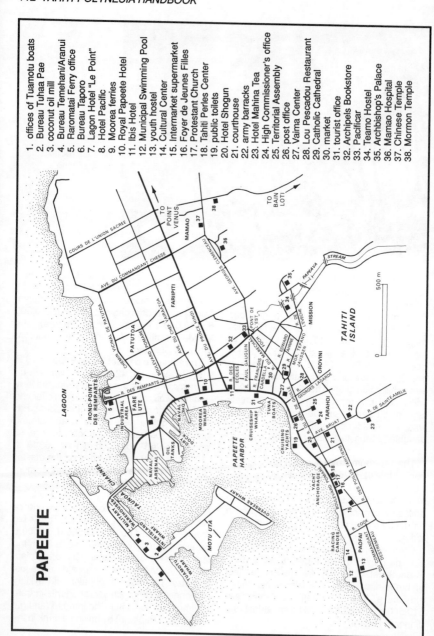

1. offices of Tuamotu boats
2. Bureau Tuhaa Pae
3. coconut oil mill
4. Bureau Temehani/Aranui
5. Raromatai Ferry office
6. Bureau Taporo
7. Lagon Hotel "Le Point"
8. Hotel Pacific
9. Moorea ferries
10. Royal Papeete Hotel
11. Ibis Hotel
12. Municipal Swimming Pool
13. youth hostel
14. Cultural Center
15. Intermarket supermarket
16. Foyer de Jeunes Filles
17. Protestant Church
18. Tahiti Perles Center
19. public toilets
20. Hotel Shogun
21. courthouse
22. army barracks
23. Hotel Mahina Tea
24. High Commissioner's office
25. Territorial Assembly
26. post office
27. Vaima Center
28. Lou Pescadou Restaurant
29. Catholic Cathedral
30. market
31. tourist office
32. Archipels Bookstore
33. Pacificar
34. Teamo Hostel
35. Archbishop's Palace
36. Mamao Hospital
37. Chinese Temple
38. Mormon Temple

bar (closed Mon.) on the 7th floor.

The **Royal Tahitien Hotel** (B.P. 5001, Papeete; tel. 42-81-13) at PK 3.5, Pirae, is a peaceful two-story building with rooms facing beautifully kept grounds on a black-sand beach. The windsurfing offshore is good. For f.12,500 s, f.13,500 d, f.16,000 t you may just find here the Tahiti you imagined. Breakfast and dinner are f.3500 pp extra.

The **Tahara'a Hotel** (B.P. 1015, Papeete; tel. 48-11-22) at PK 8, Mahina, takes the award for charging the highest prices on the island. The 200 rooms begin at f.20,500 s or d, f.23,900 t (children under 12 free). Their breakfast and dinner meal plan is f.4000 pp extra. The Tahara'a, built by Pan American Airways two decades ago, has now been taken over by the Hyatt Regency chain, which plans to develop the property for Japanese tourism. Chances are you'll be on a package tour if you stay here and the isolation won't matter much. Built on a hillside overlooking Matavai Bay, this is one of the only hotels in the world where you take an elevator down to your room. The views from the balconies are superb. A black-sand beach is at the foot of the hill.

Accommodations Around The Island

The only reasonably inexpensive place to stay on the far side of the island is **Fare Nana'o** (B.P. 7193, Taravao; tel. 57-18-14), operated by sculptor Jean-Claude Michel. It's on the lagoon side in a colorful compound overflowing with vegetation and fragments of sculpture, very near the PK 52 marker a km north of the old French fort at Taravao (no sign). One of the two thatched bungalows on stilts (f.3500 s or d, f.4000 t) has cooking facilities. Advance reservations are essential.

The **Te Anuanua Hotel** (B.P. 1553, Papeete; tel. 57-12-54) just west of the church in Pueu at PK 10, Tahiti Iti, is f.10,000 s, f.11,000 d, f.12,000 t, for a garden bungalow, breakfast included—a lot for a place that doesn't even have a beach. Residents of Tahiti get 25% off. Credit cards are not accepted. A nice seafood restaurant faces the lagoon and locally made Tahitian handicrafts are sold at the hotel.

A more distant choice would be the **Hotel Puunui** (B.P. 7016, Taravao; tel. 57-19-20), four km up a steep paved road off the Teahupoo road, seven km from Taravao. You'll have to rent a car if you stay here. At f.10,000 for a four-bed bungalow and f.16,800 for a six-bed villa, the Puunui is overpriced unless you're in a small group. A breakfast and dinner meal plan is f.2600 pp extra, though the units have kitchenettes. They do offer horseback riding at f.1500 an hour (tel. 57-19-20 for reservations), so it may be worth dropping by for a ride and the view.

In contrast to these **Le Petit Mousse** (B.P. 12085, Papara; tel. 57-42-07), on the lagoon opposite Restaurant Nuutere at PK 32.5 Papara, is highly recommended. The six duplex bungalows (12 units) go for f.4000 d or t, f.24,000 a week, and monthly rates are available. Unfortunately there are no cooking facilities, but adjacent to the motel restaurant is a pleasant terrace overlooking the lagoon. Le Petit Mousse would make a convenient base for surfers, and the snorkeling's also good here.

FOOD

Papeete Restaurants

Papeete's most famous restaurant is **Acajou** (closed Sun., tel. 42-87-58), corner of rue Georges Lagarde and boulevard Pomare near the Vaima Center. This is *the* place for a coffee (f.240) on the sidewalk or a gourmet meal in the elegant dining room. House specialties include onion soup (f.600), slices of mahi mahi *au gratin* (f.1350), and filet mignon with mustard sauce (f.1390). The plates are individually prepared so allow some time. A cheaper branch of Acajou (open for breakfast and lunch only) is at 7 rue Cardella by the market, half a block from the tourist office.

For a taste of the Mediterranean, **La Pizzeria** (closed Sun. and holidays; tel. 42-98-30) on boulevard Pomare near the Tahiti Pearl Center prepares real pizza in a brick oven. The price is surprisingly reasonable for the waterfront location—it's all spelled out in a big tabloid menu.

Pizzeria Lou Pescadou (open Mon. to Sat. 1130-1400/1830-2230, closed Sun.; tel. 43-74-26) on rue Anne-Marie Javouhey behind the cathedral is friendly, unpretentious, breezy, and inexpensive. Their pizza pescatore (f.520) makes a good lunch and a big pitcher of ice water comes in the price. Owner Mario Vitulli may be from Marseille but you won't complain about his spaghetti—a huge meal for about f.650. Drinks are on the house if you have to stand and wait for a table. The service is excellent and Lou Pescadou is very popular among local French, a high recommendation.

La Baie d'Along (Le Restaurant La Saigonnaise, closed Sun., tel. 42-05-35) on Ave. du Prince Hinoi has moderately expensive Vietnamese food. Saigonese soup (f.780) makes a good lunch.

Many Chinese restaurants in Papeete specialize in chicken and Hinano beer, but none are special bargains. The most popular is the **Waikiki Restaurant** (open daily 1100-1300/ 1800-2100, closed Sun. lunch; tel. 42-95-27) on rue Leboucher near the market. At **Te Hoa Restaurant** (closed Sun., tel. 43-54-85), 30 rue du Marechal-Foch behind the market, the furnishings aren't as neat but the portions are bigger and the prices slightly lower than at Waikiki.

Self-service Cafeterias

The **Foyer de Jeunes Filles de Paofai** (tel. 42-87-80) has a good modern cafeteria (closed Sat. and Sun.) with a fixed menu including a small salad, main plate, bread, and dessert for f.890 lunch or dinner. Alcohol is not available here. **Snack Paofai Self Service** (open Mon. to Sat. 1000-1300 only) near Clinique Paofai is another inexpensive cafeteria.

Self-Service Le Brasilia (tel. 42-46-24) upstairs in the Vaima Center offers excellent plats du jour for f.1000 or less on their breezy terrace with a view of Tahiti. Only lunch is available Mon. to Sat. from 1100-1400; the bar/cafe is open the same days from 0900-1700. This place can be hard to find: if you stand in front of the Catholic cathedral and look directly above the Air New Zealand office across the street you'll see the sign RESTAURANT BAR BRASILIA CLUB on the roof.

Snack Bars

The snack bar at the **Cultural Center** is good for breakfast or lunch (plat du jour) from 0600-1600 weekdays. An airy restaurant and snack bar are above the Municipal Swimming Pool.

The plat du jour at **Big Burger** (closed Sunday; tel. 43-01-98) beside Aline is often big value (f.1100), and it's not fast food as the name implies.

Snack Roger, 3 rue Jaussen next to the cathedral, offers good plate lunches, plats du jour, cheap salads, real espresso coffee, and ice cream. It's a good place to catch your breath, so locate it early in your visit!

To sample the local cuisine repair to **Cafe Snack Ella,** 23 rue Cardella right beside the market. Try maa tinito, a melange of red beans, pork, macaroni, and vegetables on rice (f.500). A large Hinano beer is f.350. Check out their Tahitian toilet (two treads and one squat) through the door below the blackboard in back.

If you're catching an interisland ship, it's good to know about the **Restaurant Motu Uta** near the wharf where the Temehani and Taporo dock. Lunch is good—especially with big bottles of cold beer. Indulge before you embark (if they're open).

Food Trailers

Take a stroll along the waterfront near the Moorea ferry landing in the early evening. After 1730 the scene changes completely with dozens of gaily lit vans known as les roulettes or les brochettes forming a colorful night market selling everything from couscous and pizza to steak with real pommes frites (f.700). Sailors promenade with their vahines as the city lights wink gently across the harbor, adding a touch of romance and glamor. The food and atmosphere are excellent but be prepared for regular restaurant prices. Even if you're not dining, it's a scene not to miss.

On boulevard Pomare across the park from the Moorea ferry landing are a row of side-

The food trucks along the Papeete waterfront near the Moorea ferry wharf are about the best place in the city to eat.

walk cafes frequented by French servicemen, happy hookers, gays, and assorted groupies. Some even have a happy hour. This is a good place to sit and take in the local color of every shade and hue.

Supermarkets

Intermarket (open Mon. to Sat. 0715-1230/1445-1845) is a large supermarket on rue du Commandant Destremeau. Get whole barbecued chickens (f.700) and chow mein at the small deli section.

At PK 8 Punuuai just south of the junction of the autoroute to Papeete is the **Centre Moana Nui,** Tahiti's first enclosed shopping mall, with a large adjoining supermarket, the **Euromarche.** The restaurant on the mall is rather poor; a barbecued chicken from the deli in the supermarket (f.650) is a better deal.

Restaurants Around The Island

A good place for lunch on your way around the island might be **Snack Guilloux** (closed Mon.), a hundred meters down the road to Tautira from the Banque Indosuez in Taravao. It's a regular restaurant, not a snack bar as the name implies.

The pretentious **Gauguin Museum Restaurant** (tel. 57-13-80) is half a km west of the museum. Circle-Island tour groups lunch here and you can join them for a steep f.3000 for the meal.

ENTERTAINMENT

Ask for the monthly program of activities at the Departement Fetes et Manifestations upstairs in the **Cultural Center** at "Te Fare Tauhiti Nui" (tel. 42-88-50) on the waterfront. Recitals by well-known classical musicians take place here Fri. and Sat. at 2000 (admission f.2000).

Five Papeete cinemas show B-grade films dubbed in French (admission f.600). The Concorde is in the Vaima Center; Hollywood I and II are on rue Lagarde beside the Vaima Center; Liberty Cinema is on rue Marechal Foch near the market; and the Mamao Palace is near Mamao Hospital.

Nightlife

Papeete after dark is not just for the tourists! Lots of little bars crowding the streets around rue des Ecoles are full of locals. The places with live music or a show generally impose a f.1000 cover charge which includes one drink. Nothing much gets going before 2200 —by 0100 everything is very informal for the last hour before closing.

The **Piano Bar** (tel. 42-88-24) on rue des Ecoles is the most notorious of Papeete's *mahu* (transvestite) discos; **Lido Nightclub** (tel. 42-95-84) next door offers striptease (both f.1000 cover). Young French service-men are in their element in these places. To dance rock with a rough-and-ready crowd try the **Bounty Club** (closed Mon.; tel. 42-93-00) just up the street.

Cafe des Sports (tel. 42-51-33) on the corner across the street from the Piano Bar has beer on tap and usually no cover. More locals than tourists patronize this pleasant, inexpensive establishment, which has music on weekends.

For more earthy interplay try the **Bar Kiki-riri** (no cover; tel. 43-58-64) on rue Colette. The **Champagne Club Bar Americain** (tel. 43-71-70) beside Liberty Cinema on rue du Marechal Foch is another place where you can get a beer without paying a cover.

French soldiers and sailors out of uniform patronize the bars along boulevard Pomare opposite the Moorea ferry landing, such as **La Cave** (tel. 42-01-29) at the Royal Papeete Hotel (entry though the lobby) which has live Tahitian music for dancing on the weekends (closed Sun. to Tues.; cover charge).

The **Tiki d'Or Bar Americain** (no cover; tel. 42-07-37) on the back street near the Vaima Center gets lively around happy hour. You'll locate it by the ukuleles and impromptu singing.

Le Jonque (no cover; tel. 42-47-34), a floating bar on the waterfront opposite the end of Ave. Bruat, is a quiet, safe place to drink. The **Pitate Bar** (cover charge; tel. 42-80-54), on the corner of Ave. Bruat beside the UTA office, is loud and dark, but there's often Tahitian-style music you can dance to. Check out the Pitate on Sunday afternoon. **Club 106** (closed Sun. and Mon.; cover charge; tel. 42-72-92) nearby on boulevard Pomare is the disco for the "in" set.

Polynesian Shows

A Tahitian dance show takes place in the Bougainville Restaurant downstairs at the **Maeva Beach Hotel** (tel. 42-80-42) Mon., Wed., Fri., and Sat. at 2000. If you're not interested in having dinner, a drink at the Bar Moorea by the pool will put you in position to see the action (no cover charge). The first and third Sun. of each month this hotel puts

a Tahitian dancer at a Papeete hotel

on a full Tahitian feast at 1200, complete with earth oven *(ahima'a)* and show (f.3700).

Every evening at 2030 the **Beachcomber Hotel** (tel. 42-51-10) presents one of the best Tahitian dance shows on the island; attend for the price of a drink at the bar near the pool (no cover charge). For something special take in the barbecue (on Wed.) and the Tahitian feast (on Sun.)—f.3300 each.

More convenient if you're staying in town is the Tahitian dancing Sun. at 1200 at the **Matavai Hotel** (tel. 42-67-67), a five-minute walk from the Cultural Center. You can see it for the price of a drink at the bar (no cover charge).

Le Tamure Hut at the Royal Papeete Hotel (tel. 42-01-29) on the waterfront opposite the Moorea ferry landing is one of the few down-town Papeete clubs designed for visitors. Through entertainment and decor they've at-tempted to recapture the nightlife milieu of a decade or more ago, before Quinn's Tahitian

Hut closed in 1973. You can dance to '50s and '60s music here! The Tahitian floor show is Thurs., Fri., and Sat. at 1930 (f.3900 pp including dinner and the show). Daily except Sun. from 1600 to 0200 the Hut operates as a bar. If you don't mind spending a little money Le Tamure is a good choice for a night out.

SPORTS AND RECREATION

Tahiti Plongee (B.P. 2192, Papeete; tel. 43-62-51 or 41-00-62) offers scuba diving several times daily from its base at the Hotel Belair, Punaauia. The charge is f.3000 per dive all-inclusive, or f.13,000 for a five-dive card, f.22,000 for 10 dives. Night dives are double price. Ocean dive at 0800 daily (except Mon. and Fri.) and at 1400 on Saturday. Lagoon diving is at 1000 daily (except Mon. and Fri.) and 1400 weekdays. Night diving is at 1815 Thursdays. To dive with this company you must join the **Club Corail-Sub** (f.4800) which includes a medical examination and an

insurance policy. Credit cards are not accepted.

Divemaster Henri Pouliquen was one of the first to teach scuba diving to children. The youngest person Henri has taken down was aged two years, nine months—the oldest was a woman of 78 on her first dive. Since 1979 Tahiti Plongee has arranged over 10,000 dives with children, certainly a unique accomplishment. Most diving is on the Punaauia reef. Other favorite scuba locales include a scuttled Pan Am Catalina PBY seaplane near the airport, its upper wing 12 meters down, and a schooner wreck 10 meters down about 45 meters from the breakwater at the entrance to the harbor.

Tahiti Aquatique (B.P. 6008, Faaa; tel. 42-80-42) at the Maeva Beach Hotel also offers scuba diving. Ask for Dick Johnson at the office by the hotel wharf. Their prices are higher than those of Tahiti Plongee (f.5000 for scuba diving) but you don't have to pay the club membership fee. For f.700 pp roundtrip they'll shuttle you out to their offshore sunbathing pontoon anchored above a fine snorkeling locale (no lifeguard or shade). Rental of mask, snorkel, and fins is f.800 extra. Underwater photography equipment is available.

Scuba diving can also be arranged at the **Yacht Club of Tahiti** (B.P. 1456, Papeete; tel. 42-78-03) at PK 4, Arue. Outings are offered at 0900 and 1400 daily except Sun. (f.4500 a dive, or f.36,000 for 10 dives).

If you only want to rent tanks (f.1000 a day, f.1500 a weekend), go to **Marine Corail** (B.P. 40, Papeete; tel. 42-98-63) at Fare Ute. They can be a little slow understanding what you want—persist.

The **Municipal Swimming Pool** (tel. 42-89-24) is open to the public Tues. to Fri. 1130-1700, Sat. and Sun. 0730-1700 (f.200). The pool on the roof of the **Vaima Center** next to Self-Service Le Brasilia has more class. It's open weekdays from 0900-1700; get a f.250 ticket from Vaima Sports (tel. 42-62-70) by the stairway up to the restaurant. In the evening after 1800 **football** is practiced in the sports field near the Municipal Swimming Pool.

SHOPPING

Papeete's largest shopping complex is the **Vaima Center,** where numerous shops sell black pearls, designer clothes, cheap souvenirs, books, etc. It's certainly worth a look, then branch out into the surrounding streets. **Anuraro Pearls,** 7 rue Jeanne d'Arc next to the Vaima Center, is a good place to examine the famous Gambier black pearls. **Galerie Winkler,** 17 rue Jeanne d'Arc beside American Express, sells contemporary paintings of Polynesia.

Don't overlook the local fashions. **Tahiti Art** on boulevard Pomare just west of the Vaima Center has expensive block-printed fabrics: a men's short-sleeved shirt is f.4500. **Marie Ah You** on the waterfront between the Vaima Center and the tourist office sells very chic island clothing—also with prices to match.

a Marquesan woodcarving

For reproductions of authentic Marquesan woodcarvings have a look in **Manula Curios** on the east side of the cathedral. Also try **Manula Junior,** corner of rues Albert Leboucher and des Ecoles opposite the Cafe des Sports.

If you're a surfer **Shop Tahiti Surf and Skate,** 10 rue Edouard Ahnne near the market, sells boards (f.59,000 and up) plus all attendant gear. **Caroline,** 41 rue Colette, and **Waikiki Beach,** 9 rue Jeanne d'Arc, also have surfing gear.

You can pick up a T-shirt (f.800) bearing the double spiral emblem of the Polynesian independence movement from the Secretariat at **la Mana Te Nunaa,** corner of rues Cook and Commandant Destremeau, two blocks from the Cultural Center. Only small sizes are available.

The **T-Shirt Center** on Ave. Georges Clemenceau between the Chinese Temple and Cours de l'Union Sacree on the way to Bain Loti has the cheapest and best selection of Tahitian T-shirts.

SERVICES

To change money patronize the **Banque Socredo** with over a dozen branches on Tahiti and no f.300 commission. The only place to get a cash advance on a Mastercard is UAP Assurances Chichong, 16 rue Jaussen, opposite Restaurant Bougainville back behind the cathedral.

The main **post office** is on boulevard Pomare across from the yacht anchorage. Aerograms and large mailing envelopes/boxes are sold at the counters up the escalators (closes at 1500). Pick up poste restante (general delivery) mail at window 15 downstairs (f.40 per piece). The Philatelic Bureau at the post office sells the stamps and first-day covers of all the French Pacific territories. Some are quite beautiful and inexpensive. The post office is also the place to place a long-distance telephone call.

If you have an **American Express** card or travelers cheques you can have your mail sent c/o Tahiti Tours, B.P. 627, Papeete. Their office (tel. 42-78-70) is at 15 rue Jeanne d'Arc next to the Vaima Center. They charge f.500 to forward mail.

For those uninitiated into the French administrative system, the **police** station (in emergencies tel. 17) opposite the War Memorial on Ave. Bruat deals with Papeete matters, while the gendarmerie (tel. 42-02-02) at the head of Ave. Bruat is concerned with the rest of the island. The locally recruited Papeete police wear blue uniforms, while the para-military French-import gendarmes are dressed in khaki.

Visa extensions are handled by the **Police de l'Air et des Frontieres** (open weekdays 0800-1200/1400-1700; tel. 42-67-99) at the airport (up the stairs beside the snack bar). Extensions cost f.3000 and you must show your money, ticket to leave Tahiti-Polynesia, and provide two photos. North Americans are limited to three months total; it's far better to ask for a three-month stay on arrival making this formality unnecessary. Be patient and courteous with these officials if you want good service.

The honorary consul of West Germany is Claude-Eliane Weinmann (B.P. 452, Papeete; tel. 42-99-94), rue Tihoni Te Faatau off Ave. du Prince Hinoi in Afareru on the far east side of the city. Other countries with **honorary consuls** at Papeete are Austria, Belgium, Chile, Denmark, Finland, Holland, Italy, Monaco, Norway, South Korea, and Sweden. There's no U.S. diplomatic post in Tahiti-Polynesia. All visa applications and requests for replacement of lost passports must be sent to Suva, Fiji, where it can take up to five weeks to get through the paperwork. Australia, Britain, Canada, Japan, and New Zealand are also *not* represented.

Yachts pay US$9 a day to moor Mediterranean-style (stern-to, bow anchor out) along the quay on boulevard Pomare. For half the price you can anchor farther west along the boulevard. A one-time entry fee and optional daily electricity hookup are charged. Public toilets and showers are on the waterfront near the end of Ave. Bruat. The port captain, customs, and immigration are all in a building behind the tourist office near the market. The **Yacht Club of Tahiti** (B.P. 1456, Papeete; tel. 42-78-03) at PK 4, Arue, charges visiting boats f.4500 a month to use one of their anchor buoys.

L'Office Territorial d'Action Culturelle (OTAC), B.P. 1709, Papeete; tel. 42-88-50) at the Cultural Center (Te Fare Tauhiti Nui) offers Tahitian courses for those spending longer periods in Papeete. The charge is f.10,000 a month for an hour and a half of lessons twice a week.

The **French University of the Pacific** (B.P. 4635, Papeete; tel. 42-16-80) created in 1987 has campuses in Tahiti-Polynesia and New Caledonia.

There's no coin laundry in Papeete but **Central Pressing,** 72 rue Albert Leboucher (the street behind the Royal Papeete Hotel), offers a special service to visitors: for f.580 they'll wash, dry, and fold one kg of laundry.

HEALTH

If you need a doctor, the **Clinique Paofai** (B.P. 545, Papeete; tel. 43-77-00) accepts outpatients weekdays and Sat. mornings, emergencies anytime. The facilities and attention are excellent, but be prepared for fees of around f.3500. The **Clinique Cardella** (tel. 42-81-90) on rue Anne-Marie Javouhey is also open day and night.

Dr. Vincent Joncker and Dr. J.-M. P. Rosenstein in the building above the pharmacy opposite the Catholic cathedral operate a clinic, S.O.S. Medecins (tel. 42-34-56), open daily. They charge US$20 for a consultation if you were referred by IAMAT (the International Association for Medical Assistance to Travellers).

Get cholera (f.400) and yellow fever (f.1200) **vaccinations** from the Service d'Higiene (open weekdays 0800-0900; tel. 42-97-95) on rue des Remparts.

INFORMATION

The **Tahiti Tourist Promotion Board** (OPATTI) at Fare Manihini (B.P. 65, Papeete; tel. 42-96-26), a neo-Polynesian building on the waterfront not far from the market, can answer basic questions and supply maps. Ask about special events here, but check their information carefully. They have detailed accommodation lists for all the outer islands. They're open weekdays 0730-1700, Sat. 0800-1100/1300-1600.

The **Institute Territorial de la Statistique** (B.P. 395, Papeete; tel. 43-71-96), 2nd floor, Bloc Donald (behind Voyagence Tahiti, opposite the Vaima Center), puts out a quarterly *Statistical Bulletin* (f.500).

La Boutique Klima (B.P. 31, Papeete; tel. 42-00-63) behind the cathedral sells old topographical maps, nautical charts, and many interesting books on Polynesia.

Newer topographical maps (f.1200) of some islands are available from the **Service de l'Amenagement** (B.P. 866, Papeete; tel. 42-46-50), 4th floor, Administrative Building, 11 rue du Commandant Destremeau.

For the best selection of French nautical charts, visit O.C.I. (Ouverages Cartes et Instruments) in the white Marine Nationale building next to the UTA office on the waterfront.

A small **public library** (open Mon. to Thurs. 0800-1600, Fri. 0800-1500; tel. 42-88-50) is located in the Cultural Center. To take books out you must buy an annual card for f.2000. You can sometimes watch videos on the Pacific in the library "discotheque."

Papeete's largest French bookstore is **Hachette Pacifique** (B.P. 334, Papeete; tel. 42-84-60), 14 Ave. Bruat. You'll find a much better selection of English books at **Librairie Archipels**, 68 rue des Remparts (B.P. 1689, Papeete; tel. 42-47-30). Archipels is about the only place you can find books and guides to the Pacific. There's a **newsstand** with magazines in English in front of the Vaima Center by the taxi stand on boulevard Pomare.

Airline Offices

Reconfirm your international flight at your airlines' Papeete office:

Air France (B.P. 4656, Papeete; tel. 43-43-00) is in Room 94 upstairs on the third floor of the Vaima Center.

Air New Zealand (B.P. 73, Papeete; tel. 43-01-70) is in the Vaima Center off rue Gen. de Gaulle.

Continental Airlines (B.P. 314, Papeete; tel. 43-39-39) uses Air Tahiti as their general agent.

Hawaiian Airlines (B.P. 1699, Papeete; tel. 42-15-00) is represented by Vahine Tahiti Travel below the Vaima Center, at street level off boulevard Pomare.

LAN Chile (B.P. 1350, Papeete; tel. 42-64-55) is upstairs in the Centre Bruat at 8 Ave. Bruat.

Minerve Corail Polynesie (B.P. 398, Papeete; tel. 43-25-25) is at Bloc Donald in the back courtyard behind Voyagence Tahiti on rue Jeanne d'Arc.

Qantas (B.P. 1695, Papeete; tel. 43-06-65) is on the plaza level in the Vaima Center.

UTA French Airlines (B.P. 4468, Papeete; tel. 43-63-33) is on boulevard Pomare near Ave. Bruat.

GETTING AROUND

Le Truck

You can go almost anywhere on Tahiti by *le truck,* converted cargo vehicles with long benches and loadspeakers in back. *Trucks* run from Papeete to Faaa Airport and the Maeva Beach Hotel every few minutes during the day, with sporadic service after dark until 2200, then again in the morning from 0500 on. On Sundays long-distance *trucks* run only in the very early morning and evening; weekdays the last trip to Mahina, Paea, and points beyond is around 0500.

Trucks don't run right around the island. Although a couple go as far as Tautira and Teahupoo on Tahiti Iti, you could have difficulty getting a *truck* back to Papeete from those remote villages in the afternoon. To go around the island by *truck,* start early and travel clockwise. Get out at Taravao and walk down to the Gauguin Museum (three km). With lots of traffic along the south coast, it'll be easy to find a ride back this way, though the last Papeete-bound *truck* leaves around 1300. Luckily, so far, hitching is usually no problem.

The eastbound *trucks* park on the north side of Papeete market and face the waterfront, westbound *trucks* are on the south side and face inland. Destinations and fares are posted on the side of the vehicle: f.110 to Punaauia, f.130 to Mahina, f.140 to Paea, f.160 to Papara, f.210 to Mataiea or Papeari, f.300 to Teahupoo. After dark all *truck* fares increase. Outside Papeete you don't have to be at a stop: *trucks* stop anywhere if you wave. There's no charge for luggage on *le truck*.

Others

Taxis in Papeete are a ripoff. Don't get in unless there's a rate card you can check; or at least agree on the price beforehand. Fares are 25% more on Sundays and holidays; from 2200 to 0600 they double. They also charge extra for luggage at these times. The taxis don't have (and don't want) meters which might limit their gouging. *Trucks* can't run to Mahina after 1700 due to protests from greedy taxi drivers. The three taxi stands are at the Vaima Center, the market, and at the airport. If you are cheated by a taxi driver take down the license number and complain to the tourist office.

Hitching *(autostop)* on Tahiti is fairly easy and relatively safe. It's great adventure because the local people are quite receptive to visitors. Your chances are better if it's obvious you're not French. Treat yourself to a circle-island tour by thumb!

Car Rentals

To rent a car you must be 21 (or 25 with Avis and Budget) and have held a driver's license for at least a year. Check the car as carefully as they check you. Comment on dents, scratches, flat tires, etc. All the car rental agencies include third-party public liability insurance in the basic price, but collision damage waiver (CDW) varies from f.350 to f.1200 extra per day. Some agencies charge the client for damage to the tires, insurance or no insurance. Tahiti insurance isn't valid if you take the car across to Moorea. Of course the car comes full of gas (f.100 a liter) and you're supposed to return it that way. You'll see Mobil and Total gas stations all around Tahiti, but an outer island may only have one.

There's no way you can whiz around Tahiti in a rental car for less than US$50. If you choose a per-km rate (instead of unlimited mileage) it's better value to take several days to go around the island. You'll need two days minimum anyway if you want to explore Tahiti Iti. A trip around the island in two days, one of the roads on Tahiti Iti included, would be just under US$75 (based on the cheapest per-km rental from the cheapest agency without insurance). Some agencies impose a 50-km daily minimum on their per-km rentals to prevent you from traveling *too* slowly; most rentals are for a minimum of 24 hours. If you want to circle the island in one day and pack as many sidetrips in as you can, an unlimited mileage rental may be for you (from US$60). With four people sharing the costs it's not a bad deal.

Check with Avis and Budget for Tahiti specials before leaving home. Sometimes you can reserve a car with unlimited kilometers from Australia or the U.S. for less than you'd pay upon arrival.

Of the eight car rental agencies on Tahiti, **Hertz** (tel. 42-04-71), beside Peugeot near Uranie Cemetery, is the most expensive (from f.2250 a day, plus f.32 a km, or f.6990 with unlimited mileage). Their CDW insurance is valid only on paved roads. Not recommended.

The cheapest rates on a per-km basis are offered by **Pacificar** (B.P. 1121, Papeete; tel. 42-43-64) on Pont de l'Est at the east end of rue Paul Gauguin. Their smallest car is f.1300 a day, plus f.26 a km, plus f.800 insurance. They're open 24 hours a day—if the main office is closed the watchman in the parking lot can give you a car. Pacificar doesn't have unlimited mileage rentals.

Avis, (B.P. 1683, Papeete; tel. 42-96-49), 35 rue Charles Vienot, offers the lowest rates with unlimited mileage (f.5600, minimum two-day rental), although their insurance charges are the highest (f.1200). **Tahiti Car Rental** (B.P. 1724, Papeete; tel. 42-46-16), in the back of the Renault showroom on boulevard Pomare opposite the Moorea ferry landing, also has good deals on unlimited mileages. Their two-day 300-km "weekend special" is f.9500, insurance included. Recommended.

On a per-km basis compare prices at **Robert** (B.P. 1047, Papeete; tel. 42-97-20), rue du Commandant Destremeau, **Andre** (tel. 42-94-04), boulevard Pomare opposite naval headquarters, **Budget** (B.P. 306, Papeete; tel. 43-80-79), in the flashy Mobil Oil Australia building north of downtown, and **Points Oranges** (tel. 42-14-14), Ave. du Prince Hinoi at rue des Remparts with a branch in Puna-auia (tel. 42-44-22) opposite the Maeva Beach Hotel.

Garage Daniel (B.P. 1445, Papeete; tel. 42-98-41) at PK 5.5 across the highway from the airport terminal has competitive per-km rates, but no unlimited mileages. Many car rental companies have kiosks inside Faaa Airport, and most offer a free pickup and dropoff service to the hotels and airport for clients.

Due to insurance problems and kamakaze traffic, it's not possible to rent a motorcycle or bicycle on Tahiti. **Garage Bambou** (B.P. 5592, Papeete; tel. 42-80-09) on Ave. Georges Clemenceau just beyond Hospital Mamao sells new bicycles for f.20,000 and does repairs.

Local Tours
Aroma Tours (B.P. 4477, Papeete; tel. 42-95-50) at Hotel Tahiti offers a half-day circle-island tour, including visits to Point Venus, Faarumai Falls, and the Gauguin Museum for f.3000 pp (admissions extra). The manager, Jean-Paul Aromaiterai, also specializes in making arrangements for film crews shooting in Polynesia.

William Leeteg of **Tahiti Rainbow Tours** (B.P. 6719, Faaa) takes visitors to the top of Mt. Marau (1,372 meters) by four-wheel-drive jeep for f.5000 pp at 0930 and 1430 (four hours). If it's raining the tour is cancelled. William speaks good English; contact him through the tourist office.

GETTING AWAY

The **Air Tahiti** office (tel. 43-39-39) is upstairs in Fare Tony, the building behind Acajou off boulevard Pomare. **Air Moorea** (tel. 42-44-29) is at Faaa Airport. Interisland services by air and sea are covered in the main Introduction to this book.

The ferry to Moorea departs from the landing just north of the tourist office downtown. The *Raromatai Ferry* to the Leeward Islands also leaves from there, as do cruise ships and a few other small boats. All other interisland ships, including the popular *Taporo IV* and *Temehani,* leave from the interisland wharf or Tuamotu wharf in Motu Uta across the harbor from downtown Papeete. You can catch a *truck* directly to Motu Uta from rue Albert Leboucher beside Papeete market. The ticket offices of some of the vessels are in Fare Ute just north of downtown (addresses given in the Main Introduction to this book).

cultivating sugar cane

MOOREA

Moorea, Tahiti's heart-shaped sister island, is clearly visible across the Sea of the Moon just 16 km northwest of Papeete. This enticing island offers the white-sandy beaches rare on Tahiti, plus long, deep bays, lush volcanic peaks, and a broad blue-green lagoon. Dino de Laurentis filmed *The Bounty* here in 1983. Tourism is concentrated along the north coast around Paopao and Club Med; most of the locals live in the south. Much more than Tahiti, Moorea is the laidback South Sea isle of the travel brochures. With a population of just 8,801 (1988), Moorea lives a quiet, relaxed lifestyle; coconut, pineapple, and vanilla plantations alternate with pleasant resorts and the vegetation-draped dwellings of the inhabitants.

Tourism in Moorea is highly competitive and you can often get good deals by shopping around for rooms, car rentals, tours, etc. When things are slow (such as in Sept. and from mid-Jan. to Feb.) some hotels really slash their rates. Even if you're staying at one of the luxury hotels, you'll do better dealing with a kiosk on the highway for rental cars and circle-island tours; reservations desks inside the hotels are run by exactly the same companies but tack on a commission for the hotel. *Le truck* circles this easily accessible island. The accommodations are good and plentiful, while weekly and monthly apartment rentals make even extended stays possible. Don't try to see it as a daytrip: this is a place to relax!

Orientation

If you arrive by ferry you'll get off at Vaiare, four km south of Temae Airport. Your hotel may be at Maharepa (Bali Hai Hotel, Coconut House), Paopao (Bali Hai Club, Motel Albert), Pihaena (Moorea Lagoon Hotel, Chez Marie Blandine), or Tiahura (Club Med, Chez Nelson et Josiane, Moorea Village Hotel), all on the north coast. The Paopao hotels enjoy better scenery, but the beach is far superior at Tiahura.

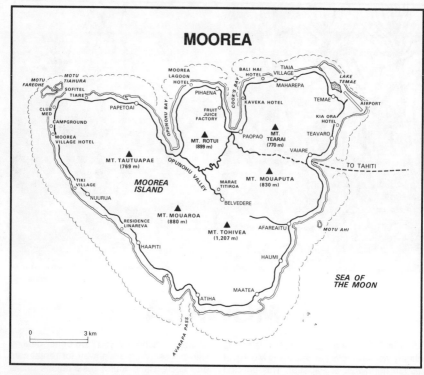

MOOREA

The PKs (kilometer stones) on Moorea begin at the post office opposite the access road to Temae Airport. They're numbered up to PK 35 along the north coast via Club Med and up to PK 24 along the south coast via Afareaitu, meeting at Haapiti halfway around the island. Our circle-island tour below begins at Temae Post Office and travels counterclockwise. The Moorea accommodations and restaurant listings below begin at Vaiare wharf and also go counterclockwise in each category.

THE LAND

This triangular island is actually the surviving south rim of a volcano once 3,000 meters high. Moorea is twice as old as its Windward partner Tahiti, and weathering is noticeably advanced. The two spectacular bays cutting into the north coast flank Mt. Rotui (899 meters), once Moorea's core. The jagged grandeur of the crescent of peaks facing these northern bays is scenically superb.

Shark-tooth-shaped Mouaroa (880 meters) rising behind Cook's Bay is a visual triumph, but Mount Tohivea (1,207 meters) is higher. Polynesian chiefs were once buried in caves along the cliffs. Moorea's peaks protect the north and northwest coasts from the rain-bearing southeast trades; the drier climate and scenic beauty explain the profusion of hotels along this side of the island. Moorea is surrounded by a coral ring with several passes into the lagoon. Three motus enhance the lagoon, one off Afareaitu and two off Club Med.

Moorea's interior valley slopes are unusually rich, with large fruit and vegetable plantations and human habitation. At one time or another coconuts, sugar cane, cotton, vanilla, coffee, rice, and pineapples have all been grown in the rich soil of Moorea's plantations. Stock farming and fishing are other occupations. Vegetables like taro, tomatoes, cucumbers, pumpkins, and lettuce, and fruit such as bananas, oranges, grapefruit, papaya, star apples, rambutans, avocados, mangos, limes, tangerines, and breadfruit, make Moorea a veritable garden of Eden.

HISTORY

Legend claims that Eimeo (Moorea) was formed from the second dorsal fin of the fish that became Tahiti. A hole right through the summit of Mt. Mouaputa (830 meters) is said to have been made by the spear of the demigod Pai, who tossed it across from Tahiti to prevent Mt. Rotui (899 meters) from being carried off to Raiatea by Hiro, the god of thieves. The name Moorea supposedly means "Yellow Lizard" from a onetime chiefly family.

Captain Samuel Wallis was the European discoverer of the Windward Is. in 1767. After leaving Tahiti he passed along the north coast of Moorea without landing. He named it Duke of York's Island. The first European visitors were botanist Joseph Banks, lieutenant Gore, the surgeon William Monkhouse, Herman Sporing, and half a dozen sailors sent over there by Capt. Cook on 1 June 1769 to observe the transit of Venus. (The main observatory was, of course, on Point Venus, but it was also observed by officers on Moorea and on a small islet off the east coast of Tahiti.) The telescope was set up on the small Motu Irioa, halfway between Club Med and Opunohu Bay, and the observation duly made on 3 June. Banks landed several times on the north coast at Papetoai. The party returned to Tahiti on 4 June. Captain Cook anchored in Opunohu Bay for one week in 1777, but he never visited the bay which today bears his name! His visit was uncharacteristically brutal as he smashed the islanders' canoes and burned their homes when they refused to return a stolen goat.

In 1792 Pomare I conquered Moorea using arms obtained from the *Bounty* mutineers. Moorea had long been a traditional place of refuge for defeated Tahitian warriors, thus in 1808 Pomare II fled into exile here with a party of English missionaries after his bid to bring all Tahiti under his control failed. Moorea has a special place in the history of Christianity: here in 1812 the missionaries finally managed to convert Pomare II after 15 years of trying. On 14 Feb. 1815 Patii, high priest of Oro, publicly accepted Protestantism and burned the old heathen idols at Papetoai, where the octagonal church is today. Shortly afterward the whole population followed Patii's example. The *maraes* of Moorea were then abandoned and the Opunohu Valley depopulated. The first Tahitian Bible was printed on Moorea in 1817. From this island Protestantism spread throughout the South Pacific.

In June 1769 a party led by Captain Cook's botanist Joseph Banks became the first Europeans to land on Moorea. This fictitious engraving by a contemporary London artist shows "Mr. Banks receiving a Visit from the King of Duke of York's Island."

After Pomare II finally managed to reconquer Tahiti in 1815, Moorea again became a backwater. American novelist Herman Melville visited Moorea in 1842 and worked with other beachcombers on a sweet-potato farm in Maatea. His book *Omoo* contains a marvelous description of his tour of the island.

Cotton and coconut plantations were created on Moorea in the 19th century, followed by vanilla and coffee in the 20th, but only with the advent of the travel industry has Moorea become more than a beautiful backdrop for Tahiti.

SIGHTS

Around Cook's Bay
On the grounds of the American-owned **Bali Hai Hotel** at PK 5 are historic anchors lost by captains Bougainville and Cook in the 18th century. On the mountain side of the road just past the Bali Hai is the "White House," the stately mansion of a former vanilla plantation, now used as a *pareu* salesroom.

At the entrance to Cook's Bay (PK 7) is the **Galerie Aad Van der Heyde** (tel. 56-14-22), as much a museum as a gallery. Aad's paintings hang outside in the flower-filled courtyard; inside is his black-pearl jewelry, a large collection of Marquesan sculpture, and artifacts from around the Pacific.

The **Tropical Aquarium** (open daily 0900-1200/1400-1730; f.400 admission; tel. 56-19-12) at PK 7.5 near the Kaveka Beach Club has 36 aquariums full of colorful fish and corals—well worth seeing. At the **Moorea Pearls Center** (admission free; tel. 56-13-13)

opposite Club Bali Hai in Paopao (PK 8.5) are exquisite black pearls and more Polynesian woodcarvings.

A rough dirt road up to the Belvedere begins just west of the bridge at Paopao (PK 9). On the west side of Cook's Bay a km farther along is a **Catholic church** (PK 10); an interesting altar painting with Polynesian angels (1948) was done by the Swedish artist Peter Heyman.

It's possible to visit the Distillerie de Moorea **fruit-juice factory** (tel. 56-11-33) up off the main road at PK 12 Tues. to Fri. 0900-1200, the only one of its kind in Tahiti-Polynesia. Aside from the papaya, grapefruit, and pineapple juices made from local fruits, the factory produces apple, orange, and passionfruit juices from imported concentrate with no preservatives added. There're also 40-proof brandies (carambole, ginger, grapefruit, guava, mango, orange, and pineapple

an old photo of Mouaroa across Cook's Bay, Moorea

underwater attractions of Tahiti-Polynesia (all photos this page courtesy Tahiti Tourist Board)

1. WW II American gun on Bora Bora; **2.** a vanilla house, Maharepa, Moorea; **3.** *le truck* near Papeete Market, Tahiti; **4.** lighthouse, Point Venus, Tahiti; **5.** church at Pueu, Tahiti Iti; **6.** Chinese temple, Papeete, Tahiti (all photos this page by D. Stanley)

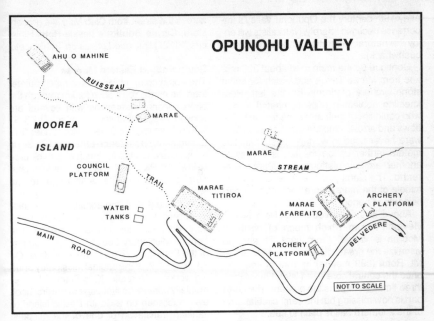

OPUNOHU VALLEY

MOOREA ISLAND

AHU O MAHINE

RUISSEAU

MARAE

MARAE

STREAM

COUNCIL PLATFORM

TRAIL

MARAE TITIROA

WATER TANKS

MARAE AFAREAITO

ARCHERY PLATFORM

MAIN ROAD

BELVEDERE

ARCHERY PLATFORM

NOT TO SCALE

flavors) and 25-proof liqueurs (coconut, ginger, and pineapple varieties) made here and sold to the public at the Accueil counter. If you look affluent enough they may invite you to sample their brews.

Opunohu Bay To Le Belvedere

The **Moorea Lagoon Hotel** at PK 14 is the only large hotel between Paopao and Tiahura. The **Shark's Tooth Boutique** at PK 17 has an intriguing array of jewelry, island clothing, and antiques.

Shrimp are bred in large basins at the head of Opunohu Bay (PK 18). A paved road up the pineapple-filled **Opunohu Valley** to the Belvedere begins here: 1.5 km to the connecting road from Cook's Bay, another two km to Marae Titiroa, then one more steep km up to the lookout. On the way pass Moorea's agricultural high school. This worthy institution with students from all the islands of Tahiti-Polynesia has hundreds of hectares planted in pineapples, vanilla, coffee, fruit trees, decorative flowers, and native vegetables.

Marae Titiroa, high up near the geographical center of Moorea, is the largest of a group of Polynesian temples restored in 1969 by Prof. Y.H. Sinoto of Honolulu. The small platform or *ahu* at the end of this *marae* (and the others) was a sacred area reserved for the gods. Stone backrests for chiefs and priests are another feature of the *marae*. Here the people offered gifts of tubers, fish, dogs, and pigs, and prayed to their gods, of whom many were deified ancestors. Just 50 meters northwest of Marae Titiroa near the watertanks is a long council platform, and 50 meters farther are two smaller *marae* surrounded by towering Tahitian chestnut trees *(mape)*. The most evocative of the group is four-tiered **Marae Ahu o Mahine,** about 250 meters down a deteriorating trail.

Some 500 ancient structures have been identified in this area and, if you're keen, you should be able to find a few in the forest across the stream, evidence of a large population with a highly developed social system. With the acceptance of Christianity in the early 19th century the Opunohu Valley's importance declined sharply. Naturalists will enjoy the natural vegetation in there (you must bushwhack).

Continue up the main road about 300 meters from Marae Titiroa and watch for some stone archery platforms on the left. Here kneeling noblemen once competed to see who could shoot their arrow the farthest. The bows and arrows employed in these contests were never used in warfare. Less than 100 meters farther up on the left is access to another archery platform and **Marae Afareaito.** The slabs you see sticking up in the middle of the *marae* were backrests for participants of honor.

Above is the **Belvedere** or Roto Nui, a viewpoint from which much of northern Moorea is visible. From here it's easy to visualize the great volcano that was Moorea. Mt. Rotui (899 meters) in front of you was once the central core of an island more than three times as high as the present. The north part is now missing but the semi-circular arch of the southern half is plain to see.

Papetoai To Club Med
Return to the main circuminsular highway and continue west. The **octagonal Protestant church** behind the post office at Papetoai (PK 22) was built on the site of the temple of the god Oro in 1822. Despite having been rebuilt several times the church is known as "the oldest European building still in use in the South Pacific."

As the road begins to curve around the northwest corner of Moorea one passes a number of large resort hotels, the **Sofitel Tiare** (PK 24), **Club Med** (PK 27), and the **Moorea Village Hotel** (PK 28); only Club Med forbids you to walk through their grounds to the beach. It's possible to snorkel out to Tarahu and Tiaharu *motus* from this beach. The recreation people at the Sofitel Tiare and Moorea Beach Hotel could also ferry you over for f.500 pp roundtrip. Try feeding bread to the fish. There's excellent reef break surfing here, too. In **Le Petit Village** shopping mall across the street from Club Med is a grocery store. **Carole Boutique** beside Hotel Hibiscus (PK 27) lists good prices on T-shirts, etc.

Southern And Eastern Moorea
The south coast of Moorea is much quieter than the north. You'll drive for km through the open coconut plantations with several unspoiled villages and scenic vistas. At PK 31 is **Tiki Theater,** described below under "Entertainment." **Residence Linareva** (PK 34) is a nice place to stop for lunch or a drink (see below). At PK 35/24, Haapiti, the kilometer numbering begins its descent to Temae Airport.

Afareaitu (PK 9), the administrative center of Moorea, has a hospital, police station, etc. Tiny Motu Hahi lies just off Afareaitu. The London Missionary Society had its Academy of the South Seas here in the early days. On 30 June 1817, at the original missionary printing works at Afareaitu, King Pomare II ceremonially printed the first page of the first book ever published on a South Pacific island, a Tahitian translation of one of the gospels. Before the press was moved to Huahine a year later over 9,000 books with over half a million pages were printed at Afareaitu!

Hike an hour up the **Afareaitu Valley** from the old Protestant church (1912) to a high waterfall which cascades down a sheer cliff into a pool. Keep straight on the main track till it becomes a footpath, and you're almost there. Tohivea (1,207 meters) towers to one side.

Vaiare Wharf (where you may have landed) is at PK 4, then comes the **Sofitel Kia Ora** (PK 1.5). If you have your own transport stop for a look around Moorea's most sophisticated resort. It's enjoyable to walk north along the beach from this hotel or even to go snorkeling. At PK 1 on the main road high above the Kia Ora ia a fine **lookout** over the deep passage romantically named the Sea of the Moon between Tahiti and Moorea. Temae Post Office (PK 0) and the airport mark the end of our 59-km circle-island tour.

Hiking

An excellent three-hour hike along a shaded trail takes you from Vaiare up across the mountains to Paopao. The way, partly marked by red paint dabbed on tree and rock, is easier to follow from the Vaiare side. Take the road inland about 50 meters south of the first bridge just south of the Vaiare ferry wharf. At the fork, cross a creek on the right and look for the first red marks. The way requires a little concentration to follow, but all the locals know it.

When you reach the divide, go a short distance south along the ridge to a super viewpoint over the pineapple plantations behind Paopao. On a clear day the rounded double peak of Orohena, Tahiti's highest, is visible, plus the whole interior of Moorea. If you're fresh off the ferry, no other introduction to the island could be more spectacular. This hike is also worth doing simply to see a good cross section of the vegetation. Don't miss it.

Moorea's Rotui rises above a country road.

PRACTICALITIES

ACCOMMODATIONS

Inexpensive Accommodations

The **Tiaia Village** (Chez Gisele et Raymond, B.P. 266, Moorea; tel. 56-16-84) near Maharepa has four bungalows with cooking facilities on the mountain side facing the highway. Each bungalow (up to four persons) is f.5000 daily, f.50,000 monthly. There's a store nearby.

Syd Pollock's **Coconut House** (B.P. 2329, Papeete; tel. 56-18-98) at PK 5 Maharepa just west of the Bali Hai Hotel has a lively resort atmosphere without Bali Hai prices. Syd offers 16 bungalows at f.1500 pp in a shared four-bed unit with private bath; pay f.4500 and you get the whole bungalow to yourself. If required, sheets and pillows are f.200 extra for your entire stay. Camping on the premises is f.700 pp. Rental of mask, snorkel, and fins is f.200, although the nearby beach can't compare with those at Tiahura. There's a swimming pool, washing machine

(f.400), and communal kitchen. The male staff resides in a bungalow near the kitchen here and they tend to kick up quite a ruckus when they get off work around midnight, especially if any single females are around. Happy hour at the bar is 1800-1900 and there's a special meal deal at the snack bar for the dorm/camper crowd. Coconut House is well known for its seafood restaurant specializing in mahimahi. Recommended.

Motel Albert (Albert Haring, tel. 56-12-76), up on the hill above Club Bali Hai at Paopao (PK 8.5), catches splendid views across Cook's Bay. The eight older units with double bed are f.3000 s or d, f.4000 t (two-night minimum stay). The 11 larger houses accommodating up to four persons are f.6000. Monthly rates are f.70,000, a good deal if you can stand Paopao for a month. Each unit has cooking facilities and several stores are nearby. No reservations are accepted. Don't ask Albert for permission to pitch your tent on the grounds—he doesn't care for campers. Giant cockroaches take over the motel at night.

The three bungalows behind **Boutique Dina** (tel. 56-10- 39) a km east of the Moorea Lagoon Hotel are f.4000 t; subtract f.500 a day for the weekly rate. Cooking facilities are provided and the bathroom is communal.

Several places near the Moorea Lagoon Hotel (PK 14) rent more expensive bungalows. **Chez Nani** (B.P. 67, Papeete; tel. 42-79-37) on the west side of the hotel has three thatched bungalows with kitchenettes for f.6000 s or d. The signposted **Faimano Village** (B.P. 1676, Papeete; tel. 56-10-20) next to Chez Nani has four bungalows at f.5000 d without kitchen, f.6500 t with kitchen. **Chez Francine** (tel. 56-13-24) 400 meters farther west has one house with kitchenette at f.5000 d. There's no grocery store near the Moorea Lagoon—the nearest is by the bridge in Paopao.

Chez Marie-Blandine (Mesmin Bernard, B.P. 257, Moorea), half a km west of the Moorea Lagoon Hotel, offers camping on the front lawn for f.300, a foam mattress in one of the dorms for f.1000. A public beach is near this friendly place on Opunohu Bay. Cooking facilities are available. At last report they were having licensing problems so ask around before heading out to make sure they're still open.

Motel Maeva (tel. 56-20-51), all by itself at PK 20 on the north side of Opunohu Bay, has a couple of studios with cooking facilities at f.4000 for up to three people.

Hotel Residence Tiahura (B.P. 1068, Papetoai; tel. 56-15-45), at PK 25 Tiahura on the mountain side just east of Club Med, is only a short walk to the beach. One of the six bungalows without kitchenette is f.3500 d, one of the 18 with kitchenette f.4000 d, f.5500 t. Monthly rates are f.65,000 d, f.75,000 t. All units have fridge and private bath. Their res-

taurant is reasonable—nice people, friendly service, good reports.

If you have a tent *the* place on Moorea to pitch it is **Chez Nelson et Josiane** (tel. 56-15-18), beside the Hibiscus Hotel just south of Club Med (PK 27). This campground is beautifully set in a coconut grove right on the beach. The charge is f.500 pp, toilets, showers, refrigerator, and basic cooking facilities provided. No tents are for rent but a bunk in the six-bed hostel is f.1000. Small rooms with shared bath are f.3000 d the first night, f.2500 d thereafter. Ask about getting one free day if you stay over a week. Every backpacker in Tahiti-Polynesia knows Chez Nelson et Josiane.

Billy Ruta Bungalows (tel. 56-12- 54) is at the south end of the west coast strip, right on the beach at PK 28, Tiahura. The thatched A-frame bungalows begin at f.4000 d without kitchenette, f.5000 d with kitchenette.

Fare Matotea (B.P. 1111, Papetoai; tel. 56-14-36) on the beach just south of Billy Ruta (PK 29) is OK if you're in a group: f.7200 for four, f.8300 for six (minimum stay two nights). All seven bungalows on spacious grounds have full cooking facilities and private bath.

Chez Pauline (Pauline Teariki, tel. 56-11-26) at PK 9, Afareaitu, is between the two stores opposite the gendarmerie. One of the seven rooms with double beds and shared bath in this old colonial house runs f.2500 s, f.3500 d or t. You may get a discount if you arrive late or leave early! A picturesque restaurant, with Pauline's *tikis* on display, rounds out this establishment which would have great atmosphere if it weren't for the abrupt manner of the proprietress. Dinner here is around f.2000 (fish and Tahitian vegetables).

profile of Moorea

Chez Coco's Madou (B.P. 371, Papeete; tel. 56-17-16) is on Motu Temae, 1.5 km down the road opposite the post office near Temae Airport. The contact person is at the Chez Helene shop nearby. Camping is f.700 pp and sleeping in the dorm is f.1000 pp with cooking facilities provided. It's a little off the beaten track; in fact, the easiest way to get there from the wharf is to walk north along the beach from the Sofitel Kia Ora. Coco's is a good base for surfers awaiting those big righthanders on the nearby Temae reef.

Expensive Accommodations

The **Sofitel Kia Ora** (B.P. 6008, Moorea; tel. 56-12-90) at PK 1.5 between Vaiare and the airport is *the* place if you want absolute luxury and don't give a damn about the price. Deluxe thatched bungalows begin at f.19,200 s, f.21,200 d, f.24,700 t (children under 12 free). This French-owned hotel has class! Breakfast and dinner are f.2900 pp extra together. The Kia Ora's La Perouse Restaurant is the finest French restaurant in Tahiti-Polynesia—mahimahi for f.1300. See Tahitian dancing in this restaurant Mon., Wed., and Sat. at 2030. On the shore is another restaurant-cum-disco in a converted interisland schooner. The beach (topless) is one of the best on the island, with a splendid view of Tahiti.

The **Bali Hai Hotel** (B.P. 26, Moorea; tel. 56-13-59) at PK 5, Maharepa, caters mainly to American tour groups staying three, four, or seven nights. The cheapest rooms are f.8500 s, f.10,000 d, f.12,500 t (children under 12 free), bungalows two or three times that. The rooms near the highway are noisy. For breakfast and dinner add f.3400 pp extra. There's a Tahitian feast with Polynesian dancing Sundays at lunchtime (f.3600)—see it all for free from the bar. This hotel and its namesakes on Huahine and Raiatea were founded by the so-called "Bali Hai Boys," Hugh, Jay, and Muk. The happy-go-lucky tale of this gang of three's arrival on Moorea in 1959 is posted in the lobby, if you're interested.

The **Hotel Baie de Cook** (tel. 56-10-50), formerly the Ibis Moorea, is a mock-colonial building by the highway at the entrance to Cook's Bay. The 76 rooms are f.10,500 s or d, f.13,000 t (children under 12 free). It has a false-front Waikiki feel. Neither this hotel nor the two mentioned below are on the beach.

The **Kaveka Beach Club** (B.P. 13, Moorea; tel. 56-18-30) nearby at PK 7.5, Paopao, is better. Thatched garden bungalows run f.5950 s, f.8500 d, f.10,200 t; the breakfast and dinner meal plan is f.2600 pp extra. Some nautical activities such as windsurfing, snorkeling, and paddling are offered free, and scuba diving is available nearby.

Club Bali Hai (B.P. 26, Moorea; tel. 56-13-68) at PK 8.5, Paopao, is f.11,000 s, f.12,500 d, f.15,000 t for a room with a view of spectacular Cook's Bay. The Club's restaurant is worth checking out, but many of the units with cooking facilities have been sold to affluent Americans on a time-sharing basis with each owner getting two weeks a year at the Club.

The Tahitian-owned **Moorea Lagoon Hotel** (B.P. 11, Moorea; tel. 56-14-68) at PK 14 is f.11,000 s, f.12,000 d, f.15,000 t for one of the 41 garden bungalows. The beach is fine —have fun if your tour company dropped you here.

The **Sofitel Tiare** (B.P. 1019, Papetoai; tel. 56-19-19) at PK 24 takes the cake as the most expensive hotel on Moorea. Rooms in the main building start at f.22,000 s, f.24,000 d, f.28,000 t—much too much. For an overwater bungalow tack on an additional 50%. It will take years before the surrounding vegetation lends any warmth to this lifeless place, and their beach will always be artificial.

The **Moorea Beach Club** (B.P. 1017, Papetoai; tel. 56-15-48), formerly the Climate de France, is the first hotel on the white sandy shores of Tiahura tourist strip. The 40 a/c rooms with fridge go for f.5600 s, f.8000 d, f.9600 t, plus f.2600 pp extra for breakfast and dinner (if desired). A four-person garden bungalow with kitchenette is f.13,000; the same for six persons is f.16,500. Outrigger canoes, windsurfing, tennis, snorkeling, and fishing gear may be loaned free.

Residence Les Tipaniers (B.P. 1001, Moorea; tel. 56-12-67) is cramped around the reception but better as you approach the beach. Rooms are f.7500 s, f.10,000 d, f.11,700 t. A thatched bungalow with kitchen is a few thousand francs extra. They'll shuttle you over to a *motu* for snorkeling free. The hotel's Italian restaurant is not recommended.

Club Mediterranee (B.P. 1010, Moorea; tel. 56-15-00) at PK 27 has been renovated and expanded to 350 bungalows. Club Med's for you if non-stop activity amid an "ambience indigene" is your aim. Otherwise, all the canned entertainment can be to the detriment of peace at night. Clocks inside the village are set ahead to give guests an extra hour in the sun. Join them by paying f.11,000 pp per day (double occupancy) at the Club Med office in the Vaima Center, Papeete (B.P. 575, Papeete; tel. 42-96-99). The price includes all meals and a wide range of activities, but no transfers. If you're not a member the Club Med initiation fee (US$30) and annual dues (US$50) are extra. No visitors are allowed. In North America for information on Club Med call tel. 1-800-258-2633. If you only want to crash "Le Club" for food, water-skiing, or men/women, remove all watches and jewelry—that's how they identify outsiders.

The **Hibiscus Hotel** (B.P. 1009, Moorea; tel. 56-12-20) right beside Club Med might be a good choice for families. Two adults and two children can stay in a garden bungalow beneath the coconut palms for f.7500. Weekly rates are available and there's a two-night minimum stay. Canoes and snorkeling gear are extra.

The **Moorea Village Hotel** (B.P. 1008, Moorea; tel. 56-10-02) at PK 28 has nice thatched bungalows for f.4000 s, f.4500 d, f.6500 for up to four people. For a kitchen in your unit add f.3500 to the price. To be on the beach is another f.1000. The kitchenless garden bungalows are one of the best buys on Moorea. Nudism is possible on a small offshore *motu*. Saturdays at 1900 there's a veal barbecue; the Tahitian feast with Polynesian dancing is Sunday at 1300. For those seeking a resort with middle-range prices, this is a good choice.

Residence Linareva (B.P. 205, Moorea; tel. 56-15-35), amid splendid mountain scenery at PK 34 on the wild side of the island, is designed for long stays. Reservations are recommended. Prices begin at f.5800 s, f.6800 d, f.7800 t, with weekly discounts. Each of the 11 housekeeping units is unique. Large cozy rooms are available for groups (for example, a very pleasant eight-bed bunkroom with kitchenette is f.22,000). The scuba facilities make this residence a natural for divers. Linareva's floating seafood restaurant, the *Tamarii Moorea I,* is an old ferryboat which once plied between Moorea and Tahiti. Colorful reef fish are kept in an enclosure by the dock. It's a good place to have lunch (1200-1400) on the way around the island; specials are marked on a blackboard. Other times the restaurant has a pub atmosphere.

FOOD

Aside from the hotel restaurants, a mixed bag of eateries caters to table hoppers. **Restaurant Chez Michel et Jackie** (closed Mon.; tel. 56-11-08) on the main road just east of the Bali Hai Hotel features French cooking and big two-person pizzas (f.2000).

The **Manava Nui Restaurant** (Chez Marare and Marguerite, tel. 56-22-00) on the east side of Cook's Bay serves Cantonese and European dishes. No comment.

Le Bonne Table du Hakka Restaurant (closed Thurs. or Fri.; tel. 56-12-19) on the island side of the road by Cook's Bay a few hundred meters south of Club Bali Hai (PK 8.5) is one of the old established places. Its moderately expensive French cooking with a Chinese air is reputed to be the best on the island. Fresh fish and shrimp are specialties.

Snack Te Honu Iti at PK 9 near the head of Cook's Bay dispenses inexpensive hamburgers and a *plat du jour* (f.900) on their airy terrace.

Restaurant Fare Manava (Chez Marguerite-Marere, tel. 56-14-24) opposite the Pharmacie in Paopao has a pleasant dining room overlooking Cook's Bay. Prices are reasonable with mahimahi under f.1000. Check this one out!

Restaurant L'Escargot "Restobeach" (tel. 56-14-09) at the Hibiscus Hotel (PK 27)

a charming Polynesian woman

is a rather expensive French restaurant with good views of the *motus* off Club Med—the place for a sunset drink or a staging area for Club Med jumpers (the boundary of the resort is here).

Snack Eimeo (tel. 56-20-14) just south of Pauline's at Afareaitu (PK 9) has hamburgers, omelettes, salads, steak frites (f.500), and lobster specials (f.1800). They're open for lunch and dinner daily.

ENTERTAINMENT

Most of the hotel bars have happy hour from 1800-1900.

Moorea has its own instant culture village, the **Tiki Theater** (B.P. 1016, Moorea; tel. 42-34-81 or 56-18-97) at PK 31, Haapiti (admission f.1000; closed Wed.). Doors open at 1030, with traditional dances performed at 1130. Line fishing on the reef from a pirogue takes place at 1330 and is included in the price. Lunch is f.2000 extra and features local foods, with beer and wine on the house. Tuesday and Sat. nights there's a big sunset show with an open bar (f.4000 without transport). Pirogue transportation from the hotels to Tiki Theater is f.1000. If you've got US$995 to blow, a royal Tahitian wedding can be arranged at the village (bring your own wife). The ceremony lasts two hours, from 1600 to sunset, and is a private party with the village closed to the public. The bridegroom arrives by canoe and the newlyweds are carried around in procession by four warriors. Yes, it's kinda tacky, but that's show biz.

SPORTS AND RECREATION

M.U.S.T. Plongee Scuba Diving or "Moorea Underwater Scuba-diving Tahiti" (B.P. 336, Moorea; tel. 56-17-32 or 56-15-83), on the dock behind the Hotel Baie de Cook, offers diving at 0900 and 1400 daily except Mondays. Prices are f.4500 for one dive, f.20,000 for five dives. Rental of snorkeling gear is f.300. A scuba certification course with four dives costs f.30,000. Divemaster Philippe Molle knows 15 different spots in and outside the reef. He also runs a guesthouse, **M.U.S.T. Herbergement,** at PK 15, 1.5 km west of the Moorea Lagoon Hotel. Only divers are accommodated: f.30,000 pp for six nights with all meals and free transfers to the dive shop. Philippe's slogan is: "Diving with M.U.S.T. is a must!"

The "Activities Nautiques" kiosk (tel. 56-19-19, extension 1140) on the wharf at the **Sofitel Tiare** has a glass-bottom boat (f.1200 pp) which leaves at 0900 and 1400. For more excitement hire a lagoon jet boat for f.6000 an hour (maximum four passengers). A tour of both bays on northern Moorea is f.9000 by lagoon jet; a trip around the island f.15,000. Bernard Begliomini's "Bathy's Club" (B.P. 1019, Papetoai; tel. 56-21-07) at the Sofitel Tiare offers scuba diving for f.5000.

Diving is also offered by Catherine and Jean-Luc of **Scubapiti** at Residence Linareva (B.P. 1072, Moorea; tel. 56-20-38), Haapiti. They go out daily (except Wed.) at 0900 and 1430. Linareva guests get a 10% discount on the f.4000 tariff (f.30,000 for 10 dives). Child divers aged five and up are welcome.

For some horseback riding try **Rupe-Rupe Ranch** (tel. 56-22-10 or 56-15-31) on the mountain side just south of the Hibiscus Hotel. To take one of their 16 horses along the beach for an hour is f.2000. Rides commence at 0800, 1000, 1430, and 1600, but it's best to call ahead.

The 21-meter luxury yacht *Seer* (B.P. 160, Moorea; tel. 56-25-01) sails right around Moorea every Wed. with a picnic stop at a *motu* (f.9000 pp including lunch and drinks).

Windsurfers acclaim Cook's Bay.

SERVICES

Most of the banks (Banque Socredo included) are near the Bali Hai Hotel at Maharepa, although a branch of the Banque Indosuez is in Le Petit Village shopping mall opposite Club Med. **Lav'matic** laundromat, also in Le Petit Village, is absurdly expensive at f.800 to wash, f.800 to dry.

The **Moorea Visitors Bureau** has an office (usually padlocked) opposite Club Bali Hai. A newsstand opposite Club Bali Hai has books and magazines in French. The pharmacy is near the bridge at Paopao.

TRANSPORT

Air Moorea (tel. 56-10-34) is based at Moorea Temae Airport. Details of the air and ferry services from Tahiti are given in the main Introduction to this book. *Trucks* (f.200 to anywhere on the island) meet the ferries at Vaiare. Although they don't go right around the island the northern and southern routes meet at Club Med, so you could theoretically effect a cimcumtrucknavigation by changing there provided you caught the last boat *truck* back (around 1400).

Hitching is wearing thin with Moorea motorists, although still possible. If you really need the ride you'll probably get it. Taxis on Moorea are actually minibuses with a white letter "T" inside a red circle. The maximum speed limit is 60 km an hour.

Arii Rent-A-Car (B.P. 104, Moorea; tel. 56-11-03), the Hertz representative on Moorea, has eight locations along the north coast of Moorea including Vaiare Wharf and opposite the Bali Hai Hotel. Their scooters are f.2500 for four hours, f.3000 for eight hours; f.3500 for 24 hours; unlimited mileage cars are f.5000 for eight hours, f.6100 for 24 hours, plus f.1100 insurance. Gas is extra. Bicycles are overpriced at f.1000 for four hours, f.1500 for the whole day. Arii doesn't rent to people under age 25.

Pierre Rent-A-Car (Pierre Danloue, tel. 56-12-58), which represents Avis, has an office at the Total service station on the airport access road (and elsewhere). Unlimited mileage cars are f.4100 for four hours, f.5400 for eight hours, f.6600 for 24 hours, plus f.950 insurance.

The lowest rates for rental cars, bicycles, and circle-island tours (f.1500) are obtained at **Albert Activities Center** (B.P. 77, Moorea; tel. 56-13-53), with locations opposite the Bali Hai Hotel, Club Bali Hai, and the Moorea Lagoon Hotel. Unlimited mileage cars begin at f.5500 for eight hours including insurance and 10 liters of gasoline. Their island tour (f.1500) is recommended but the other rolling stock is in rough shape, so check carefully before turning the key.

Airport

Moorea Temae Airport (MOZ) is at the northeast corner of the island. No *trucks* serve the airport, so unless you rent a car you'll be stuck with a high taxi fare in addition to the airfare: f.700 to the Bali Hai Hotel or Vaiare wharf, f.1300 to the Moorea Lagoon Hotel, f.2300 to Club Med. You could also walk out to the main highway and wait for the boat *truck* (f.200) or hitch. The Moorea Visitors Bureau has a brochure counter at the airport.

SOCIETY ISLANDS

The Leeward Islands

Huahine, Raiatea, Tahaa, Bora Bora, Maupiti

Mount Temanu, Bora Bora

an early 19th century view of Fare, Huahine

HUAHINE

Huahine, 170 km northwest of Papeete, is the first Leeward Island encountered on the ferry ride north from Tahiti. This friendly, untouristed island, a taste of times gone by, is an easy escape from busy Papeete. In many ways lush, mountainous Huahine has more to offer than overcrowded Bora Bora. The variety of scenery, splendid beaches, archaeological remains, and characterful main town all call on you to visit. Huahine is a well-known surfing locale with excellent lefts and rights in the passes off Fare.

It's claimed that the island got its name because, when viewed from the sea, Huahine has the shape of a reclining woman—very appropriate for such a fertile, enchanting place. *Hua* means "phallus" (from a rock on Huahine Iti) while *hine* comes from *vahine* (woman). The almost entirely Polynesian population numbers 4,479 (1988). Some of

the greatest leaders in the struggle for the independence of Polynesia, Pouvanaa a Oopa among them, have come from this idyllic spot.

Orientation
The little town of Fare, with its tree-lined boulevard along the quay is joyfully peaceful after the roar of Papeete. A beach runs right along the west side of the main street. There isn't a lot to do in Fare so you're able to stop and relax. The seven other villages on Huahine are joined by winding, picturesque roads. For bicycle riders the roads of Huahine are fairly flat and easily managed. A narrow channel crossed by a bridge slices Huahine into Huahine Nui and Huahine Iti (Great and Little Huahine, respectively). The story goes that the demigod Hiro's canoe cut this strait. The airstrip sits on an elevated barrier reef

HUAHINE

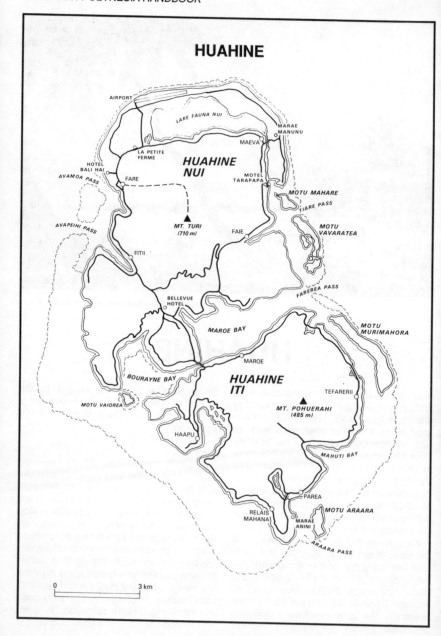

AIRPORT

LAKE FAUNA NUI

MARAE MANUNU

MAEVA

LA PETITE FERME

HOTEL BALI HAI

AVAMOA PASS

FARE

HUAHINE NUI

MOTEL TARAPAPA

MOTU MAHARE

TIARE PASS

AVAPEIHI PASS

MOTU VAVARATEA

MT. TURI (710 m)

FAIE

FITII

BELLEVUE HOTEL

FARAREA PASS

MAROE BAY

MOTU MURIMAHORA

BOURAYNE BAY

MAROE

MOTU VAIOREA

HUAHINE ITI

TEFARERII

MT. POHUERAHI (485 m)

HAAPU

MAHUTI BAY

PAREA

MOTU ARAARA

RELAIS MAHANA

MARAE ANINI

ARAARA PASS

0   3 km

north of Lake Fauna Nui. White beaches line this cantaloupe- and watermelon-rich north shore.

HISTORY

Archaeologists have found that human habitation goes back 1,300 years on Huahine. In 1925 Dr. K.P. Emory of Hawaii's Bishop Museum recorded 54 *marae* in Huahine, most of them built after the 16th century. In 1968 Professor Yosihiko Sinoto found another 40. Huahine Nui was divided into 10 districts with Huahine Iti as a dependency. As a centralized government complex for a whole island, Maeva is unique in Tahiti-Polynesia. Both the great communal *maraes* at Maeva and Parea have two-stepped platforms *(ahu)* which served as raised seats for the gods. About 16 *marae* have been restored and can be easily visited today. The archaeological area on the south shore of Lake Fuana Nui is one of the five most important in Oceania (along with those on Easter I., Tongatapu, Pohnpei, and Kosrae). Maeva was occupied as early as A.D. 900.

History Of The Leeward Islands

Roggeveen, coming from Makatea in the Tuamotus, discovered (but did not land on) Bora Bora and Maupiti on 6 June 1722. Captain Cook discovered the other Leeward Islands in July 1769, which was quite easy since the Tahitians knew them well. Cook had the Raiatean priest Tupaia on board the *Endeavour* as a pilot. Cook wrote: "To these six islands, as they lie contiguous to each other, I gave the names of Society Islands." In 1773 a man named Omai from Huahine sailed to England with Cook's colleague, Capt. Furneaux, aboard the *Adventure;* he returned to Fare in 1777.

The Leeward Islands remained independent until 1887; armed resistance to France was only overcome in 1897. The French sent packing the English missionary group which had been there 88 years. Today 80% of the population of the Leewards remains Protestant.

SIGHTS

Near Fare

After you've had a look around Fare, walk inland on the road which begins beside the third house east of the post office to see the beautiful *mape* (chestnut) forest up the valley. After the road becomes a trail follow the small stream into a forest laced with vanilla vines. By the stream is a long bed-like rock known as Ofaitere, or "Traveling Rock." With a guide you could continue right to the summit of Mt. Turi (710 meters) in about three hours, but it's rough going.

Maeva

Maeva is one of the few Tahitian villages to retain its ancient pattern. In round-ended **Fare Potee** (1974), a replica of an old communal meeting house on the shores of Lake Fauna Nui, is a historical exposition providing much information on the Maeva archaeologi-

Marae Fare Miro at Huahine's Maeva

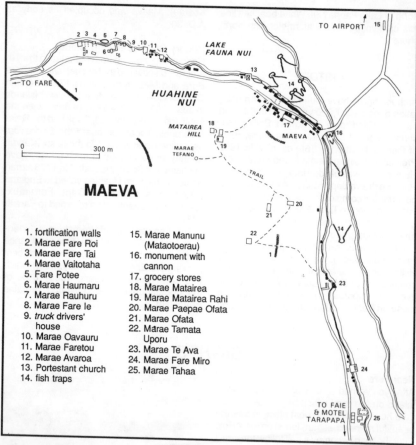

MAEVA

1. fortification walls
2. Marae Fare Roi
3. Marae Fare Tai
4. Marae Vaitotaha
5. Fare Potee
6. Marae Haumaru
7. Marae Rauhuru
8. Marae Fare Ie
9. *truck* drivers' house
10. Marae Oavauru
11. Marae Faretou
12. Marae Avaroa
13. Portestant church
14. fish traps
15. Marae Manunu (Mataotoerau)
16. monument with cannon
17. grocery stores
18. Marae Matairea
19. Marae Matairea Rahi
20. Marae Paepae Ofata
21. Marae Ofata
22. Marae Tamata Uporu
23. Marae Te Ava
24. Marae Fare Miro
25. Marae Tahaa

cal site. Each of the 10 district chiefs of Huahine Nui had his own *marae;* many are strewn along the lakeshore and in the nearby hills. The plentiful small fish in the lake were able to support large chiefly and priestly classes. Under the bridge at the east end of the village are ancient stone fish traps. Huge stone walls were erected to defend Maeva against invaders from Bora Bora and (later) France. Many of the structures were restored by Prof. Y.H. Sinoto of Hawaii in the 1970s.

One way to organize a visit to Maeva is to follow the road around to **Marae Te Ave,** then cut up into the foothills on a trail which leads

between stakes planted with vanilla (follow the map). **Marae Ofata** gives a magnificent view over the whole northeast coast of Huahine. The ruins of **Marae Tefano** are engulfed by an immense banyan tree. **Marae Matairea Rahi** was the most sacred place on Huahine, dedicated to Tane, god of light. The backrests of Huahine's eight principal chiefs are in the southernmost compound of the *marae,* where the most important religious ceremonies took place.

When you get back down to the road return to the bridge, across which is a monument guarded by seven cannon. Underneath are buried the French soldiers killed in the Battle of Maeva (1846) when the islanders successfully defended their independence against French marines sent to annex the island. A few hundred meters farther along toward the ocean and to the left is two-tiered **Marae Manunu,** the community *marae* of Huahine Nui. In its base is the grave of Raiti, the last great priest of Huahine. When he died in 1915 a huge stone fell from the *marae.*

Maeva is easily accessible by *truck* from Fare (six km, f.150), and there are two small stores where you can get cold drinks. The Hawaiian artist/singer Bobby Halcomb resides here. His stylish neo-Polynesian paintings inspired by pre-European mythology are available at the Bali Hai Hotel in postcard form. From Faie, south of Maeva, a steep track crosses the mountains, making a complete circuit of Huahine Nui possible.

Huahine Iti

Though a bridge joins the two islands, Huahine Iti is far less accessible than Huahine Nui. *Trucks* to **Parea** (f.400) run only once a day, so you'll have to stay the night unless you rent a bicycle, scooter, or car. The one hotel is expensive so you may want to bring a tent.

On a golden beach on Point Tiva one km south of Parea is **Marae Anini**, the community *marae* of Huahine Iti. Look for petroglyphs on this two-tiered structure dedicated to the god Oro where human sacrifices once took place. If you decide to camp near the *marae*, don't leave a mess. Search for the water tap by the road at the end of the path (search). Be aware of theft by dogs at night and small boys by day. The only grocery store on Huahine Iti is at **Haapu**, but a grocery truck circles the island several times daily; the locals can tell you when to expect it. Another nice beach with better swimming is a couple of km west. Surfing is possible in Araara Pass beside the *motu* just off Marae Anini.

Haapu village was originally built entirely over the water for lack of sufficient shoreline to house it. Over the centuries the move has gone ashore. From the water Bourayne Bay to the west of the inter-island bridge is one of the loveliest spots on the island.

This bridge links Huahine Nui to Huahine Iti.

PRACTICALITIES

ACCOMMODATIONS

Several inexpensive hotels await you in Fare. Cheapest are the rooms above the post office (f.2500 s or d) at **Pension Rine** (B.P. 19, Fare; tel. 68-82-79). Inquire at Ah Foussan, the large Chinese store on the waterfront with the Coke signs. They have water problems.

Guynette's Lodging (tel. 68-83-75), on the waterfront to the left as you get off the boat, has a 12-bed f.1000 dorm (single night f.1500), three shared four-bed rooms for f.1250 pp, and three doubles for f.3000, minimum two nights, maximum one month. On departure day you can use the hostel facilities all day for an extra f.300 (the Papeete boat leaves in the evening).

Guynette serves a big chicken dinner with wine for f.1000 (notice the chicken coop behind the hostel). You can also cook your own meals. Mask and snorkel may be rented at f.550 a day. It's a clean place: no shoes or radios allowed in the house. Upon arrival peruse the list of rules and rates—applied rigorously. Guynette, a Belgian expat who speaks good English and German, is a bit of a character. Her overhead exceeds US$1000 a month so she can't make exceptions. Highly recommended.

Nearby on the waterfront is decrepit three-story **Hotel Huahine** (tel. 68-82-69), overpriced at f.2500 s, f.4000 d, f.5000 t. The price drops to f.2000 s, f.3000 d, f.4000 t if you stay three nights. They have water problems, and don't order any meals here as the food is lousy and far too expensive.

Pension Martial et Enite (B.P. 37, Fare; tel. 68-82-37) is a six-room boarding house at the west end of the waterfront beyond the snack bar. A room here with breakfast and dinner is f.4800 s, f.8400 d (two-day minimum stay, shared bath). Middle-of-the-night arrivals mustn't knock on the door before 0700. They're often full or closed. Martial and Enite also serve meals to outsiders in their thatched cookhouse on the beach for f.2200, or f.3000 if shellfish are on the menu. Advance notice must be given, but the food is good (closed on Sundays).

In a pinch you could **camp** free in the coconut plantation on the beach 300 meters north of town near the Bali Hai Hotel. Take care with your gear as there have been many thefts from campers, surfers, and sunbathers

the back porch at Guynette's Lodging, Fare, Huahine

the view across the bay from Guynette's Lodging, Fare, Huahine

along this beach. It's probably too risky to go off and leave your tent unattended.

Chez Lovina (tel. 68-81-90 or 68-81-11) a km beyond the Bali Hai toward the airport has four oversized ramshackle bungalows with cooking and bathing facilities at f.5500 for up to four persons.

Motel Tarapapa (Franchi Napoleon, B.P. 80, Fare; tel. 68-81-23) is just south of the archaeological area at Maeva. A room in a long block of units with cooking facilities is f.3000 s, f.4000 d or t, or f.50,000 a month. Airport transfers are f.400.

Expensive Hotels

The American-owned **Bali Hai Hotel** (B.P. 2, Fare; tel. 68-82-77) is probably the nicest of the four-hotel Bali Hai chain. The 10 rooms in the main building begin at f.8500 s, f.10,000 d, f.12,500 t (children under 18 free), the 34 lakeside bungalows about double. The Bali Hai's tour around the island lasts 2.5 hours for f.2400. The sunset cruise Tues. and Fri. or Sat. (varies) aboard the *Liki Tiki II* is free. If you're in Fare Monday at 2000 don't miss the Tahitian dancing at the hotel. They don't mind if strangers wander in and add to the ambience. Splurge for dinner with the elderly or watch the show from the bar. The dancers often begin late, so hang loose.

Even if you're not staying the Bali Hai is a kind of museum with a showcase in the lobby displaying artifacts found here by Dr. Yosihiko H. Sinoto of the Bishop Museum, Hawaii, who excavated the site during construction of the hotel in 1973-75. Marae Tahuea has been reconstructed on the grounds.

The **Hotel Bellevue** (B.P. 21, Huahine; tel. 68-82-76), six km south of Fare, offers eight rooms in the main building at f.3500 s, f.4500 d, f.5000 t, 15 bungalows for twice that. There's an expensive restaurant (meals f.2500 each) with a view of Maroe Bay. Roundtrip airport transfers are f.600. Considering the expense, isolation, and absence of a beach (there is a swimming pool), the Bellevue has little going for it.

The **Relais Mahana** (B.P. 30, Huahine; tel. 68-81-54) on a wide white beach at Parea is a hideaway for the affluent. A garden bungalow for up to three persons is f.11,500. For all meals add another f.4000 pp; roundtrip airport transfers are an extra f.1200 pp. If price isn't everything, Relais Mahana should be your choice.

OTHER PRACTICALITIES

Food

Fare doesn't have a good, cheap eatery. The only reasonable places to fill your stomach are the food trailers, which congregate at the wharf when a ship is due in. One trailer is there every afternoon making *crepes breton.* The numerous Chinese stores sell groceries and cold beer. What you'd pay for the cheapest item on the menu at the "snack bar" will get you the makings of fine sandwiches. The tap water on Huahine can be clouded after heavy rains.

Snack Te Marama (tel. 68-81-76) at the west end of the waterfront charges similar prices to the restaurant at the Bali Hai Hotel, which is a little ridiculous. It's the only place in town serving regular meals and they know it. Te Marama does have an unpretentious terrace built over the lagoon, so drop in for an afternoon coffee or a sunset beer. And there your choice ends on Huahine!

Services

The **Mairie de Huahine** (town hall) provides an excellent free ice water fountain to the left in the courtyard. Public toilets and wash basins are in one of the yellow buildings on the waterfront (if open). The **Banque Socredo** branch (tel. 68-82-71) is on the first street back from the Fare waterfront. The **gendarmerie** is opposite the hospital at the south end of town over the bridge. Yachts anchor just off the Bali Hai. Don't leave valuables unattended on the beach on Huahine.

Transport

The **Air Tahiti** agent (tel. 68-82-65) is wedged in between the Chinese stores on the Fare waterfront. For information on flights to Huahine from Papeete, Moorea, Raiatea, and Bora Bora see the main Introduction to this book.

The Papeete ships tie up to the wharf in the middle of town. *Taporo IV* and *Temehani* arrive from Papeete around 0200 on Tues., Thurs., and Sat., returning from Raiatea on

their way to Papeete Tues., Thurs., Fri., and Sun. afternoons. The *Raromatai Ferry* arrives from Papeete at the more convenient hour of 0600 on Wed. and Sat., departing for Papeete again at 2000 on Thurs. and Sunday. Tickets are sold on the wharf as the ships are loading.

Getting around Huahine is not easy. You'll find *trucks* to anywhere on Huahine when a ship arrives; otherwise they're irregular. Only one truck a day runs to Maeva, leaving Fare at 0830 (f.150).

Kake Rent-A-Car (B.P. 34, Fare; tel. 68-82-59) beside the entrance to the Bali Hai Hotel rents small cars (f.5500 plus f.1000 for insurance and f.1000 for gas for eight hours), scooters (f.3500 plus f.700 insurance for eight hours), and bicycles (f.800 for eight hours). If you can get a small group together consider renting a six-passenger Subaru minibus from Kake for f.6700, plus f.1000 insurance, plus f.1000 gas for eight hours. This would work out to around f.1500 pp for a complete island tour at your own pace.

Le Petite Ferme (B.P. 12, Huahine; tel. 68-82-98), between Fare and the airport, offers riding with Jerome, Connie, and their 10 small, robust Marquesan horses. A two-hour ride along the beach is f.2600 (offered at 0800 and 1600). They also offer a two-day ride and camp-out in the mountains for f.12,500, meals included. A three-day ride right around the island is f.18,500. Call up to let them know you're coming. This is the best horseback riding operation in Tahiti-Polynesia.

Airport

The airport (HUH) is four km north of Fare. Make arrangements for the airport minibus (f.300 pp) at Pension Enite.

RAIATEA

Raiatea is the second largest and perhaps the friendliest high island of Tahiti-Polynesia. Uturoa is a pleasant, unspoiled town, much like Papeete was long ago. Yet this relaxed port is the business and administrative center of the Leeward Islands. The rest of the population of 8,560 (1988) lives in eight flower-filled villages around the island: Avera, Opoa, Puohine, Fetuna, Vaiaau, Tehurui, Tevaitoa, and Tuu Fenua. The west coast of Raiatea south of Tevaitoa is old Polynesia through and through. Raiatea is traditionally the ancient Havai'i, the sacred isle from which all of Eastern Polynesia was colonized.

Orientation
Everything is easy to find in Uturoa (population 3098). The double row of Chinese stores along the main drag opens up onto a colorful market. On Wed. and Fri. mornings the Tahaa people sell their products here; the Sun. market is over by 0700. Beyond this is the harbor, with a pleasant park alongside. By the souvenir stalls opposite the wharf is a tourist information stand. All of the stores in Uturoa close for lunch from 1200-1400.

THE LAND AND HISTORY

Raiatea, 220 km northwest of Tahiti, shares a protected lagoon with Tahaa three km away. Legends tell how the two islands were cut apart by a mythical eel. About 30 km of steel-blue sea separates Raiatea from both Huahine and Bora Bora. Mount Temehani on mountainous Raiatea rises to 772 meters, and some of the coastlines are rugged and narrow. The highest mountain is Toomaru (1,017 meters). All of the people live on a coastal plain planted in coconuts where cattle graze. No beaches are found on hulking big Raiatea itself. Instead, picnickers are taken to picture-postcard *motus* in the lagoon. Surfing is possible at the eight passes which open onto the Raiatea/Tahaa lagoon, and windsurfers are active. The Leeward Islands (Iles Sous le Vent) is the most popular sailing area in Tahiti-Polynesia and most of the charter boats are based at Raiatea.

In the old days Raiatea was the religious, cultural, and political center of Tahiti-Polynesia. Tradition holds that the great Polynesian

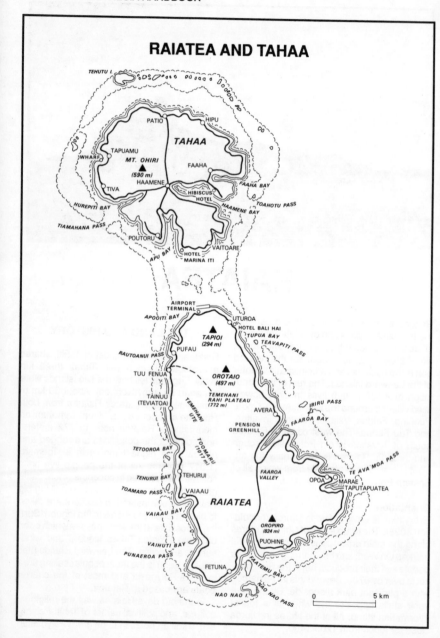

RAIATEA AND TAHAA

TEHUTU I.

PATIO   HIPU

TAHAA

TAPUAMU

WHARF   MT. OHIRI
         (590 m)
         HAAMENE   FAAHA

TIVA   FAAHA BAY

HUREPITI BAY   HIBISCUS
                          HOTEL   TOAHOTU PASS
TIAMAHANA PASS   HAAMENE BAY

         POUTORU   VAITOARE
APU BAY
              HOTEL
              MARINA ITI

AIRPORT
TERMINAL
APOOITI BAY   UTUROA
                   HOTEL BALI HAI
            TAPIOI   TUPUA BAY
            (294 m)   TEAVAPITI PASS
         PUFAU
RAUTOANUI PASS
                   OROTAIO
TUU FENUA   (497 m)
                                    IRIRU PASS
TAINUU   TEMEHANI
(TEVIATOA)   RAHI PLATEAU   AVERA
                   (772 m)   FAAROA BAY
            TEMEHANI
            UTE   PENSION
                                GREENHILL
TETOOROA BAY   TOOMARU   TE AVA MOA PASS
                (1017 m)   FAAROA
TEHURUI BAY   TEHURUI   VALLEY   OPOA
                                                MARAE
TOAMARO PASS   VAIAAU   TAPUTAPUATEA

VAIAAU BAY   RAIATEA

VAIHUTI BAY   OROPIRO
                         (824 m)
PUNAEROA PASS   PUOHINE

         FETUNA   FAATEMU BAY

            NAO NAO I.   NAO NAO PASS   0   5 km

voyagers to Hawaii and New Zealand parted from these shores.

Raiatea was Capt. Cook's favorite island; he visited three times. During his first voyage in 1769 he called first at Opoa from 20 to 24 July. After having surveyed Bora Bora from the sea, he anchored for a week in the Rautoanui Pass on the northwest coast of Raiatea, near the village of Tuu Fenua. During his second voyage Cook lay at anchor twice, first from 8 to 17 Sept. 1773 and again from 25 May to 4 June 1774, both times at Rautoanui. His third visit was from 3 Nov. to 7 Dec. 1777, again at Rautoanui. It can therefore be said that Rautoanui (which he calls "Haamanino Harbour" in his journals) was one of Cook's favorite anchorages.

The last resistance to the French takeover on Raiatea lasted until 1897 when French troops and warships used arms and guns to conquer the island. The native leader of the resistance, Teraupoo, was deported to New Caledonia.

SIGHTS

For a view of four islands climb **Tapioi Hill** (294 meters), the one topped by a TV antenna behind Uturoa. Take the road beside the Gendarmerie Nationale up past the locked gate and ignore any bad dogs you encounter: visitors are allowed. The fastest time on record for climbing Tapioi is 17 minutes! There's good swimming in a large pool open to the sea at the Centre Nautique *("la piscine")* on the coast north of Uturoa.

It takes four to 10 hours to ride a bicycle around Raiatea (97 km), depending on how fast you go. A **waterfall** may be visited up the valley from the Chinese store near PK 9, Avera. The road down the east coast circles fjord-like **Faaroa Bay,** associated with the legends of Polynesian migration. The Apoomau River, which drains the Faaroa Valley, is the only navigable river in Tahiti-Polynesia (for two km by dinghy). From the popular yacht anchorage in the middle of the bay there's a fine view of Toomaru, highest peak in the Leeward Islands.

On the point just beyond Opoa, 32 km from Uturoa, is **Marae Taputapuatea**, one of the largest and best preserved in Polynesia. Its mighty *ahu* is 43 meters long, 7.3 meters wide, and between two and three meters high. Before it is a rectangular courtyard paved with black volcanic rocks. A small platform in the middle of the *ahu* once bore the image of Oro, god of war; backrests still mark the seats of high chiefs on the courtyard. Marae Taputapuatea is directly opposite Te

Marea Taputapuatea on Raiatea is among the most sacred sites Polynesia.

Ava Moa Pass, and fires on the *maraes* may have been a beacon to ancient navigators. Human sacrifices and firewalking once took place on the *marae*.

Marae Taputapuatea is said to retain its psychic power. Test this by writing down all your negative emotions, bad habits, unhappy memories, and self-doubts on a piece of paper. Then burn the paper(s) on the *marae*. The catharsis works best when done solo, beneath a full moon or the three following nights. The *tupapau* (spirits) are most active at this time, often taking the form of dogs, cats, pigs, etc.

The setting of the village of **Fetuna** on the south coast is attractive and there are two Chinese stores.

Tevaitoa church, on the west side of Raiatea, is the oldest on the island. Petroglyphs on a broken stone by the road at the entrance to the church show a turtle and some other indistinguishable figure. Behind the church is **Marae Tainuu** dedicated to the ancient god Taaroa.

HIKING

According to Polynesia mythology the fertility god Oro was born from the molten rage of **Mt. Temehani** (772 meters), the cloud-covered plateau that dominates the north end of the island. *Tiare apetahi*, a sacred white flower which not only exists nowhere else on Earth but also resists transplantation, grows on the slopes around the summit. The fragile blossom represents the five fingers of a beautiful Polynesian girl who fell in love with the handsome son of a high chief, but couldn't marry him due to her lowly birth. These flowers are now rare, so don't pick any! Small pink orchids also grow by the way.

Temehani can be climbed from Pufau, the second bay south of Marina Apooiti. Note a series of concrete benches by the road as you come around the north side of the bay. The jeep track inland is about 200 meters south of the bridge. You climb straight up through pine reforestation till you have a clear view of Temehani Rahi and Temehani Ute, divided by a deep gorge. Descend to the right and continue up the track you see on the hillside opposite. It takes about three hours from the main road to the Temehani Rahi Plateau. A guide up Temehani should charge about f.5000 for the group. Friday and Sat. are the best days to go, long pants and sturdy shoes required.

Poedoora, daughter of a chief of Raiatea, as painted by Capt. Cook's artist John Webber

PRACTICALITIES

ACCOMMODATIONS

Places Near Uturoa

The budget traveler's best headquarters on Raiatea is **Pension Marie-France** (B.P. 272, Uturoa; tel. 66-37-10) by the lagoon just beyond Chez Andre Chinese store, a km south of the Bali Hai Hotel (yellow sign). There's a clean modern dormitory with full cooking facilities at f.1200 pp for two or more nights (f.1500 if you stay only one night). Four neat private rooms with shared bath are f.3600 d, f.4400 t. Campers pay f.800 but cannot use the dormitory facilities. Bicycles are free for guests. There's even hot water. The lagoon off Pension Marie-France is good for windsurfing and minibus tours of the island can be arranged.

If you're into **scuba diving** be sure to stay at this pension; Marie-France's husband, Patrice Philip, is the local divemaster. Resi-

dents get reduced rates: f.3000 for a one-tank dive (regular f.4000), f.5000 for two tanks (regular f.6000). He'll take you to the century-old, 100-meter wreck of a Dutch coal boat sunk off the Bali Hai, the top of which is 18 meters down. Snorkelers are dropped on a *motu* for f.600 (gear included). A trip right around Tahaa by motorized canoe with visits to two *motus* is f.3500 (minimum of three persons).

Hotel Le Motu (B.P. 549, Raiatea; tel. 66-34-06) is above the noisy pool hall on the main street in the center of Uturoa. At f.5500 s or d, f.6500 t, it's medium-priced. The seven rooms have private bath, but cross your fingers for hot water. The location is convenient, the adjoining restaurant excellent, and the management convivial, which helps compensate for the tariff. If you're here on business it's ideal. Le Motu arranges picnics on a reef island for f.5000 pp and waterskiing across the lagoon.

Expensive Hotel

The American-owned **Bali Hai Hotel** (B.P. 43, Uturoa; tel. 66-31-49) just south of Uturoa is Raiatea's only luxury hotel. The nine over-water bungalows run f.17,000 s, f.18,500 d (rooms half that). A breakfast and dinner meal plan is f.3400 pp extra. Unlike the accommodations, the hotel bar (shaped like a Polynesian canoe) is reasonable and a great place to stop for coffee or a drink. One or two ukulele-strumming Tahitians might host happy hour.

Places Around Raiatea

Hotel Apooiti (Jean and Elianne Boubee, B.P. 397, Uturoa; tel. 66-33-47) is in a coconut grove five km from Uturoa (no sign). Look on the point across the bay from Marina Apooiti, about two km west of the airport. The seven well-spaced bungalows have cooking facilities and private bath (hot water) at f.5000 s or d, f.6000 t. This would be good for families.

Pension Ariane Brotherson (B.P. 236, Uturoa; tel. 66-33-70) is a km up the valley from PK 8 near Avera School. The two rooms with shared bath go for f.4000 s, f.7000 d, but that includes breakfast and dinner, airport transfers, and sightseeing excursions. (The meals are too spicy and the trips short.)

Pension Yollande Roopinia (B.P. 298, Uturoa; tel. 66-35-28), near the Raiatea Village Hotel at PK 10, Avera, is a large thatched bungalow with four rooms at f.4000 d (private bath). Cooking facilities are provided but you may be asked to take demi-pension.

The locally owned **Raiatea Village Hotel** (B.P. 282, Uturoa; tel. 66-31-62) at the mouth of Faaroa Bay (PK 10) is laid out like a real Tahitian village. A garden bungalow with kitchenette is f.5885 s, f.8239 d, f.9416 t. Airport transfers are f.1000 pp extra.

Pension Greenhill (B.P. 598, Raiatea; tel. 66-37-64), at PK 12 overlooking serene Faaroa Bay, is an exquisite little hideaway nestled among flowers and birds. Greenhill caters to a select crowd. Cheerful rooms with private bath are f.6000 s, f.8000 d including all meals at the host's table (minimum stay two nights). Sightseeing trips and occasional boat rides are also included, though a minimum of four persons is required before they'll go. Getting into town is no problem—the pension minibus makes several trips a day and will arrange to pick you up later. Bicycles are at your disposal. Gourmet chef Jason makes dining a delight, while hostess Marie-Isabelle loves to sit and chat with guests. They'll pick you up free at airport or wharf if you call ahead. Recommended.

FOOD, ETC.

Restaurant Au Motu (closed Sun., tel. 66-34-06) is up a stairway overlooking the park in the center of Uturoa. Their specialty is seafood, cooked as only the French can. Fish of the day is an entire reef fish grilled and served with rice (f.1000). Proprietor Roger Bardou adds to the breezy, informal atmosphere by trading gossip with his clientele.

The **Jade Garden Restaurant** (open Wed. to Sat.; tel. 66-34-40) on the main street serves exquisite Chinese dishes at about f.1000 a plate (reasonable for Polynesia), but it's pretentious. Climb to the upstairs dining room for more privacy.

Le Quai des Pecheurs (tel. 66-36-83) on the wharf offers pizza with a view of the port. If you stick to the pizza this is one of the cheapest places to eat, and large Hinano beer is available (f.450). They don't mind if you linger all evening (the informative cook might join you at your table now and then).

To escape the tourist scene try **Bar Restaurant Maraamu** (Chez Remy; tel. 66-31-08) in what appears to be an old Chinese store between the park and the small boat harbor. The few minutes it takes to locate will net you the lowest prices in town. Coffee and omelettes are served in the morning, while the lunch menu tilts toward Chinese food. There's also poisson cru and a good selection of other dishes—even cheap carafes of wine!

Snack Moemoea on the harbor in the former Hotel Hinano building has hamburgers (f.300). **Coconut's Restaurant** at the south end of the waterfront has a complete daily menu for f.1100 and ice cream.

Entertainment
Firewalking, once commonly practiced on Raiatea, is now a dying art. The pit is just across the street from the Bali Hai Hotel, so ask there if they'll be lighting anyone's fire.

Cockfights are staged in the pit at PK 9, Avera, Sundays at 1400, a good chance to give your baser instincts free reign. The cockfighting season is June to December—you place a bet on the bird of your choice.

Services
Of Uturoa's four banks only Banque Socredo (tel. 66-30-64) doesn't levy a f.300 commission. The large modern post office is just north of town, with the **gendarmerie** about 50 meters beyond on the left. There are free public washrooms *(sanitaires publics)* on the wharf behind Le Quai des Pecheurs restaurant.

TRANSPORT

Getting There And Away
The **Air Tahiti** office (tel. 66-32-50) is at the airport. Flights operate from Raiatea to Maupiti (f.4865) three times a week. For information on flights from Papeete, Huahine, and Bora Bora see the main Introduction to this book.

You can catch the *Temehani, Taporo IV,* and *Raromatai Ferry* to Bora Bora or Huahine twice weekly. Consult the schedule in the main Introduction. Several village boats run between Raiatea and Tahaa on Wed. and Fri. mornings (f.300).

The *Taporo I,* a small cargo/passenger ship, shuttles weekly between Raiatea and Maupiti, departing Raiatea Tues. or Thurs. at midnight (f.850 deck, f.1450 berth). Once every three months the *Taporo I* makes a six-day roundtrip Raiatea-Scilly-Bellingshausen-Mopelia-Raiatea (f.8000 deck). Meals

are not included. For information write: Societe Taporo Teaotea, B.P. 68, Uturoa, Raiatea (tel. 66-32-30). Exact times of all boats should be verified locally as they change constantly.

Bareboating
The Moorings (B.P. 165, Uturoa; tel. 66-35-93), a bareboat charter operation with 19 yachts, is based at Marina Apooiti two km west of the airport. Rates begin at f.25,500 a day, f.178,500 a week, for an 11-meter yacht without crew for use around the Leeward Islands. Food and drink are extra. This may seem like a lot but split among a nautical-minded group it's a much better deal than hotel rooms. Charterers are given a complete briefing on channels and anchorages, and provided with a detailed set of charts. All boats are radio-equipped and a voice from The Moorings is available to talk nervous skippers in and out. Travel by night is forbidden, but by day it's easy sailing.

Another yacht charter operation, **A.T.M. South Pacific** (B.P. 331, Uturoa; tel. 66-23-18), is slightly cheaper than The Moorings. The huge power-cruiser *Manavaroa* (B.P. 377, Uturoa) is also based at Marina Apooiti. This monster rents for US$1250 a day, plus US$100 per cruising hour, plus US$50 a day pp for room and board.

Getting Around
Trucks depart Uturoa for Fetuna (f.200) and Opoa every afternoon, but never on Sunday.

Mr. Charles Brotherson (B.P. 99, Uturoa; tel. 66-32-15 or 66-39-04), the gentleman barber, rents mopeds out of his barbershop (open Mon., Wed., and Fri.) adjacent to the jeweler beside Hotel Le Motu *(not* the one directly below the hotel beside the pool hall). Other times find Charles at the Mobil service station between Uturoa and the airport. His Vespa motorscooters are f.4000 for eight hours, f.7000 for 24 hours, insurance included (f.5000 deposit). No special motorcycle driver's license is required. Charles is the most knowledgeable person on Raiatea and speaks good English.

Garage Motu Tapu (Guirouard Rent-A-Car, B.P. 139, Uturoa; tel. 66-33-09) across the road from the airport has cars at f.7500 for 24 hours, insurance and km included. **Hotel Le Motu** (tel. 66-34-06) also rents cars at f.7500 a day, mileage and insurance included.

The **Centre Equestre** (tel. 66-22-46) at PK 7, Avera, charges f.1200 an hour for horseback riding. You must reserve 24 hours in advance and there's a two-person minimum.

Airport

The airport (RFP) is three km northwest of Uturoa. A taxi from the Uturoa market taxi stand to the airport is f.500 (double tariff late at night). Most of the hotels pick up clients at the airport free upon request.

frangipani (Plumeria obtusa)

TAHAA

Raiatea's lagoonmate, 90-sq-km Tahaa is shaped like an hibiscus flower. It's a quiet island with little traffic and few tourists. Mt. Ohiri (590 meters), highest point on the island, gets its name from the demigod Hiro who was born here. There aren't many specific attractions other than a chance to escape the crowds and hurried life on the other Society islands. Notice the vanilla plantations. Beaches are scarce on the main island so the pension owners arrange picnics on *motus* such as Tautau off Tapuamu. The *motus* off the northeast side of Tahaa have the finest white-sand beaches. The 4,005 (1988) Tahaa islanders are a little wary of outsiders. It's well off the beaten track.

Orientation
The administrative center is at Patio on the north coast, where the post office, *mairie* (town hall), and police station share one compound. The ship from Papeete ties up to the wharf at Tapuamu. There's a large covered area at the terminal where you could spread a sleeping bag in a pinch. A new road crosses the mountains from Patio direct to Haamene.

Sights
Several large sea turtles are held captive in a tank by the lagoon behind the community hall near the church in Tiva. You could walk right around the main part of Tahaa in about eight hours with stops passing villages every couple of km. Haamene Bay, the longest of Tahaa's four fjords, catches the full force of the southeast trades.

ACCOMMODATIONS AND FOOD

Lodging With The Inhabitants
The most convenient place to stay is **Chez Pascal** (tel. 65-60-42). From the Tapuamu ferry wharf you'll see a small bridge at the head of the bay. Turn left as you leave the dock and head for this. Chez Pascal is the first house north of the bridge on the inland side. Bed and breakfast is f.1500 pp, dinner another f.1500. Pay f.5000 pp and you'll get accommodations with all meals, plus a boat trip to a *motu*. You can cook and they may loan you the family bicycle.

About two km south of the Tapuamu ferry wharf is **Chez Anna** (tel. 65-61-18), also known as the Tahaa Village Hotel, operated by Mr. Petit Tetuanui. There are five small bungalows on the lagoon at f.4000 each (up to five persons), with a 50% reduction if you stay a week. You can cook. A trip to a *motu* is f.2000 for a group or f.1000 for one person.

In Patio ask for Simeon Chu (B.P. 1, Tahaa; tel. 67-73-13) in the Conseiller Technique office behind the post office. If his house is full he'll direct you to Madame Mama Marae (tel. 65-64-08) who lives near the large Protestant church nearby. Both rent rooms with shared bath at about f.2500 s or d, half pension another f.1500 pp.

Hotels

The **Hotel L'Hibiscus** (B.P. 184, Tahaa; tel. 65-61-06) or "Tahaa Lagon" is run by Leo and Lolita on the northeast side of windy Haamene Bay. Get there on the Haamene launch (Wed. and Fri. mornings) and ask to be dropped near the hotel. Other days call Leo from Raiatea and he'll come over to pick you up in his motorized canoe for f.1000 pp. L'Hibiscus has two classes of accommodations: nice bungalows with private bath at f.5000 s or d, f.6000 t, or a hostel nearby called Le Moana with dorm beds at f.1500 pp for one to three nights, f.1000 pp for four nights and up (no camping).

Although the accommodations are satisfactory, the trick is that virtually everything you consume—even the water you drink— is charged extra at resort prices. Common drinking water is not available at L'Hibiscus; bottled water is f.250. The prices of the meals are fixed at f.500 for breakfast, f.1500 for lunch, f.1750 for dinner (not possible to order a la carte). Don't accept a "free welcome drink" from Leo or Lolita unless you don't mind having it added to your bill. There are no cooking facilities and the nearest store is three km away in Haamene (bring food and bottled water). The running water in the hostel may be turned off, although you can usually use the communal shower behind the restaurant. Lighting in the hostel could consist of a kerosene lamp.

The **Hotel Marina Iti** (B.P. 888, Uturoa, Raiatea; tel. 65-61-01) on the isolated south tip of Tahaa opposite Raiatea offers clean pleasant garden bungalows on Tahaa's only sandy beach at f.5000 s, f.7000 d, f.9000 t. Use of bicycles, canoe, and snorkeling gear

in included, but meals are extra: breakfast f.700, lunch and dinner f.2500 each. Scuba diving is f.5000. Roundtrip transfers from Raiatea are f.3500 pp. A package including accommodations, food, and transfers from Raiatea is US$110 pp. Credit cards are not accepted. Numerous cruising yachts anchor in the calm waters offshore (f.500 a day to use the facilities).

The Marina offers yacht cruises within the Tahaa-Raiatea lagoon for US$110 pp a day including meals (minimum four participants). Bareboat yacht rentals begin at US$260 a day, plus US$100 a day extra for a skipper (if required). There are discounts in the off yachting season Oct. to May. In the U.S. these charters can be arranged through The Moorings and Ocean Voyages (see page 78).

Food

No real restaurants are to be found on Tahaa. A grocery truck passes the L'Hibiscus around 1000 on Mon., Tues., Thurs., and Sat.; the same truck calls at the Marina Iti about noon daily except Sundays.

TRANSPORT

There's no airport on Tahaa. Seven of the eight villages on Tahaa have small passenger launches which leave for Raiatea at 0500 on Wed. and Fri. only, returning to Tahaa at 1100 these same days (f.300 OW). Make sure your boat is going exactly where you want to go.

Temehani and *Taporo* call at Tahaa on Tues. and Thurs., the *Raromatai Ferry* on Wed. (northbound) and Sun. (southbound). There's a telephone booth at Tapuamu wharf where you could call your hotel to have them come pick you up.

Trucks on Tahaa are for transporting school children only, so you may have to hitch to get around. It's not that hard to hitch a ride down the west coast from Patio to Haamene, but there's almost no traffic along the east coast. Even car rentals are difficult on Tahaa.

BORA BORA

Bora Bora, 260 km northwest of Papeete, is everyone's idea of a South Pacific island. Dramatic basalt peaks soar 700 meters above a gorgeous, multi-colored lagoon. Slopes and valleys blossom with hibiscus. Some of the most perfect beaches you will ever see are here, complete with topless sunbathers. Among the population of 4,225 (1988) are many skilled dancers. To see them practicing in the evenings follow the beat of village drums to their source.

The uncontrolled expansion of tourism continues to throw up luxury resorts around the island, creating the illusion of Hawaii or some West Indies hot spot. Yet many of the US$250-a-night hotels stand almost empty and the Bora Bora Club Med has closed. Construction of a huge Hyatt Regency proceeded on a swampy shore at the far north end of the island opposite the airport, until halted by skyrocketing costs. Today the crumbling Hyatt ruins stand as a monument to bad planning and the perils of high-impact development.

Orientation

You can arrive at Motu Mute airport and be pleasantly carried to Vaitape wharf by launch, or disembark from a ship at Farepiti wharf, three km north of Vaitape. Most of the stores, banks, and offices are near Vaitape wharf. The best beaches are at Matira at the south tip of the island. *Trucks* link these places and you'll have the choice of staying at a hotel near Vaitape or at Matira.

The Land

Seven-million-year-old Bora Bora is made up of a 10-km-long main island, a few smaller high islands in the lagoon, and a long ring of *motus* on the barrier reef. Pofai Bay marks the center of the island's collapsed crater with Toopua and Toopuaiti as its eroded west wall. Mt. Pahia's gray basalt mass rises 649 meters behind Vaitape and above it soar the sheer cliffs of Otemanu's mighty volcanic plug (727 meters). The wide-angle scenery of the main island is complemented by the surrounding coral reef and numerous *motus*,

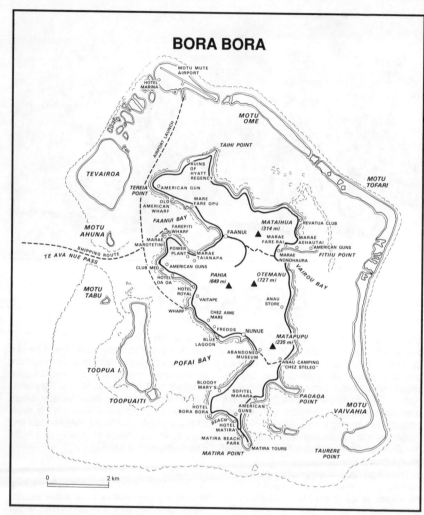

BORA BORA

one of which bears the airport. Tiny Motu Tabu of the travel brochures was popularized in Murnau's 1928 film *Tabou*. Teavanui Pass is the only entry through the barrier reef. Watch for dolphins near this channel as your ship enters Bora Bora's lagoon. Whole colonies sometimes race the boats.

History

The letter "B" doesn't exist in Tahitian, so Bora Bora is actually Pora Pora (First Born). Bora Borans of yesteryear were indomitable warriors who often raided Maupiti, Tahaa, and Raiatea. "Discovered" by Roggeveen in 1722, Bora Bora was visited by Capt. James

Cook in 1777. Charles Darwin came aboard the *Beagle* to study Bora Bora's barrier reef, and he developed part of his theory of atoll formation here. In 1895 the island was annexed by France.

In Feb. 1942 the Americans hastily set up a refueling and regrouping base code-named "Bobcat" on the island to serve shipping between the U.S. west coast or Panama Canal and Australia/New Zealand. You can still see remains from this time, including eight huge naval guns to defend the island against a surprise Japanese attack which never materialized. The big lagoon with only one pass offered a secure anchorage for as many as 100 U.S. Navy transports at a time. A road was built around the island and an airfield constructed. The 4,400 American army troops also left behind 130 half-caste babies, 40% of whom died when the base closed in 1946 and the abandoned infants were forced to switch from their accustomed American baby formulas to island food. The survivors are now approaching ripe middle age. Novelist James A. Michener, a young naval officer at the time, left perhaps the most enduring legacy by modeling his "Bali Hai" on this "enchanted island," Bora Bora.

SIGHTS

South of Vaitape

Behind the Banque de Tahiti at Vaitape Wharf is the **monument to Alain Gerbault**, who sailed his yacht, the *Firecrest,* around the world from 1925-29—the first Frenchman to do so solo. Gerbault's first visit to Bora Bora was from 25 May to 12 June 1926. He returned to Polynesia in 1933 and stayed until 1940. To get an idea how the Bora Borans live take a stroll through the village: go up the road that begins beside the Banque Socredo nearby.

The good, level 32-km road around the island makes it easy to see Bora Bora by rented bicycle. On the north side of Pofai Bay is a large white mansion built as the residence for the governor of American Samoa for the Dino de Laurentis film *Hurricane* starring Mia Farrow. At the head of Pofai Bay notice the odd assortment of looted war wreckage across the road from **Boutique Alain Linda,** remnants of an abandoned A-frame museum. The seven-inch American gun dragged here from Tereia Point is hard to miss. The locations of the other seven MK II naval guns remaining on Bora Bora are given below. An overgrown track up over the saddle and across the island departs from opposite the forlorn, violated gun.

From **Bloody Mary's Restaurant** there's a spectacular view across Pofai Bay to the island's soaring peaks. An unmarked road near the restaurant leads up to a TV tower with a spectacular view (ask). Photographer Erwin Christian's **Moana Art boutique** just north of Hotel Bora Bora has a good selection of postcards. The finest beach on the island stretches east from Hotel Bora Bora to Matira Point. Off the small point at **Hotel Bora Bora** is some of the best snorkeling in the world, with a varied multitude of colorful tropical fish. **Martine's Creations** just east of Hotel Bora Bora has finely crafted black-pearl jewelry and designer beachwear.

Two naval guns sit on the ridge above Hotel Matira. The trail behind the hotel leads right to them (10 minutes): keep straight ahead up to the top of the ridge for good views of the lagoon and neighboring islands. A **public beach** is opposite the **Moana Beach Hotel** on Matira Point. At low tide you can wade from the end of Matira Point right out to the reef.

The East Coast

Continue north to the **Sofitel Marara,** a good place for a beer. Farther up the east side of Bora Bora past Anau is Vairou Bay. An unmarked jeep track crosses the mountains from behind Francois Temanua's house at the head of Vairou Bay to Faanui.

Just a little farther along, the *ahus* of three *maraes* can be seen by the water. A short distance down a side track off the main road

one of eight U.S. naval guns left behind in 1945

is the best of these, **Marae Aehautai**, from whence there's a stupendous view of Otemanu. From here you'll be able to pick out Te Ana Opea cave far up on the side of Otemanu. It's possible to climb up to the cave in about three hours.

Two more American **seven-inch guns** sit atop Fitiiu Point. To get to them continue east along the shore from Marae Aehautai till the way becomes constricted and you are forced onto a black rocky outcrop. Go back just a little and look for a trail up to the ridge and guns. Once again, the view alone makes the visit worthwhile. Other than the Hyatt Regency ruins, little of interest is found farther north on this side of the island. Stop at the **Revatua Club** for a drink at the bar.

North of Vaitape
One American **naval gun** remains on the hillside above the rectangular water tank at Tereia Point. The housing of a second gun, vandalized in 1982, is nearby. The remains of several American concrete wharfs can be seen along the north shore of Faanui Bay. **Marae Fare Opu**, just east of a small boat harbor, is notable for petroglyphs of turtles carved into the stones of the *ahu*. Turtles, a favorite food of the gods, were often offered to them on the *marae*.

Most of the wartime American occupation force was billeted at Faanui, and Quonset

huts can still be found in the bush. Just east of the coconut husk-fueled electricity-generating plant between Faanui and Farepiti wharf is **Marae Taianapa**; its long *ahu* is clearly visible from the road.

The most important *marae* on Bora Bora was **Marae Marotetini** on the point near Farepiti wharf—west of the wharf beyond a huge banyan tree. The great stone *ahu,* 50 meters long and up to three meters high, was restored by Prof. Sinoto in 1968 and is visible from approaching ships.

The last **two American guns** are on the ridge above Club Med, a 10-minute scramble from the main road. At the end of the ridge there's a good view of Te Ava Nui Pass, which the guns were meant to defend. Maupiti is farther out on the horizon.

HIKING

If you're experienced and determined, it's possible to climb **Mt. Pahia** in about three hours. Take the road inland beside the Banque Socredo at Vaitape and go up the depression past a series of mango trees, veering slightly left. Circle the cliffs near the top on the left side, and come up the back of Snoopy's head and along his toes. (These directions will take on meaning if you study Pahia from the end of Vaitape's wharf.) There's no set trail; you must bushwhack.

1. Tetiaroa atoll (Tahiti Tourist Board); 2. sunset over Moorea (Paul Bohler)

1. pier at Residence Linareva, Moorea (D. Stanley);
2. tents at Chez Nelson et Josiane, Moorea (Don Pitcher)

Avoid rainy weather when the way will be muddy and slippery. Note that Otemanu has *never* been climbed because clamps pull right out of the vertical, crumbly cliff face. It's name means "Sea of Birds."

EVENTS

The *Fetes de Juillet* are celebrated at Bora Bora with special fervor. The canoe and bicycle races, javelin throwing, flower cars, singing and dancing competitions run until 0300 nightly. A public ball goes till dawn on the Sat. closest to 14 July. Try to participate in the 10-km foot race to prove that all tourists aren't lazy, but don't take the prizes away from the locals. If you win, be sure to give the money back to them for partying. You'll make good friends that way and have more fun dancing in the evening. The stands are beautiful because the best decorations win prizes, too.

PRACTICALITIES

ACCOMMODATIONS

Nearly a quarter of Tahiti-Polynesia's hotel rooms are on Bora Bora and overbuilding has produced a glut. Except at holiday times, it's not necessary to book a room in advance. In the off season many hotel owners meet the boats. If there isn't anyone from the hotel of your choice at the dock when you arrive get on the blue *truck* marked VAITAPE-ANAU (f.150-300).

Stay in Vaitape if you're interested in observing the life of the inhabitants, hiking, or frequenting the local bars. You're better off at Matira if the beach is what you came for and you prefer the company of other travelers/ tourists. Since most travelers choose to stay at the beach, the budget places at Matira may be overcrowded while those in Vaitape are almost empty, a factor to consider. Bora Bora suffers from serious water shortages, so use it sparingly.

Inexpensive Places Near Vaitape
As you disembark you may be offered a room by someone from the **Hotel Royal Bora Bora** (B.P. 202, Vaitape; tel. 67-71-54). Their minibus meets all boats. This establishment consists of nine bungalows with private bath on the lagoon beside Ets. Loussan supermarket, a few hundred meters north of the wharf in Vaitape. At last report they were asking f.4500 pp in a bungalow including breakfast and dinner, though the price fluctuates according to what the traffic will bear. Avoid the bungalows near the restaurant or shower block—noisy. Hotel Royal also offers beds in small double rooms with shared bath near the restaurant at f.1400 pp with reductions if you stay two or more nights, worth considering only if everything else is full up. No cooking facilities are available. Unfortunately, the elderly Tahitian hotel owner has a rather unpleasant manner and manages to cast a shadow over this hotel.

A better choice would be **Chez Aime Mare** (tel. 67-71-46), a km south of Vaitape pier. They offer simple shared rooms at f.1500 if you stay only one night, f.1000 a night if you stay two nights, f.800 a night if you stay three or more nights. A private room is f.1400 a night. With good cooking facilities and bicycles for rent at f.300 per half day, this place is recommended. The owners live across the street. Once the budget traveler's favorite, since the places at Matira Beach opened up it's been largely deserted, which is rather unfair.

Four or five houses south down the road from Chez Aime past the Jehovah's Witnesses Church is **Chez Alfredo Doom** (tel. 67-70-31; no sign) with a f.1000 pp dorm (minimum stay two nights). Fredo also has a few duplex bungalows with kitchens (f.5000 d, f.6000 t) if you want more privacy. Cooking and bicycles are available.

Marama Bungalows (B.P. 11, Vaitape; tel. 67-72-97) is by the lagoon between Chez Aime and Vaitape wharf. The two units have private bath and fridge but no kitchens (f.5500 d). The distance from the beach and its high price put this place at the bottom of the list.

Inexpensive Places On The Beach
On the Matira peninsula are two excellent alternatives to the hotels. **Chez Nono** (Noel Leverd, B.P. 12, Vaitape; tel. 67-71-38) is beside the beach park across from the Moana Beach Hotel. A room in the three-bedroom guesthouse with shared kitchen is f.3000 s, f.5000 d. Bungalow accommodations are f.1000 more.

Chez Robert et Tina (tel. 67-72-92) has two houses with cooking facilities at the tip of Matira Point beyond the Moana Beach Hotel. Rooms are f.3000 s, f.5000 d. Robert's company Matira Tours (see below) offers excellent lagoon trips, but Robert himself has acquired a taste for female visitors so let him know right away if you're not interested.

Fare Toopua (Annie Muraz, B.P. 87, Vaitape; tel. 67-70-62) is only inexpensive if you're part of a small group. The main feature is the location—near a white-sand beach on Toopua Island across the lagoon from Vai-

tape. The four thatched bungalows with cooking facilities are f.8300 d, f.9500 t, or f.10,700 for four, and that includes an aluminum dinghy with outboard motor for shopping or exploring the lagoon (f.15,000 security deposit). The minimum stay is three nights and monthly rates are available. If you can afford it, this is a great little get-away.

Camping
Most backpackers stay at **Chez Pauline** (Pauline Youssef, B.P. 215, Vaitape; tel. 67-72-16), a perfect campsite in a coconut grove right on a white-sand beach. It's between the Moana Beach and Sofitel Marara hotels, eight km from Vaitape. Pauline charges f.700 pp to camp (own tent) or f.1500 s, f.2500 d in one of her four simple beach cabins. The two thatched bungalows with kitchens are f.4000 s, f.6000 d. The cooking facilities are rudimentary and it's quite a hike to the nearest grocery store, although a food truck circles the island daily. Pauline's experiences water shortages and you must drink bottled water. It can also get crowded here.

The other popular campground is **Chez Steleo** (tel. 67-71-32) at Anau on the east side of the island. Look for the blue VAITAPE-ANAU *truck* at the wharf—transfers are f.300 pp. Steleo, a helpful, laid-back sort of guy, owns the *truck* so once you're staying there additional rides are free. Camping is f.550 pp and there's a dormitory at f.800 pp. You can cook. Unlike Pauline's there are no water problems, but it's not on the beach. Steleo owns land on idyllic Motu Vaivahia: for f.800 pp he'll drop you off there for a few days (take food and water). If you know how to swim ask him about renting an outrigger canoe (*pirogue*). He also rents bicycles. A shortcut trail straight across the island begins opposite the campground (follow the power lines). Freelance camping on public land is prohibited. Bora Bora is overrun by land crabs, funny little creatures which make camping exciting.

Yachties Special

Cruising yachties are catered to by two hotels on Bora Bora, both with atmospheric restaurants serving good food, but no beaches. The **Hotel Oa Oa** (B.P. 10, Vaitape; tel. 67-70-84) between Farepiti and Vaitape has long been a yachtie hangout. For visiting boats the eight moorings, hot showers, garbage disposal, and 20 gallons of water a day are free. The hotel's eight thatched bungalows are f.9000 s, f.11,400 d, f.14,000 t. Their breakfast and dinner meal plan is f.3000 pp extra. Sailing, windsurfing, snorkeling, and outrigger are free. Captains and crews congregate at the Oa Oa's bar to watch the sun set in the west. Owners/managers Greg and Elaine Claytor make you feel right at home.

The newly opened **Bora Bora Yacht Club** (B.P. 17, Vaitape; tel. 67-70-69) near Farepiti Wharf allows boats free use of their 17 moorings and provides fresh water and showers. Their three floating bungalows with cooking facilities and solar electricity (f.20,000 for four persons) can be towed out and moored off a *motu*. A garden bungalow is f.9000 for four.

Expensive Hotels

Stuffy **Hotel Bora Bora** (B.P. 1, Vaitape; tel. 67-70-28) is f.42,500 s or d for an overwater bungalow or one-bedroom suite—the most hyperpriced set-up in the South Pacific. Standard rooms in this snobs' paradise begin at f.23,600 s or d, f.28,300 t. Breakfast and dinner are f.4400 pp extra. Though you may

not wish to shell out those funds, it's worth dropping into this oasis to watch the privileged few consuming—a sightseeing experience. Some 257 coconut trees surround the hotel and any of the gardeners will be happy to crack a nut.

Hotel Matira (B.P. 31, Vaitape; tel. 67-70-51) is one of the only deluxe places offering cooking facilities. Their 29 thatched bungalows with kitchenettes on the mountain side of the road are f.8600 s, f.10,200 d, f.12,200 t. The hotel annex is more attractive: thatched bungalows with kitchenettes right on the lagoon at the neck of Matira peninsula (f.9000 s, f.11,500 d, f.13,500 t). The Matira's Chinese restaurant (closed Mon.) is moderately priced. The beach is excellent.

It's hard to recommend the **Hotel Moana Beach** (B.P. 156, Bora Bora; tel. 67-73-73) on Matira Point, a sterile, lifeless luxury resort on a white-sand beach. A beachfront bungalow will set you back f.28,500 s or d; overwater bungalows an additional f.11,000 (children under 19 free). Even the meals are overpriced: f.4950 pp extra for breakfast and dinner. Skip the Moana Beach until it develops a little character (and an extra zero is added to the end of your weekly paycheck).

The **Bora Bora Beach Club** (B.P. 252, Nunue; tel. 67-71-16), which in previous incarnations has been the Climate de France and Ibis Bora Bora, shares the same white beach with the Sofitel Marara and charges half the price. Nine four-unit shingle-roof blocks total 36 rooms at f.10,500 s or d (garden), f.12,000 s or d (beach). A breakfast and dinner package is f.2800 pp extra. This hotel loans outrigger canoes, windsurfing, fishing, and snorkeling gear to guests free. Their restaurant serves Mexican food. We'll give this one a cautious recommendation in the middle-price bracket.

Hotel Sofitel Marara (B.P. 6, Bora Bora; tel. 67-70-46) is in the same top-end price range as Hotel Bora Bora, but it's a lot more open and informal. Instead of the boring types you hear at Hotel Bora Bora, the Marara caters to an international mix of tourists. Their bar and restaurant are fairly reasonable for such a swank place and the beach doesn't have the policed look of the Bora Bora's. The Marara was built in 1978 to house the crew filming Dino de Laurentis' *Hurricane*; the name means "Flying Fish." This is the place to stay if you don't give a damn how much it costs: from f.21,700 s, f.23,700 d, f.27,200 t. It's the only hotel on the island with a swimming pool. Bicycles rent for f.500. Happy hour is 1700-1800 daily.

The **Revatua Club** (B.P. 159, Vaitape; tel. 67-71-67) on the northeast side of the island is isolated, beachless, and (thus) expensive: f.9500 for up to three persons. The mock-Victorian architecture is right out of Hollywood. Its only draws are the excellent over-water French restaurant **Chez Christian** which offers free transport for diners and the bar. Boat transfers airport/hotel are f.1500 pp roundtrip.

FOOD AND DRINK

The assorted snack bars in Vaitape need no introduction. **Bar Teave** (no sign) opposite the Banque de Polynesie near Vaitape wharf is a great place to mix with the locals (open daily till midnight). Beer prices here are the cheapest on the island and Fri. and Sat. afternoons you can get steak frites and poisson cru to go with the brew. This place has been going for 50 years now, so it should still be around when you get there.

Chez Madam Chou next to the pharmacy in Vaitape has Chinese and Tahitian dishes at reasonable prices. You dine on a pleasant outdoor terrace (open daily till 2200).

The **Blue Lagoon Restaurant** (B.P. 27, Bora Bora; tel. 67-70-54) on the north side of Pofai Bay claims to be "the leading French restaurant on Bora Bora," which is something of an overstatement. The French owner, Marcien Navarro, mascarades as a Spaniard and will prepare paella Valenciana (f.2500 pp) if given two-hours' advance notice. It's all a bit of a come-on, but American tourists with thick wallets eat it up. Marcien fetches clients with reservations from their hotels at 1845. He also offers a six-hour reef tour with shark feeding and lunch on a *motu* for f.4500 pp (f.4000 pp for campers). With Marcien along

it's sure to be a good show.

Bloody Mary's Seafood Restaurant (closed Sun.; tel. 67-72-86) used to be the "in" spot on Bora Bora: a board outside lists "famous guests" including Jane Fonda and Baron George Von Dangel. It's still good, with pizza for lunch (1100-1500) and dinner (1830-2100). Sample prices are f.1000 for pizza, filet of fish f.2300, lobster f.4000, and a vegetarian plate f.1500. Free transportation for diners is available at 1830 or 1930 if you call for pick-up. Beer is on tap all day, so it's worth a stop at any time on your way around the island.

On the inland side of the road opposite Musee Jean Masson at Matira look for the sign "Cuisine Vietnamiene." The lady in this tiny hut serves delicious meals for about f.1000 afternoons from 1200-1700. The handwritten menu changes daily. A snack bar near Pauline's also serves good cheap meals (but no beer).

Entertainment

Witness the Polynesian dancing at **Hotel Bora Bora** (tel. 67-70-28) for free by grabbing a barside seat before it starts at 2100 on Wed., Fri., and Sun. nights. This hotel has a "tropical hour" with free hors d'oeuvres and exotic cocktails for half price on Tues., Thurs., and Sat. from 1700-1800.

You'll feel more at home watching the Tahitian dance show at the **Hotel Sofitel Marara** every night at 2030; see it all for the price of a draught beer. On Sat. at 1830 they open the earth oven and a Tahitian feast begins.

Le Recife Bar (B.P. 278, Vaitape; tel. 67-73-87) between Hotel Oa Oa and Farepiti wharf is Bora Bora's after-hours club, open Fri. and Sat. from 2230. Disco dancing continues almost until dawn and there are rooms for rent (f.3000 d) if you can't make it back to your hotel or just want to be near the action.

SPORTS AND RECREATION

Scuba diving can be arranged through Erwin Christian of **Moana Adventure Tours** (B.P. 5, Bora Bora; tel. 67-70-33) at the Moana Art boutique just north of Hotel Bora Bora, f.6000 in the lagoon, f.7000 in the ocean. The Moana Beach Hotel (tel. 67-73-73) charges f.5300 for lagoon diving, f.6500 for ocean diving.

Claude Sibani's **Bora Bora Calypso Club** (B.P. 6, Bora Bora; tel. 67-70-46) at the Sofitel Marara offers scuba diving at normal prices: f.4800 for a lagoon dive, f.6000 for an ocean dive. They go out daily at 0900.

Matira Tours (B.P. 118, Bora Bora; tel. 67-70-97) runs a round-the-island boat trip (f.5000 pp) departing Matira Point daily at 0900. The price includes a seafood picnic lunch on a *motu,* reefwalking, and snorkeling gear, plus a chance to see giant clams, manta rays, and the hand feeding of small lagoon sharks.

Lagoon trips with other companies vary in price from f.2000 to f.6500 depending on whether lunch is included, the length of trip, luxury of boat, etc., so check around. Also see the Blue Lagoon Restaurant listing above. An excursion of this kind is an essential part of the Bora Bora experience, so splurge on this one.

SERVICES

Air Tahiti and a tourist information office are beside the Banque de Tahiti on the wharf at Vaitape. Local handicrafts are sold in the **Centre Artisanal** hut nearby. The post office, gendarmerie, and health clinic *(infirmerie)* are within a stone's throw of the wharf. The Banque Socredo branch (tel. 67-71-11) is behind the basketball court across the street from the clinic. Pharmacie Fare Ra'au is farther north.

Also north of Vaitape wharf is the largest store, Magasin Chin Lee, and the island's Mobil gas station. Chin Lee and another well-stocked grocery store in Vaitape open Mon. to Sat. 0600-1730. The Total service station is north again, just south of Hotel Oa Oa. The only other place to buy groceries is the general store at Anau, half way 'round the island. It closes from 1200-1330 and on Sunday. No grocery store is found at Matira although a grocery truck passes this way around 1100 daily (except Sundays).

TRANSPORT

The Air Tahiti office (tel. 67-70-35) is opposite the Town Hall *(mairie)* adjoining the wharf. A useful transversal flight direct from Bora Bora to Rangiroa (f.15,600) operates twice a week. For information on flights to Bora Bora from Papeete, Huahine, and Raiatea see the main Introduction to this book.

Ships from Raiatea and Papeete tie up at Farepiti wharf, three km north of Vaitape. The shipping companies have no representatives on Bora Bora, so for departure times just keep asking. Drivers of the *trucks* are the most likely to know. You buy your ticket when the ship arrives.

Officially the *Taporo IV* leaves at 1300 on Tues. and 0800 on Sun., while the *Temehani* departs at Fri. at 0900. The *Raromatai Ferry* is supposed to leave Thurs. and Sun. at 1200. Beware of ships leaving early.

Truck fares between Vaitape and Matira vary between f.150 and f.300. *Trucks* usually meet the boats. Some of the *trucks* you see around town are strictly for guests of the luxury hotels—avoid those operated by Hotel Bora Bora. Taxi fares are high so check before getting in.

Mautara Rent-A-Bike (tel. 67-73-76) near Chez Aime rents bicycles at f.400 a half day, f.800 a full day, f.500 for additional days.

If you have to rent a car, **Bora Rent-A-Car** (B.P. 246, Vaitape; tel. 67-70-03) south of Vaitape wharf rents Renaults at f.5500 for an 0800-1700 day, f.6500 for 24 hours. The price includes unlimited km, insurance, and gasoline, valid driver's license required. They also have motorscooters for f.4000 from 0800-1700 or f.4500 for 24 hours. For service and price they're the best on the island. If driving at night watch out for scooters and bicycles without lights.

Otemanu Rent-A-Car (B.P. 250, Vaitape; tel. 67-70-94) has two locations: opposite Vaitape wharf and by the road between Hotel Oa Oa and Club Med. But best is to dispense with motorized transport on little Bora Bora.

The **Bora Bora Yacht Club** (tel. 67-70-69) rents small, two-person dinghies with six-horse power outboard motors for f.3500 a half day, f.6000 a whole day (gas extra). With an early start you could circumnavigate the island.

Mrs. Vaea of **Otemanu Tours** (tel. 67-70-49) between Hotel Oa Oa and Club Med offers a tour around the island by *truck* daily at 1400 (2.5 hours—f.1500).

Airport

Bora Bora's vast airfield (BOB) on Motu Mute north of the main island was built by the Americans during WW II. Until 1961 all international flights to Tahiti-Polynesia arrived here; passengers were then transferred to Papeete by Catalina amphibious or Bermuda Flying Boat seaplanes. Today, arriving air passengers are taken to Vaitape wharf by launch (included in the plane ticket). If you're flying to Bora Bora from Papeete go early in the morning and sit on the left side of the aircraft for spectacular views—it's only from the air that Bora Bora is the most beautiful island in the world.

strand morning glory (Ipomoea pes-caprae)

scorpion fish

MAUPITI

Majestic Maupiti (Maurua), 44 km west of Bora Bora, is the least known of the accessible Society Islands. Maupiti's mighty volcanic plug soars from a sapphire lagoon. Vegetation-draped cliffs contrast with magnificent *motu* beaches. Almost every bit of level land on the main island is taken up by fruit trees, while watermelons thrive on the surrounding *motus*. Maupiti abounds in native sea birds including frigate birds, terns, and others. The absence of Indian mynahs allows you to see native land birds almost extinct elsewhere.

The 963 (1988) people live in the adjacent villages of Vaiea, Farauru, and Pauma. Tourism is not promoted because there aren't any hotels, which can be an advantage! Maupiti was once famous for its black basalt stone pounders and fishhooks made from the seven local varieties of mother-of-pearl shell.

Sights

It takes only three hours to walk right around the island. The nine-km crushed coral road lined with breadfruit, mango, banana, and hibiscus passes crumbling *maraes,* freshwater springs, and a beach.

Marae Vaiahu by the shore a few hundred meters beyond Hotuparaoa Massif is the largest *marae*. Once a royal landing opposite the pass into the lagoon, the king's throne and ancient burials are still on the *marae*. Nearby is the sorcerers' rock: light a fire beside this rock and you will die. Above the road are a few smaller *marae*.

Terei'a Beach at the west tip of the Maupiti is the only good beach on the main island. At low tide you can wade across from Terei'a to Motu Auira in waist-deep water. **Marae Vaiorie** is a double *marae* with freshwater springs between.

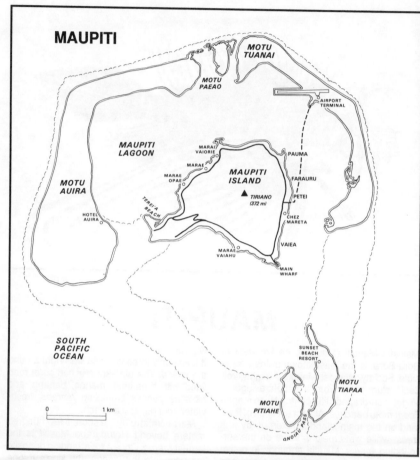

As many as two dozen large *marae* are hidden in Maupiti's mountainous interior and the island is known for its ghosts. A local guide will lead you to the 372-meter summit of Maupiti for around f.2500. With the proper encouragement he/she may show you the *marae* and tell the legends.

Accommodations

Several of the 963 inhabitants take paying guests at about f.3000 pp, including all meals. The guest house owners meet the flights and boats in search of clients. The absence of a regular hotel on Maupiti throws together an odd mix of vacationing French couples, backpackers, and "adventuresome" tourists in the guest houses. You could camp on the white sands of Terei'a Beach but water and *nonos* (insects) would be a problem. If you're set on camping get across to the airport *motu* and hike south looking for a campsite there— you'll have to befriend someone to obtain water. Maupiti, like Bora Bora, experiences serious water shortages during the dry season.

Chez Mareta (Tinorua and Mareta Anua, tel. 67-80-25) is in the center of Vai'ea village, the house with the sloping blue roof a few-minutes' walk from the Mairie. They offer mattresses on the floor in the upstairs double rooms for f.2500 pp including breakfast and dinner. A very pleasant sitting room faces the lagoon downstairs. Upon request they'll drop you on a *motu* for the day (beware of sunburn). It's OK for a couple of days, but not an extended stay. Agree on the price beforehand and check your bill when you leave.

Sunset Beach Resort (B.P. 1, Maupiti; tel. 67-80-63), on Motu Tiapaa beside the pass into the Maupiti lagoon, is quiet and offers superb food. It's f.3600 pp with breakfast and dinner in a shared four-room bungalow. For information on this place ask for Floriette, Augusta, or Vilna in the house next to Chez Mareta in the village. Reservations are required to ensure airport pick-up and a bed. This may be the closest thing to experiencing the true flavor of Polynesia.

Hotel Auira (Edna Terai and Richard Tefaatan, B.P. 2, Maupiti; tel. 67-80-26) on Motu Auira, the *motu* opposite Terei'a Beach, has eight thatched bungalows. The garden variety with shared bath are f.5840 pp a day including all meals; those on the beach, with private bath, are f.6910 pp. Both food and beach are excellent. Boat transfers from the airport are f.1000 pp.

Services

No bank exists on Maupiti, so bring money. The post office is at the Mairie. There's a village disco in Fararuru village Fri. and Sat. nights with no cover charge, and canned beer is sold.

Getting There

Air Tahiti has flights to Maupiti from Raiatea (f.4865 OW) three times a week. Reconfirm with the Air Tahiti agent (tel. 67-80- 20) at the Mairie. Here you board the launch to the airport (f.400 pp OW).

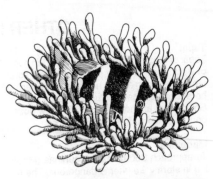

A clown- or damselfish (Amphiprion clarkii) nestles among the venomous tentacles of an anemone. A mucous secretion protects the fish from the creature's stinging cells, providing it with a safe refuge. Anemones gather plankton from the water, but also feed on mussels, snails, or barnacles which fall their way

The small interisland boat *Taporo I* motors weekly between Raiatea and Maupiti, leaving Raiatea around 2300 on Tues. or Thurs. (f.850 deck, f.1450 *couchette*). The boat returns to Raiatea from Maupiti in the afternoon of arrival day. The pass into Maupiti is narrow. When there's a southeast wind it can be dangerous—boats have had to turn back. Ships must enter the channel during daylight, thus the compulsory morning arrival and afternoon (or morning) departure. *Taporo I* has only six bunks and in rough weather it can be a rough trip. The coming and going of this tiny ship is a major event in the otherwise unperturbed weekly life of the Maupitians. If you arrive by boat you'll be treated with more respect than if you arrive by plane.

Airport

Like Bora Bora, Maupiti's airport (MAU) is on a small *motu*. You must take a launch to the main island (f.400).

OTHER ISLANDS

Tupai

Tupai or Motu Iti ("Small Island"), 13 km north of Bora Bora, is a tiny privately owned coral atoll measuring 1,100 hectares. The facing horseshoe-shaped *motus* enclose a lagoon. Ships must anchor offshore. The few dozen people here live from making copra.

Maupihaa

To approach 360-hectare Maupihaa (Mopelia) in stormy weather is dangerous. The unmarked pass is a mere 10 meters wide and can only be found by searching for the strong outflow of lagoon water at low tide. No fresh water is available on the uninhabited atoll. Cruising yachts and copra cutters sometimes call.

In 1917 the notorious German raider *Seeadler* was wrecked on Maupihaa. Count Felix von Luckner was able to carry on to Fiji where he was captured at Wakaya Island. Count von Luckner's journal, *The Sea Devil,* became a bestseller after the war.

Manuae

Manuae (Scilly) is the westernmost island of the Society Islands. This atoll is 15 km in diameter but totals only 400 hectares. Pearl divers once visited Manuae. In 1855 the three-masted schooner *Julia Ann* sank on the Manuae reef. It took the survivors two months to build a small boat which carried them to safety at Raiatea.

Motu One

Motu One (Bellingshausen) got its second name from a 19th-century Russian explorer. Tiny 280-hectare Motu One is circled by a guano-bearing reef with no pass into the lagoon.

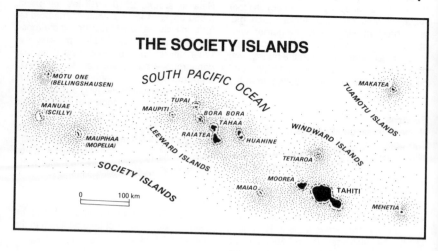

THE SOCIETY ISLANDS

OUTER ISLANDS

Australs, Tuamotus, Gambiers, Marquesas

LES MARQUISES

Ils parlent de la morte comme tu parles d'un fruit
Ils regardent la mer comme tu regardes un puits

Les femmes sont lascives au soleil redouté
Et s'il n'y a pas d'hiver cela n'est pas l'été

La pluie est traversière elle bat de grain en grain
Quelques vieux chevaux blancs qui fredonnent Gauguin

Et par manque de brise le temps s'immobilise
Aux Marquises.

Du soir montent des feux et des points de silence
Qui vont s'élargissant et la lune s'avance

Et la mer se déchire infiniment brisée
Par des rochers qui prirent des prénoms affolés

Et puis plus loin des chiens des chants de repentance
Et quelques pas de deux et quelques pas de danse

Et la nuit est soumise et l'alizé se brise
Aux Marquises.

Leur rire est dans le coeur le mot dans le regard
Le coeur est voyageur l'avenir est au hasard

Et passent des cocotiers qui écrivent des chants d'amour
Que les soeurs d'alentours ignorent d'ignorer

Les pirogues s'en vont les pirogues s'en viennent
Et mes souvenirs deviennent ce que les vieux en font

Veux-tu que je te dise gémir n'est pas de mise
Aux Marquises.

Jacques Brel

THE AUSTRAL ISLANDS

The inhabited volcanic islands of Rimatara, Rurutu, Tubuai, Raivavae, and Rapa, plus uninhabited Maria (or Hull) atoll, make up the Austral Group. This southernmost island chain is a 1280-km extension of the same submerged mountain range as the southern Cook Islands, 900 km farther northwest. The islands of the Australs seldom exceed 300 meters, except Rapa which soars to 650 meters. The southerly location makes these islands notably cooler than Tahiti. Collectively the Australs are known as Tuhaa Pae, the "Fifth Part" or fifth administrative subdivision of Tahiti-Polynesia. It's still a world apart from tourism.

History

Excavations carried out on the northwest coast of Rurutu uncovered 60 round-ended houses arrayed in parallel rows, with 14 *marae* scattered among them, demonstrating man's presence here as early as 900 A.D.

The ruins of *marae* can also be seen on Rimatara, Tubuai, and Raivavae. Huge stone *tikis* once graced Raivavae, but most have since been destroyed or removed. The terraced mountain fortifications or *pa* on Rapa are unique.

The Australs were one of the great art areas of the Pacific, represented today in many museums. The best-known artifacts are sculptured sharkskin drums, wooden bowls, fly whisks, and *tapa* cloth. Offerings which could not be touched by human hands were placed on the sacred altars with intricately incised ceremonial ladles. European contact effaced most of these traditions; the carving done today is crude by comparison.

Rurutu was discovered by Capt. James Cook in 1769; he found Tubuai in 1777. In 1789 Fletcher Christian and the *Bounty* mutineers attempted to establish a settlement at the northeast corner of Tubuai. They left after only three months following misunderstand-

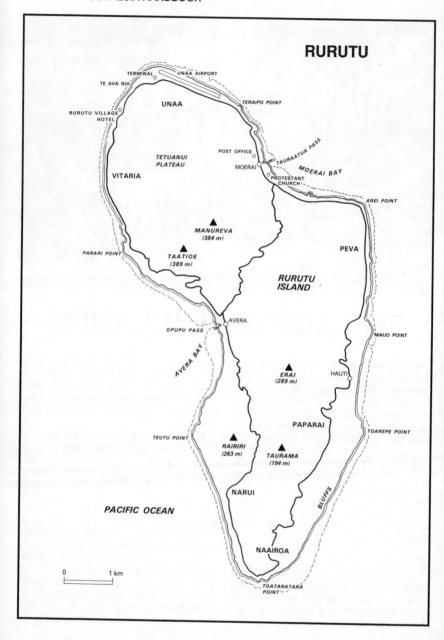

RURUTU

ings and battles with the islanders in which 66 Polynesians died. The European discoverer of Rapa was Capt. George Vancouver in 1791. Rimatara wasn't discovered until 1813 by the Australian captain Michael Fodger.

English missionaries converted most of the people to Protestantism in the early 19th century. Whalers and sandalwood ships introduced diseases and firearms which decimated the Austral islanders. The French didn't complete their annexation of the group until 1900. Since then the Australs have gone their sleepy way.

The People

The 6,509 (1988) mostly Polynesian inhabitants are fishermen and farmers who live in attractive villages with homes and churches built of coral limestone. The rich soil and temperate climate stimulate agriculture with staple crops such as taro, manioc, Irish po-

tatoes, sweet potatoes, leeks, cabbage, carrots, corn, and coffee. The coconut palm also thrives except on Rapa. Today many Austral people live in Papeete.

Getting There

Air Tahiti has flights to Rurutu and Tubuai, the only islands with airports. The twice-weekly flights alternate between a routing Tahiti-Tubuai-Rurutu-Tahiti and Tahiti-Rurutu-Tubuai-Tahiti. Rurutu gets a third weekly flight. One-way fares from Tahiti are f.16,000 to Rurutu and f.17,900 to Tubuai. Rurutu-Tubuai is f.7,300. These flights are included with the Society Islands in the Air Tahiti "Air Pass" (f.42,000).

All the other Austral Islands are accessible only by boat. For information on the twice-monthly sailings of the *Tuhaa Pae II* from Papeete, see the main Introduction to this book.

RURUTU

This island, 572 km south of Tahiti, is shaped like a miniature of the African continent. For the hiker mountainous, 32-sq-km Rurutu is a more varied island to visit than Tubuai. Taatioe (389 meters) and Manureva (384 meters) are the highest peaks. A narrow fringing reef surrounds Rurutu but there's no lagoon. The climate of this northernmost Austral island is temperate and dry. The history of Rurutu revolves around three important dates: 1821 when the gospel arrived on the island, 1970 when Cyclone Emma devastated the three villages, and 1975 when the airport opened.

In Jan. and July Rurutuans practice the ancient art of stone lifting or *amoraa ofai*. Men get three tries to hoist a 130-kg boulder up onto their shoulder, while women attempt a 60-kg stone. Dancing and feasting follow the event. The women of Rurutu weave fine pandanus hats, bags, baskets, fans, lampshades, and mats. Rurutu's famous Manureva ("Soaring Bird") Dance Group has performed around the world. The main evening entertainment is to watch dancers practicing in the villages.

Sights

The pleasant main village, Moerai, boasts a post office, four small stores, two bakeries, and two banks. Two other villages, Avera and Hauti, bring the total island population to 1,953 (1988). Electricity functions 24 hours a day. Neat fences and flower gardens surround the coral limestone houses. This is the Polynesia of 50 years ago: though snack bars have appeared, *trucks* have yet to cover the 30-km coastal road. Beaches, waterfalls, valleys, and limestone caves beckon the explorer.

At Moerai village may be seen the tomb of French navigator Eric de Bisschop whose exploits equaled but are far less known than those of Thor Heyerdahl. Before WW II de Bisschop sailed a catamaran, the *Kaimiloa,* from Hawaii to the Mediterranean via the Indian Ocean and the tip of Africa. His greatest voyage was aboard the *Tahiti Nui,* a series of three rafts, each of which eventually broke up and sank. In 1956 the *Tahiti Nui* set out from Tahiti to Chile to demonstrate the now-accepted theory that the Polynesians had

Eric de Bisschop

visited South America in prehistoric times. There, two of his four crewmen abandoned ship but Eric doggedly set out to return. After a total of 13 months at sea the expedition's final raft foundered on a reef in the Cook Islands and its courageous leader, one of the giants of Pacific exploration, was killed.

Accommodations

Chez Catherine (tel. 94-03-11), a concrete building behind the Protestant church in Moerai, has 10 rooms (f.3000 s, f.5000 d). Children under 12 are free. A restaurant and bar are on the premises.

Chez Metu Teinaore (tel. 94-03-15), across the street from Moerai's Protestant church, is a large white house with four rooms, shared cooking facilities and bath. Rates are f.50,000 a month.

Chez Maurice (tel. 94-04-48) at Avera takes guests in a large 13-bed house at f.1600-2500 a day.

The **Rurutu Village Hotel** (B.P. 6, Unaa, Rurutu; tel. 94-03-92), on a beach just west of the airport, is Rurutu's only regular hotel. The 16 bungalows go for f.5500 pp with breakfast and dinner. Facilities include a restaurant, bar, and swimming pool. The hotel owner, Iareta Moeau, is a dance leader and a very nice fellow. For reservations call tel. 42-93-85 in Papeete.

Services And Getting There

The Banque Socredo branch (tel. 94-04-75) is at Moerai.

Unaa Airport (RUR) is at the north tip of Rurutu, four km from Moerai. **Air Tahiti** tel. 94-03-57. The supply ship from Papeete ties up at Moerai.

TUBUAI

Ten-km-long by five-km-wide Tubuai, largest of the Australs, is 670 km south of Tahiti. Hills on the east and west sides of this oval 45-sq-km island are joined by low land in the middle; when seen from the sea Tubuai looks like two islands. Mount Taitaa (422 meters) is its highest point. Tubuai is surrounded by a barrier reef; a pass on the north side gives access to a wide turquoise lagoon bordered by brilliant white-sand beaches. Picnics are often arranged on the small reef *motus* amid superb snorkeling grounds.

The brisk climate permits the cultivation of potatoes, carrots, oranges, and coffee, but other vegetation is sparse. Several *marae* are on Tubuai, but they're in extremely bad condition with potatoes growing on the sites. Mormon missionaries arrived as early as 1844. Today there are active branches of the Church of Latter-day Saints in all the villages. The islanders weave fine pandanus hats and some woodcarving is done at Mahu.

Most of the 1,846 (1988) inhabitants live in Mataura and Taahuaia villages on the north

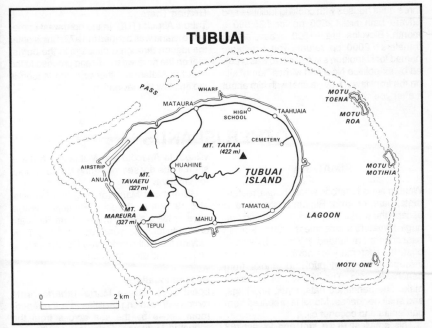

TUBUAI

coast, though houses and hamlets are found all along the 24-km road around the island. A red dirt road cuts right across the middle of Tubuai to Mahu village on the south coast.

Mataura is the administrative center of the Austral Group. The two stores at Mataura bake bread. The Banque Socredo branch (tel. 95-04-86) is also at Mataura. Restaurants and *trucks* haven't reached this island yet.

Accommodations

Several people rent rooms to visitors at about f.2500 pp, meals extra. Monthly rates are much less. **Chez Caro** (Caroline Chung Thien, B.P. 94, Mataura; tel. 95-03-46) next to Chung Tien store in Mataura may have housekeeping rooms also at this price.

Chez Taro Tanepau (tel. 95-03-82), by the lagoon near a small beach between Mataura

and the wharf, has small bungalows with cooking facilities at f.2500 pp daily or f.35,000 for the entire four-bed unit per month. On the monthly basis f.4000 extra is charged to cover electricity and gas. For advance reservations tel. 43-87-32 in Papeete.

Chez Ah Sing (tel. 95-03-52), a two-bedroom house with cooking facilities in Taahuaia, is f.2000 pp or f.32,000 d a month.

Chez Turina Victor (B.P. 7, Mataura; tel. 95-03-27) is near the beach at Taahuaia, three km east of Mataura. A room with cooking facilities is f.2000 pp or f.30,000 a month.

Chez Terii Turina behind Chez Turina Victor in Taahuaia, has two houses with cooking facilities. There's no hot water and the baths are shared. Rooms are f.2000 pp.

The **Ermitage Sainte Helene** (Madame Tehinarii Ilari, B.P. 79, Mataura; tel. 95-04-79) is at Mahu, eight km south of Mataura. The three quiet houses with cooking facilities and private bath are f.2500 pp, or f.35,000 a month. Bicycles are f.1000 a day, airport transfers f.2000 pp return. The Ermitage, named for Napoleon's isle of exile, was created by ex-politico Noel Ilari whose "tomb" sits on the front lawn. Have a chat with him about it after you check in.

Getting There
Tubuai Airport (TUB) in the northwest corner of the island was opened in 1972. Ships enter the lagoon through a passage in the barrier reef on the northwest side and proceed to the wharf at Mataura. Otherwise, the lagoon is too shallow for navigation.

OTHER ISLANDS

RIMATARA

Without airport, harbor, wharf, hotels, restaurants, bars, or taxis, Rimatara is a place to escape the world. Only a narrow fringing reef hugs Rimatara's lagoonless shore; arriving passengers are landed at Amaru by whaleboat. It's customary for newcomers to pass through a cloud of purifying smoke from beachside fires. The women of Rimatara make fine pandanus hats, mats, and bags, and shell necklaces. Monoi is prepared from gardenias and coconut oil.

This smallest (8 sq km) and lowest (83 meters) of the Australs is home to 969 (1988) people. Dirt roads lead from Amaru, the main

RIMATARA

village, to Anapoto and Mutuaura. Water is short in the dry season. Bring food and drink to Rimatara.

Uninhabited Maria (or Hull) is a four-islet atoll 192 km northwest of Rimatara, visited once or twice a year by men from Rimatara or Rururu for fishing and copra-making. They stay on the atoll two or three months, among seabirds and giant lobsters.

Accommodations
Local postmistress **Marie Taharia** rents rooms with cooking facilities in a three-bedroom house by the sea across from the school in Mutuaura. Rates are f.2000 pp a day or f.45,000 a month for the house.

The **Mairie of Amaru** offers two small rooms each with one single bed, shared bath, and cooking facilities, in Amaru Town Hall for f.500 pp a day.

RAIVAVAE

This appealing, nine-km-long and two-km-wide island is just south of the Tropic of Capricorn and thus outside the tropics. For archaeology and natural beauty, this is one of the finest islands in Polynesia. Fern-covered Mt. Hiro (437 meters) is the highest point on 16-sq-km Raivavae. A barrier reef encloses an emerald lagoon, but the 20 small coral *motus* are all located on the southern and eastern portions of the reef. The tropical vegetation is rich: rose and sandalwood are used to make perfumes for local use. A malignant fever epidemic in 1826 reduced the people of Raivavae from 3,000 to 120. The

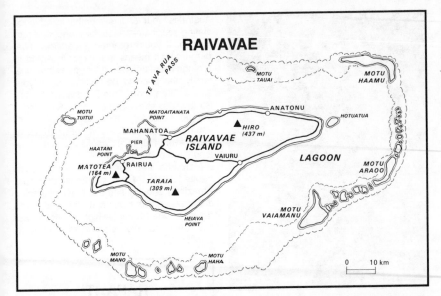

RAIVAVAE

TE AVA RUA PASS

MOTU TAUAI

MOTU HAAMU

MATOAITANATA POINT

MOTU TUITUI

MAHANATOA

PIER

ANATONU

HOTUATUA

▲ HIRO (437 m)

HAATANI POINT

RAIVAVAE ISLAND

MATOTEA (164 m) ▲

RAIRUA

VAIURU

LAGOON

MOTU ARAOO

TARAIA (309 m) ▲

HEIAVA POINT

MOTU VAIAMANU

MOTU MANO

MOTU HAHA

0   10 km

present population of 1,225 (1988) lives in four coastal villages, Rairua, Mahanatoa, Anatonu, and Vaiuru, linked by a dirt road. A shortcut route direct from Rairua to Vaiuru crosses a 119-meter saddle with splendid views of the island.

Different teams led by Frank Stimson, Don Marshall, and Thor Heyerdahl have explored the ancient temples and taro terraces of Raivavae. Many two- to three-meter-high stone statues once stood on the island, but most have since been destroyed, and two were removed to Tahiti where they can be seen on the grounds of the Gauguin Museum. One big *tiki* is still standing by the road between Rairua and Mahanatoa villages.

Annie Flores runs a two-bedroom guest house with cooking facilities next to the Gendarmerie in Rairua, the main village. The charge is f.25,000 a month for the house. A Chinese shop is nearby, but bring your own bread.

The inhabitants of Raivavae have decided they don't want an airport. If you'll be taking a boat to the Australs anyway, you may as well go to Raivavae where airborne tourists can't follow! Ships enter the lagoon through a pass on the north side and tie up to the pier at Rairua. A boat calls at the island about every 10-14 days.

RAPA

Rapa, the southernmost point in Tahiti-Polynesia, is one of the most isolated and spectacular islands in the Pacific. Its nearest neighbor is Raivavae, 600 km away. It's sometimes called Rapa Iti (Little Rapa) to distinguish it from Rapa Nui (Easter Island). Soaring peaks reaching 650 meters surround magnificent Haurei Bay, Rapa's crater harbor, the western portion of a drowned volcano. This is only one of 12 deeply indented bays around the island; the absence of reefs allows the sea to cut into the 40-sq-km island's outer coasts. Offshore are several sugarloaf-shaped islets. The east slopes of the mountains are bare, while large fern forests are found on the west. Coconut trees cannot grow in the foggy, temperate climate.

A time-worn **Polynesian fortress** with terraces is situated on the crest of a ridge at

the famous tiki *from Raivavae, now at Tahiti's Gauguin Museum*

Morongo Uta, commanding a wide outlook over the steep rugged hills. Morongo Uta was cleared of vegetation by a party of archaeologists led by Thor Heyerdahl in 1956 and is still easily visitable. About a dozen of these *pa* are found above the bay, built to defend the territories of the different tribes of overpopulated ancient Rapa. Today the young men of Rapa organize eight-day bivouacs to hunt wild goats which range across the island.

The present population of 516 (1988) lives at Area and Haurei villages on the north and south sides of Rapa's great open bay, connected only by boat. To arrange a stay on Rapa is difficult. Write to Le Maire, Rapa, Iles

Australes, four or five months in advance stating your name, nationality, age, and profession. If you're granted a *certificat d'hebergement* it means the mayor is willing to arrange room and board for you with a local family, the price to be decided upon your arrival. Then contact the Subdivision Administrative des Iles Australes, B.P. 4587, Papeete (tel. 42-20-00) which may actually grant you a permit to go. The *Tuhaa Pae II* calls at Rapa every four to six weeks, so that's how long you'll be there.

Marotiri or the "Bass Rocks" are 10 uninhabited islets 74 km southeast of Rapa. Amazingly enough, some of these pinnacles are crowned with stone platforms and round "towers." One 105-meter-high pinnacle is visible from Rapa in very clear weather. Landing is difficult.

a Tuamotu outrigger

THE TUAMOTU ISLANDS

Arrayed in two parallel northwest-southeast chains scattered across an area of ocean 600 km wide and 1,200 km long, the Tuamotus are the largest group of coral atolls in the world. Of the 78 atolls in the group 21 have one entrance (pass), 10 have two passes, and 47 have no pass at all. A total of 12,374 (1988) people live on the 45 inhabited islands. Although the land area of the Tuamotus is only 726 sq km, the lagoons of the atolls total some 6,000 sq km of sheltered water. All are atolls: some have an unbroken ring of reef around the lagoon, while others appear as a necklace of islets separated by channels.

Variable currents, sudden storms, and poor charts make cruising this group by yacht extremely hazardous—in fact, the Tuamotus are popularly known as the "Dangerous Ar-

chipelago" or "Labyrinth." Wrecks litter the reefs of many atolls. Winds are generally from the east, varying to northeast from Nov. to May and southeast from June to October. A series of hurricanes devastated these islands between 1980 and 1983.

The resourceful Tuamotu people have always lived from seafood, pandanus nuts, and coconuts. They once dove to depths of 30 meters and more wearing only tiny goggles to collect mother-of-pearl shells. This activity has largely ceased as overharvesting has made them rare. Today, cultured pearl farms operate on Aratika, Hikueru, Katiu, Kaukura, Manihi, Raroia, South Marutea, Takapoto, Takaroa, Takume, and Taenga. Cultured black pearls *(Pinctada margaritifera)* from the Tuamotus and Gambiers are world famous.

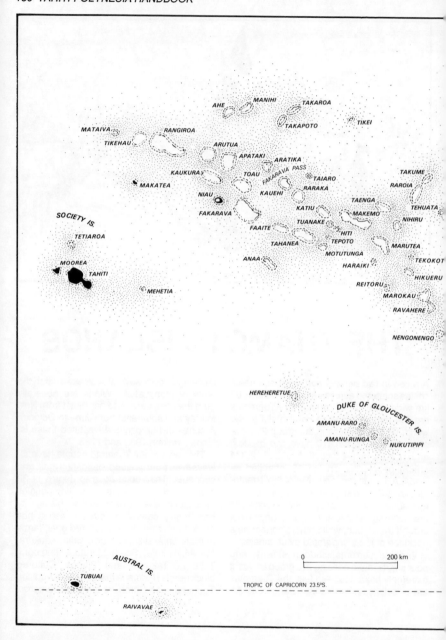

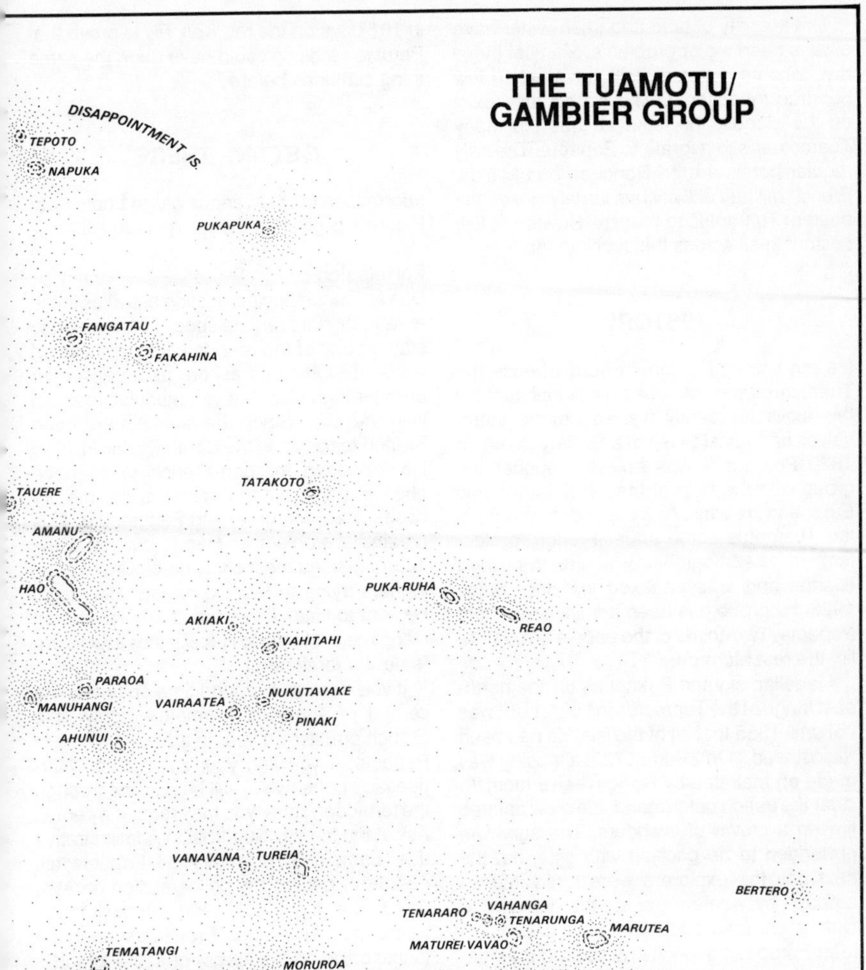

THE TUAMOTU/
GAMBIER GROUP

DISAPPOINTMENT IS.

TEPOTO

NAPUKA

PUKAPUKA

FANGATAU

FAKAHINA

TATAKOTO

TAUERE

AMANU

HAO

PUKA-RUHA

REAO

AKIAKI

VAHITAHI

PARAOA

MANUHANGI   VAIRAATEA   NUKUTAVAKE

PINAKI

AHUNUI

VANAVANA   TUREIA

BERTERO

VAHANGA

TENARARO   TENARUNGA   MARUTEA

MATUREI-VAVAO

TEMATANGI   MORUROA

MARIA

FANGATAUFA

MINERVE

GAMBIER IS.

MANGAREVA

MORANE   TEMOE

TROPIC OF CAPRICORN
23.5°S.

The scarcity of land and fresh water have always been major problems. Many of these dry, coconut-covered atolls have only a few hundred inhabitants. Though airstrips exist on 12 islands, the isolation has led many Tuamotuans to migrate to Papeete. The only regular hotels are on Rangiroa and Manihi. French military activity has largely closed the eastern Tuamotus to tourism. Beware of fish poisoning all across this archipelago.

HISTORY

It's not known for certain from whence the Tuamotus were colonized. The inhabitants of the atolls frequently warred among themselves or against those of a Society island. In 1820 Pomare II was able to conquer the group with the help of the missionaries and European firearms. As a dependency of Tahiti the Tuamotus came under French "protection" in 1842 together with the Windward Islands and was annexed in 1880. Since 1923 the group has been administered from Papeete. Two-thirds of the people are Catholic, the rest Mormon.

Magellan sighted Pukapuka on the northeast fringe of the Tuamotus in 1521, but it was not until 1835 that all of the islands had been "discovered." On 2 June 1722, a landing was made on Makatea by Roggeveen's men. To clear the beach beforehand, the crew opened fire on a crowd of islanders. The survivors pretended to be pacified with gifts, but the next day the explorers were lured into an ambush by women and stoned, leaving 10 Dutchmen dead and many wounded. Fourteen European expeditions passed the Tuamotus between 1606 and 1816, but only eight bothered to go ashore. Of these all but the first (Quiros) were involved in skirmishes with the islanders.

Centuries later, a group of Scandinavians under the leadership of Thor Heyerdahl ran aground on Raroia atoll on 7 Aug. 1947, after having sailed 7,000 km from South America in 101 days on the raft *Kon Tiki* to prove that Peruvian Indians could have done the same thing centuries before.

GETTING THERE

Information on the various cargo boats from Papeete is given in the main Introduction.

Permission

Due to French nuclear-testing activities in the area foreigners require special permission to stay on any of the islands south and east of Anaa. It's OK to go ashore as a passenger on a through ship, but you must leave again with the ship. Since the launching of overt French terrorism in the South Pacific in 1985 it's forbidden for non-French to even be aboard a ship when it stops at the military bases, Hao, Moruroa, and Fangataufa. This creates a problem as Hao is central to the Tuamotus and most ships do call there. Foreigners trying to leave a remote atoll might be sent to Hao! There aren't any ships from Rangiroa or Manihi to Hao, so those atolls are "safe" for foreigners.

If you do wish to spend time on one of the central or southern Tuamotus, apply at a French embassy a year in advance. Once in Papeete, if you find your ship (to the Marquesas or otherwise) will be passing through the forbidden zone, you may require a permit. Ask at the friendly Subdivision Administrative des Tuamotu-Gambier (B.P. 34, Papeete; tel. 42-20-00) behind the police station on Ave. Bruat. They'll probably send you back to the Police de l'Air et des Frontieres near the tourist office on the harbor or at the airport.

If the police won't help, go to the Direction Reglementation et Controle de Legalite du Haut-Commissariat, upstairs in the Bloc Donald behind Voyagence Tahiti off rue Jeanne d'Arc. With a special permit stamped and signed by them, the police at the harbor will no longer resist granting the disembarkation permit. Allow several days for these difficult formalities and don't be intimidated. You'll need to know a little French—otherwise forget it. Try to remain polite to avoid spoiling things for those who follow. On departure day get to the boat early enough to allow time for last-minute return visits to the above offices—you never know.

RANGIROA

Seventy-seven-km-long Rangiroa, 200 km northeast of Papeete, is the Tuamotus' most populous atoll and the second largest in the world (after Kwajalein in the Marshall Islands). Its 1,020-sq-km aquamarine lagoon is 78 km long, 24 km across (too far to see), and 225 km around—the island of Tahiti would fit inside its reef. The name Rangiroa means "Extended Sky." Some 240 *motus* sit on this reef.

What draws people to Rangi (as everyone calls it) is the marinelife in the lagoon. You've never seen so many fish. While lagoons in the Society Is. are often murky due to runoff from the main volcanic islands and pollution from coastal communities, the waters of the Tuamotus are clean and fresh with excellent swimming and snorkeling.

Rangiroa's twin villages, each facing a pass 500 meters wide into the lagoon, house 1,305 (1988) people. Avatoru village on Avatoru Pass is at the west end of the airport island. A 20-km paved road runs east from Avatoru to Tiputa Pass and Tiputa village, just across the water. Both villages have small post offices and stores; the town hall and gendarmerie are at Tiputa and the health clinic and marine research center at Avatoru. Avatoru has better facilities, but Tiputa is less touristed and offers the chance to escape by simply walking and wading southeast. No bank is to be found at Rangiroa, so bring money.

Budget Accommodations
The cheapest place to stay is **Chez Nanua**

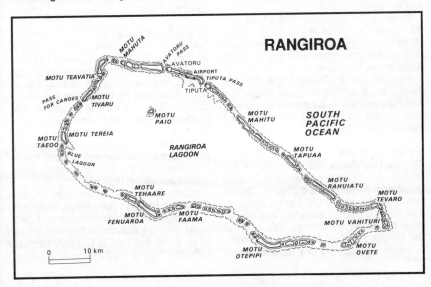

(Nanua and Marie Tamaehu, B.P. 54, Avatoru; tel. 96-03-88), between the airport and Avatoru village. The three small bungalows with shared bath are f.2500 pp including all meals (small). You eat with the owners—a little fish and rice every meal. Camping is f.500. There's no electricity and no running water. Airport transfers are free.

Chez Iris (Roger Terorotua, B.P. 21, Avatoru; tel. 96-03-24) in Avatoru has a single bungalow sleeping five, f.6000 for the unit. Snorkeling gear is f.200, bicycles f.500.

Chez Marie (Marie Bellais Richmond, B.P. 51, Avatoru; tel. 96-03-92) on Point Peretue, Avatoru, has six bungalows with private bath, f.4500 pp complete pension. Airport transfers are free.

Chez Jacqueline (Jacqueline Tevaia, tel. 96-03-56) at Point Ohutu, Avatoru, is a guesthouse with three rooms at f.2000 pp, plus another f.2000 pp for all meals. Airport transfers are free.

Chez Glorine (Glorine To'i, tel. 96-03-58) is on the airport island near Tiputa Pass. The six thatched bungalows with private bath are f.5000 pp including all meals. Airport transfers are free.

Chez Lucien (Lucien and Esther Pe'a, B.P. 69, Tiputa; tel. 96-03-55) in Tiputa village offers three traditional bungalows with private bath at f.4500 pp, including all meals. Airport transfers are f.500 pp.

Pension Estall (Ronald Estall, B.P. 13, Tiputa; tel. 96-03-16) in Tiputa village has four Polynesian-style bungalows with private bath, f.5000 pp complete pension. Airport transfers are f.500 pp.

Expensive Hotels
The **Kia Ora Village** (B.P. 1, Tiputa; tel. 96-03-84), near Tiputa Pass about two km from the airport, is Rangiroa's top resort. The 25 beach bungalows are f.20,000 s, f.26,400 d, f.30,800 t, including breakfast and dinner. Airport transfers are f.700 pp. Eric Julian at the Kia Ora organizes scuba diving (f.4500). In Papeete contact Kia Ora Tours (B.P. 706,

Papeete; tel. 42-86-72) on Boulevard Pomare for special packages to Rangiroa (f.39,000 pp including lodging and airfare but no meals).

La Bouteille a la Mer (B.P. 17, Avatoru; tel. 96-03-34), also on the airport island, has 12 thatched bungalows at f.9500 s, f.16,000 d, f.21,000 t, including breakfast and dinner. Airport transfers are f.450 pp.

The **Rangiroa Village** (B.P. 8, Avatoru; tel. 96-03-83) is a 10-bungalow resort near Avatoru village: f.8000 s, f.14,000 d, f.19,000 t, including all meals. Extras are a f.210 "bungalow tax" and f.500 pp for airport transfers.

The **Village Sans Souci** (B.P. 22, Avatoru; tel. 42-48-33) is an escapist's retreat on Motu Mahuta, an islet to the west of Avatoru Pass. It offers 14 thatched bungalows with communal shower and toilet stalls. The package rates are f.26,750 s, f.42,500 d, f.58,250 t for three nights, f.5250 pp per additional night, including transfers and all meals. The Sans Souci's restaurant specializes in seafood and there's a self-service bar. Scuba diving is possible. The San Souci is the place to get away from it all.

Sports And Recreation
The strong tidal currents *(opape)* through Avatoru and Tiputa passes generate flows of three to six knots. It's exciting to shoot these passes on an incoming tide wearing a mask and snorkel, and the hotels offer this activity (f.750-3000) using a small motorboat. The fishlife is fantastic and sharks may be seen. They're *usually* harmless black-tip reef sharks. Other popular excursions include a picnic to the "blue lagoon" at **Motu Taeoo** (f.5000 pp) and tiny mid-lagoon **Motu Paio**, a bird sanctuary (f.1500 pp).

Scuba diving is arranged by the friendly **Centre de Plongee Raie Manta Club** (B.P. 55, Avatoru; tel. 96-04-80) in Avatoru—f.3500 pp for one tank including a float through the pass. A five-dive card is f.15,000, 10 dives f.25,000. Scuba certification is required.

Every dive is different: falling, pass, undulating bottom, hollow. Humphead wrasses, manta rays, barracudas, and lots of sharks are seen. Divemaster Yves Lefevre accommodates divers only in his house, f.4000 pp with complete pension.

Jack's Rent a Boat (B.P. 61, Avatoru; tel. 96-04-69) in Avatoru also arranges scuba diving: f.3000 pp to float through the pass with a tank.

Getting There
Air Tahiti (tel. 96-03-41) flies Tahiti-Rangiroa daily (f.12,000 OW) using 46-seat ATR 42 equipment. Wed. and Sun. a flight arrives direct from Bora Bora (f.15,600). There's service three times a week from Rangiroa to Manihi (f.7400) and weekly to the Marquesas (f.28,700). All 19 seats on the plane to Hiva Oa are almost always booked in advance.

Schooners *(goelettes)* from Papeete (f.2800 OW) take 22 hours to get there from Tahiti, but 72 hours to return (not direct). Boats making the run include the *Manava II, Manava III, St. Xavier Marie Stella,* and *St. Corentin.* For more information on transport to the Tuamotus see the main Introduction to this book.

Airport
The airstrip (RGI) is about five km from Avatoru village by road, accessible to Tiputa village by boat. Some of the pensions offer free transfers; others charge f.500.

a church among the coconut palms at Anaa, Tuamotu Is., featured on this 1985 first-day cover

OTHER ISLANDS AND ATOLLS

MANIHI

Manihi is the other Tuamotu atoll commonly visited by tourists lured by its white-sand beaches and cultured black pearls. You can see right around the 10-by-22-km Manihi lagoon; Tairapa Pass is at the west end of the atoll. Many of the *motus* are inhabited. The 50,000 resident oysters outnumber the 429 (1988) local inhabitants a hundred to one. Due to the pearl industry the people of Manihi are better off than those on the other Tuamotu islands. The 50 houses of Turipaoa village, shaded by trees and flowers, share a sandy strip across the lagoon from the airstrip.

Accommodations

The **Hotel Kaina Village** (B.P. 2460, Papeete; tel. 42-75-53) is Manihi's luxury hotel, located on the airport *motu*. The 16 overwater bungalows run f.14,550 s, f.21,700 d, f.28,300 t including breakfast and dinner. A f.750 "bungalow tax" and f.350 pp airport transfer charge are additional. Scuba diving can be arranged here.

Cheaper lodging is offered by the inhabitants of Turipaoa village. Advance reservations by mail or telegram are recommended to ensure space and airport pick-ups. Bring money as credit cards and foreign currency are not accepted.

Chez Huri in Turipaoa village includes a three-bedroom house with cooking facilities and two bungalows with shared bath at f.1500 pp without food. If you want meals served it's f.3000 pp for them all. Airport transfers are free.

Chez Teiva, also in Turipaoa village, is f.4500 pp for room and board. Each of their five houses with shared bath also has cooking facilities.

Chez Rei Estall has two houses with shared bath at f.4500 pp including all meals.

Chez Marguerite Fareea is on Motu Topi-heiri, a *motu* across the lagoon from Turipaoa village. The seven bungalows are f.5000 pp including excursions and all meals. Five have private bath. This is a friendly place with better-than-average accommodations. There's no telephone at Marquerite's—you must write.

Getting There

You'll need a boat to go from Manihi airport (XMH) to Turipaoa, which can be expensive unless you've arranged to be picked up. All flights from Papeete or Bora Bora are via Rangiroa. A Twin Otter weekly flight arrives at Manihi from the Marquesas (f.26,100). Boats from Papeete also call here.

OTHERS

Makatea is an uplifted atoll with a lunar surface eight km long and 110 meters high. Gray cliffs plung to the sea. Phosphate was dug up here by workers with shovels from 1917 to 1966 and exported to Japan and New Zealand by a transnational corporation which pocketed the profits. At one time 2,500 workers were present. The mining was abandoned in 1966 but many buildings and a railway remain. Numerous archaeological remains were found during the mining.

Ahe, 13 km west of Manihi, is often visited by cruising yachts which are able to enter the 16-km-long lagoon. The village is on the southeast side of the atoll. Facilities include two tiny stores, a post office, and a community center where everyone meets at night. Despite the steady stream of sailing boats, the people are very friendly. All of the houses have solar generating panels supplied after a hurricane in the early 1980s. Only a handful of small children are seen in the village; most are away at school on Rangiroa or Tahiti. Mama Fana keeps the yachtie log. She or the mayor can arrange accommodations. Many families follow their children to the main islands while they're at school, so you may even be able to rent a whole house. A local government boat runs between Ahe and Manihi on an irregular schedule.

The shark-free lagoon at **Niau** is enclosed by an unbroken circle of land. A leper colony once on **Reao** is now closed. For information on lodging with the inhabitants on **Fakarava, Kaukura, Tikehau, Takapoto,** and **Takaroa** ask at the Tahiti Tourist Board in Papeete.

The Lost Treasure Of The Tuamotus

During the War of the Pacific (1879-83) four mercenaries stole 14 tons of gold from a church in Pisco, Peru. They buried most of the treasure on **Pinaki** or **Raraka** atolls in the Tuamotus before proceeding to Australia where two were killed by Aboriginals and the other two were sentenced to 20 years imprisonment for murder. Just prior to his death the surviving mercenery told prospector Charles Howe the story.

In 1913 Howe began a 13-year search which finally located part of the treasure on an island near Raraka. He reburied the chests and returned to Australia to organize an expedition which would remove the gold in secret. Before it could set out, however, Howe disappeared. But using Howe's treasure map, diver George Hamilton took over in 1934. Hamilton thought he found the cached gold in a pool but was unable to extract it. After being attacked by a giant octopus and moray eel Hamilton abandoned the search and the expedition dissolved.

As far as is known, the US$180,000,000 in gold has never been found. Now maverick archaeologist David Hatcher Childress is preparing a new expedition with sophisticated equipment to recover this treasure. Through a series of strange coincidences David has learned the correct name of the atoll in question! If you'd like to join up, write: Adventurers Unlimited, Box 22, Stelle, IL 60919, USA, or call tel. 815-253-6390. For more information refer to Childress' book *Lost Cities of Ancient Lemuria and the Pacific* (see Booklist).

THE NUCLEAR TEST ZONE

The nuclear test zone is at the southeastern end of the Tuamotu group, 1,200 km from Tahiti. The main site is 30-km-long Moruroa atoll, but Fangataufa atoll 40 km south of Moruroa is also being used. In 1962 the French nuclear testing sites in the Algerian Sahara had to be abandoned after the country won its independence. In 1963 French President Charles de Gaulle announced officially that France was shifting the program to Moruroa and Fangataufa. Since 1966 more than 150 nuclear bombs, reaching up to 200 kilotons, have been set off in the Tuamotus. The tests continue at the rate of eight a year. By 1974 the French had conducted 44 *atmospheric* tests, 39 over Moruroa and five over Fangataufa.

Way back in 1963 the U.S., Britain, and the USSR agreed in the Partial Test Ban Treaty to halt nuclear tests in the atmosphere. France chose not to sign. On 23 June 1973, the World Court urged France to discontinue nuclear tests, which might drop radioactive material on surrounding territories. When the French government refused to recognize the Court's jurisdiction in this matter, New Zealand Prime Minister Norman Kirk ordered the N.Z. frigate *Otago* to enter the danger zone off Moruroa. On 23 July Peru broke diplomatic relations with France. On 15 Aug. French commandos boarded the protest vessels *Fri* and *Greenpeace III,* attacking and arresting the crews.

In 1974, with opposition mounting in the Territorial Assembly and growing world indignation, French President Giscard D'Estaing ordered a switch to the *underground* tests which continue today. The French support base on Hao atoll (population 1,156), 500 km north of Moruroa, allows the French military to fly materials directly into the area without passing through Faaa Airport. Evidence of the testing is kept well away from the eyes of tourists on Tahiti—you'll find no mention of

one of 23 huge platforms where the employees at Moruroa seek refuge from hurricanes or tidal waves that sweep the atoll

these tests in any of the official tourist brochures. Most travel guides give this crime only cursory mention. The Polynesian name "Moruroa" means "Long Fish Trap" and not "Place of the Great Secret" as is often stated.

Moruroa

Obviously, an atoll, with its porous coral cap sitting on a narrow basalt base, is the unsafest place in the world to stage underground nuclear explosions. It's unlikely this was ever intended. Moruroa was chosen for its isolated location, far from major population centers which might be affected by fallout. By 1974 when atmospheric testing had to cease, the French military had a huge investment there. So rather than move to a location in France they decided to take a chance. Underground testing was to be carried out in Moruroa's basalt core, 800-1,200 meters below the surface of the atoll.

On 6 July 1979, an explosion and fire in a laboratory bunker on the reef at Moruroa killed two and injured four others. For two weeks after the accident, workers in protective suits tried to clean up the area contaminated with plutonium by the explosion. Right from the beginning of the tests contaminated debris had also carelessly been stored in plastic bags on the north side of the atoll. On 11 March 1981, a hurricane washed large quantities of this nuclear waste into the lagoon and surrounding sea. That Aug., a storm spread more material from the same dump. Enough radioactive debris to fill 200,000 44-gallon drums is still lying on the north side of the atoll.

On 25 July 1979, a nuclear device became stuck halfway down a 1,000-meter shaft. When the army engineers were unable to move the device, they exploded it where it was, causing a massive chunk of outer slope of the atoll to break loose. This generated a huge tidal wave which hit Moruroa, overturning cars and injuring seven people. After the blast, a crack 40 cm wide and two km long appeared on the surface of the island. In Nov. 1980 and March 1981 Moruroa was hit by hurricanes. As a precaution against future hurricanes and tidal waves, refuge platforms were built on the reef. For an hour before and after each test all personnel must climb up on these platforms.

By 1980 the atoll had become so fractured by drilling shafts on the reef ring that radioactivity was leaking directly into the sea from major cracks around Moruroa's 60-km coral rim. So many tests had taken place that Moruroa was punctured as a Swiss cheese, having sunk two cm after every test for a total of 1.5 meters from 1975. So, to be closer to the center of the island's core, the French switched to underwater testing in the Moruroa lagoon in 1981. Recognizing that the 108 underground blasts had severely weakened geological formations beneath Moruroa, French officials announced in 1988 that they were shifting the underground testing to nearby Fangataufa atoll. The military base remains on Moruroa and small groups of workers and technicians are sent over to Fangataufa every time a test is made there. It's believed that due to the extreme danger of continued nuclear testing on these atolls the French may eventually move the program to the Kerguelen Islands in the southern Indian Ocean.

Problems

In 1983 the French government invited a delegation of scientists from Australia, New Zealand, and Papua New Guinea to visit Moruroa. Significantly, they were not permitted to take samples from the northern or western areas of the atoll, nor of lagoon sediments. The scientists reported that "if fracturing of the volcanics accompanied a test and allowed a vertical release of radioactivity to the limestones, specific contaminants would, in this worst case, enter the biosphere within five years."

It's feared the numerous cracks and fissures have already or will eventually release contamination into the Pacific. At the very least, despite concrete plugs the drill holes will become "highways to the surface" for nuclear wastes. A 1987 film made at Moruroa by Jacques Cousteau showed a water geyser rising 60 meters into the air during a test. Radiation with a half-life of several thousand years is already suspected to be leaking from the atoll's fractured rim, but French officials will not allow independent scientists into the area to check this.

The French government claims it "owns" Moruroa and Fangataufa because in 1964 a standing committee of the Territorial Assembly voted three to two to cede the atolls to France for an indefinite period. This was never ratified by the full assembly and French troops had occupied the islands before the vote was taken anyway.

Unlike the U.S. which has paid millions of dollars to the Marshallese victims of its nuclear testing program, the French government has refused to even acknowledge the already-apparent effects of its 44 atmospheric tests. Since 1966 health statistics have been suppressed. Cases of thyroid cancer, leukemia, and brain tumors are on the upswing in Tahiti-Polynesia, and the problem of seafood poisoning *(ciguatera)* in the nearby Gambier Islands is clearly related. French non-response to these first side-effects demonstrates vividly how they plan to deal with the more serious environmental consequences still to come.

The Issue

France is the only nuclear state to have conducted tests under a Pacific island. France has not limited itself to testing atomic and hydrogen devices: numerous neutron bombs have also been exploded. The French have maintained that the tests are harmless and that every precaution has been taken. And yet, the underground tests could be carried out much more effectively, safely, and cheaply in France itself! The claim that the tests are "safe" is disproved by the very choice of the test site, on the opposite side of the globe from their homeland.

French radioactivity will remain in the Tuamotus for thousands of years and the unknown future consequences of this program are the most frightening part of it. Each successive blast continues the genocide com-

mitted by the Republic of France against the people of the Pacific.

Note

To learn more about this problem read *Poisoned Reign, French nuclear colonialism in the Pacific* by Bengt and Marie-Therese Danielsson (Penguin Books, 1986).

1. approaching Maupiti aboard *Taporo I;* **2.** deck class, *Taporo I;* **3.**the *Raromatai Ferry* at Bora Bora;
4. maintenance, *Raromatai Ferry;* **5.** *Taporo IV* arriving at Fare, Huahine
(all photos this page by D. Stanley)

1. Polynesian girl (Tahiti Tourist Board); **2.** flower vendors, Papeete Market, Tahiti (Tahiti Tourist Board photo by Tini Colombell); **3.** children, Maupiti (D. Stanley); **4.** Tahitian dancer (Tahiti Tourist Board); **5.** painter Aad Van der Heyde at his studio on Moorea (D. Stanley); **6.** Tuamotu children (Tahiti Tourist Board)

an early 19th century engraving of Mangarevans aboard a craft with sail

THE GAMBIER ISLANDS

The Gambier (or Mangareva) Islands are just north of the Tropic of Capricorn, 1,650 km southeast of Tahiti. The archipelago, contrasting sharply with the atolls of the Tuamotus, consists of 10 rocky islands enclosed on three sides by a semicircular barrier reef 65 km long. In all, there are 22 sq km of dry land. The Polynesian inhabitants named the main island and largest, Mangareva, "Floating Mountain." Unlike the Marquesas where the mountains are entirely jungle-clad, hilltops in the Gambiers are covered with tall *aeho* grass.

Aside from Mangareva, small groups of people live only on Taravai and Kamaka islands. Makaroa is a barren, rugged 136-meter-high island. In a cliffside cave on the island of Agakauitai the mummies of 35 generations of cannibal kings are interred. A local seabird, the *karako,* crows at dawn like a rooster.

A dramatic intensification of the *ciguatera* problem in the Gambiers is believed to be linked to reef damage or pollution originating at the nuclear testing facilities on Moruroa, 400 km east. Lagoon fish can no longer be eaten. During the atmospheric testing series (until 1974) Mangarevans had to take refuge in French-constructed fallout shelters whenever advised by the military. Now increasing birth defects, kidney problems, and cancer among the inhabitants are being covered up by authorities who will not allow foreigners on the islands. It's believed that a deciding reason for the French decision to launch a terrorist attack on Greenpeace's *Rainbow Warrior* in 1985 was a report indicating that the ship intended to proceed to Mangareva with doctors aboard to assess the radiation exposure of residents.

Orientation

In 1988 the population of the Gambiers was 620 (in 1797 it was 6,000). Rikitea, on 6.5-by-1.5-km Mangareva, is the main village. A post office, small shops, gendarmerie, infirmary, schools, and a cathedral three times as big as the one in Papeete make up the infrastructure of this administrative backwater. The tomb of the 35th and last king of Mangareva, Gregorio Maputeoa (died 1868), is on a plateau above the village. Nearby is a huge nuclear-fallout shelter built during the French atmospheric testing at Moruroa. Black pearls are cultured at a farm off Taku on the north coast of Mangareva.

HISTORY

Mangareva, which was originally settled from the Marquesas Islands around 1100 A.D., was shortly afterwards the jumping-off place for small groups which discovered and occupied Pitcairn and Henderson islands. In 1797 Capt. James Wilson of the London Missionary Society's ship *Duff* named the group for the English Admiral Gambier. France

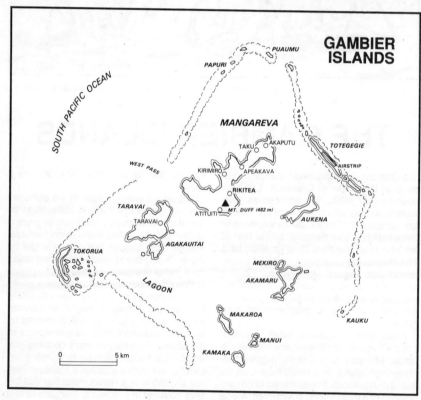

GAMBIER ISLANDS

POLYNÉSIE FRANÇAISE

EDIFICES RELIGIEUX
Intérieur de la Cathédrale S.MICHEL RIKITEA (Gambiers)

PREMIER JOUR D'ÉMISSION

EDIFICES
RELIGIEUX
EN
POLYNESIE FRANÇAISE
11 DEC. 85
PAPEETE

the mother-of-pearl-encrusted interior in Father Laval's huge cathedral at Rikitea, Mangareva, Gambier Is., featured on this first-day cover in 1985

made the Gambiers a "protectorate" in 1844 and annexed the group in 1881.

Mangareva was the area of operations for a fanatical French priest, Father Honore Laval of the Order of Picpus, who ruled here for nearly 40 years. Upon hearing whalers' tales of rampant cannibalism and marvelous pearls, Laval left his monastery in Chile and with another priest reached the Gambiers in 1834. An old Mangarevan prophecy had foretold the coming of two magicians whose god was all-powerful. Laval toppled the dreaded stone effigy of the god Tu on the island's sacred *marae* with his own hands. He single handedly imposed a ruthless and inflexible moral code on the islanders, recruiting them as virtual slaves to build a 1,200-seat cathedral, convents, and triumphal arches, with the result that he utterly destroyed this once vigorous native culture, and practically wiped out its people. During Laval's 37-year reign the population dropped from 9,000 to 500. You can still see his architectural masterpiece—the cathedral Rikitea with its twin towers of white coral rock from Kamaka and altar shining with polished mother-of-pearl—a monument to horror and yet another lost

culture. In 1871 Laval was removed from Mangareva by a French warship, tried for murder on Tahiti, and declared insane. He lies buried in a crypt before the altar of St. Michael's Cathedral, Mangareva.

For a glimpse of the Gambiers half a century ago and a fuller account of Pere Laval, read Robert Lee Eskridge's *Manga Reva, The Forgotten Islands* (see Booklist).

PRACTICALITIES

Due to the nearby French nuclear testing facilities, the entry of foreigners to the Gambier Islands is restricted. No cameras or video equipment are allowed in the islands. For information write: Subdivision Administrative des Tuamotu-Gambiers, B.P. 34, Papeete (tel. 42-20-00). Of course, this is unnecessary if you're French.

If you do get there **Chez Francois Labbeyi** near the wharf in Rikitea provides accommodations for about f.2000 pp. Mr. Jean Anania (nicknamed "Siki") offers speedboat charters and fishing trips.

The mini-cruiseship *Society Explorer* calls

at Mangareva twice a year on its way from Tahiti to Easter I. via Pitcairn. The *Explorer* also calls at Rapa in the Australs. The cheapest double-occupancy berth is US$4650 for the two-week trip, plus US$1200 airfare from the States. Contact **Society Expeditions Inc.** (3131 Elliott Ave., Suite 700, Seattle, WA 98121, USA; tel. 206-285-9400).

The airstrip (GMR) is on Totegegie, a long coral island eight km northeast of Rikitea. The weekly Air Tahiti flight from Papeete (f.41,400) is via the huge French military base at Hao, closed to non-French. The monthly supply boat from Papeete also travels via Hao.

The passion flower (passiflora) got its name from a symbolic resemblance between its flower and Jesus's wounds, crown of thorns, etc.

A Marquesan meae at Nuku Hiva in the early 19th century

THE MARQUESAS ISLANDS

The Marquesas Islands are the farthest north of the high islands of the South Pacific, on the same latitude as the Solomons. Though the group was known as Te Fenua Enata ("The Land of Men") by the Polynesian inhabitants, depopulation during the 19th and 20th centuries has left many of the valleys empty. Ten main islands form a line 300 km long, roughly 1,400 km northeast of Tahiti, but only six are inhabited today: Nuku Hiva, Ua Pou, and Ua Huka in a cluster to the northwest, and Hiva Oa, Tahuata, and Fatu Hiva to the southeast. The administrative centers, Atuona (Hiva Oa), Hakahau (Ua Pou), and Taiohae (Nuku Hiva), are the only places with post offices, banks, gendarmeries, etc. The total population is just 7,358 (1988).

The expense and difficulty in getting there has made visitors rare. Most only visit Nuku Hiva (where the plane from Tahiti lands) and Hiva Oa (where Paul Gauguin is buried). Cruising yachts from California often call on the way to Papeete, even though ocean swells reaching the shorelines make the anchorages rough. This is paradise, however, for surfers and hikers. Multitudes of waterfalls tumble down the slopes. A knowledge of French is an asset. In the smaller villages it's proper to pay a courtesy call on the mayor (or chief), who can arrange paid accommodations (if required). If you enjoy quiet, unspoiled places you'll like the Marquesas, but one month should be enough. The Marquesas have been left behind by their remoteness.

The Land

These wild, rugged islands feature steep cliffs and valleys leading up to high central ridges, sectioning the islands off into a cart-

THE MARQUESAS

others. The southern islands of the Marquesas (Hiva Oa, Tahuata, Fatu Hiva) are green and humid; the northern islands (Nuku Hiva, Ua Huka, Ua Pou) are brown and dry.

HISTORY

Pre-European Society

Marquesan houses were built on high platforms *(paepae)* scattered through the valleys (still fairly easy to find). Each valley had a ceremonial area *(tohua)* where important festivals took place. Archaeologists are still able to trace stone temples *(meae)*, agricultural terraces, and earthen fortifications *(akaua)* half hidden in the jungle, evocative reminders of a vanished civilization. Then as now, the valleys were isolated from one another by

wheel of segments which create major transportation difficulties. Reefs don't form due to the cold south equatorial current. The absence of protective reefs has prevented the creation of coastal plains, so no roads go around any of the islands. Most of the people live in the narrow, fertile river valleys. The interiors are inhabited only by hundreds of wild horses, cattle, and goats, which have destroyed much of the original vegetation. The islands are abundant with lemons, tangerines, oranges, grapefruit, bananas, mangoes, and papayas. Taro and breadfruit are the main staples. Birdlife is rich and the waters around the Marquesas are teeming with lobster, fish, and sharks.

The sub-tropical climate is hotter and drier than that of Tahiti. July and August are the coolest months. The deep bays on the west sides of the islands are better sheltered for shipping, and the humidity is lower there than on the east sides, which catch the tradewinds. The precipitation is uneven with drought some years, heavy rainfall the

stilt footrests: The Marquesans once staged races and mock battles on stilts with the participants attempting to knock one another off balance.

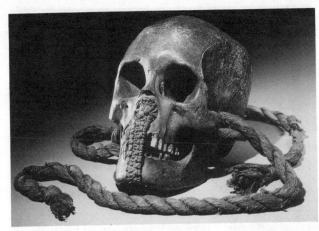

The Marquesans preserved the skulls of their ancestors.

high ridges and turbulent seas, yet warfare was vicious with cannibalism an important incentive. An able warrior could attain great power. Local hereditary chiefs exercised authority over commoners.

The Marquesans' artistic style was one of the most powerful and refined in the Pacific. The ironwood war club was their most distinctive symbol, but there were also finely carved wooden bowls, fan handles, and *tikis* of stone and wood, both miniature and massive. The carvings are noted for the faces: the mouth with lips parted, and bespectacled eyes. Both men and women wore carved ivory ear plugs. Men's entire bodies were covered by bold and striking tattoos, a practice banned by the Catholic missionaries. Stilts were used by boys for racing and mock fighting. This was about the only part of Polynesia where polyandry was common. There was a strong cult of the dead: the bodies or skulls of ancestors were carefully preserved. Both Easter Island (around 500 A.D.) and Hawaii (around 700 A.D.) were colonized from here.

European Contact

The existence of these islands was long concealed from the world by the Spanish, to prevent the English from taking possession of them. The southern group was found by Alvaro de Mendana in July 1595 during his second voyage of exploration from Peru. He named them Las Marquesas de Mendoza after his benefactor, the Spanish viceroy. The first island sighted (Fatu Hiva) seemed uninhabited, but as Mendana's *San Jeronimo* sailed nearer scores of outriggers appeared, paddled by about 400 robust, light-skinned islanders. Their hair was long and loose, and they were naked and tattooed in blue patterns. The natives boarded the ship, but when they became overly curious and bold, Mendana ordered a gun fired, and they jumped over the side.

Then began one of the most murderous and shameful of all the white man's entries into the South Pacific region. As a matter of caution, Mendana's men began shooting natives on sight, in one instance hanging three bodies in the shore camp on Santa Cristina (Tahuata) as a warning. They left behind three large crosses, the date cut in a tree, and over 200 dead Polynesians.

The northern Marquesas Islands were "discovered" by Joseph Ingraham of the American trading vessel *Hope* on 19 April 1791. After that, blackbirders, firearms, disease, and alcohol reduced the population. American whalers called frequently from 1800 onwards. Although France took possession of the group in 1842, Peruvian slavers kidnapped some Marquesans to South America

Madisonville, Nuku Hiva: On 19 Nov. 1813 Capt. David Porter of the US frigate Essex took possession of Nuku Hiva, Marquesas Is., for the United States.

in 1863 to work the plantations and mines. Those few who returned brought a catastrophic smallpox epidemic. The Marquesans clung to their warlike, cannibalistic ways until 95% of their number had died—the remainder adopted Catholicism. (The Marquesas today is the only island group of Tahiti-Polynesia with a Catholic majority.) From 80,000 at the beginning of the 19th century, the population fell to about 15,000 by 1842 when the French "protectors" arrived, and to a devastated 2,000 by 1926.

The Marquesas Today

Slowly the Marquesas are catching up with the rest of the world—VCRs are the latest introduced species. Cruise ships are also finding their ways into the group. Yet the islands remain very untouristy. Though there are many negative attitudes toward the French and in Tahiti talk for independence is heard, the Marquesans realize that without French subsidies their economy would collapse and they would become even more distant from the Tuamotus, Tahiti, and "civilization." Making copra would no longer be an economic activity and far fewer supply ships would call at the islands. Hospitalization, drugs, and dental care are provided free by the government and a monthly family allowance of US$50 is paid for each child under 16—quite a bundle if you have eight kids, as

many do! If the Marquesans had to give up their cars, videos, and U.S. frozen chicken many would abandon the already underpopulated islands.

During the Heiva or Tiurai festival in July, races, games, and dance competitions take place on the different islands. The older women prove themselves graceful dancers and excellent singers.

GETTING THERE

To visit the Marquesas requires either lots of money or lots of time. An **Air Tahiti** 46-seat ATR 42 flies to Nuku Hiva from Tahiti twice a week (f.36,700, four hours). There are also weekly flights to Hiva Oa and Nuku Hiva from Rangiroa, Manihi, and Napuka in the Tuamotus (f.28,700), but the 19-passenger plane is always full.

Twin Otter flights between Nuku Hiva, Ua Huka, Hiva Oa, and Ua Pou operate weekly, connecting with the ATR 42 flight from Papeete. Flights between Nuku Hiva, Ua Pou, and Ua Huka are f.4500 each. From Hiva Oa to Nuku Hiva, Ua Pou, or Ua Huka is f.7800.

All flights are heavily booked. Reserve your seat from Papeete to Nuku Hiva six months in advance! You can do this through your international carrier or Air France and it's not necessary to pay to make the booking. Get a through ticket to your final destination as flights to all airports in the Marquesas are the same price from Papeete. Tahuata and Fatu Hiva are without air service.

Three ships, the *Aranui, Tamarii Tuamotu,* and *Taporo V,* sail monthly from Papeete, calling at all six inhabited Marquesas Islands. The *Aranui* is the easiest to use as it follows a regular schedule and no special permission is required. To come on the *Tamarii Tuamotu* and *Taporo V* you may have to go through the procedure described under "Permission" in the Tuamotu chapter above. Air passengers are also spared these courtesies.

The freighter *Aranui* is recommended, if you can afford it. The roundtrip voyages designed for tourists flown in from the U.S. and France cost cruiseship prices. One-way fares on the *Aranui* are priced for travelers: Papeete to Ua Pou is f.21,000 deck. You can also use the *Aranui* to travel interisland in the Marquesas at about f.2000 between each island. The other main interisland boat, *Taporo V,* is cheaper at f.15,000 deck, but it's dirty and unfriendly. Food is included in the passages. It's not necessary to reserve deck passage on these boats. The ships tie up to the wharves at Taiohae, Atuona, Vaipaee, and Hakahau; at Tahauta and Fatu Hiva passengers must go ashore by whaleboat. In stormy weather landings can be dangerous. For more information on these services see the main Introduction to this book.

NUKU HIVA

Nuku Hiva is the largest (339 sq km) and most populous (2,100 inhabitants in 1988) of the Marquesas. In 1813 Capt. David Porter of the American raider *Essex* annexed Nuku Hiva for the United States, though the act was never ratified by Congress. Porter built a fort at the present site of Taiohae, which he named Madisonville for the U.S. president of his day. Nothing remains of this or another fort erected by the French in 1842. Sandalwood traders followed Porter, then whalers. Herman Melville's *Typee,* written after a one-month stay in the Taipivai Valley in 1842, is still the classic narrative of Marquesan life during the 19th century.

Taiohae (population 1,421 in 1988) on the south coast is the administrative and economic center of the Marquesas. It's a modern little town with a post office, hospital, town hall, two banks, five grocery stores, and street lighting. Winding mountain roads lead northeast from Taiohae to Taipivai and Hatiheu villages, where a few dozen families reside. In the center of the island Mt. Tekao (1,224 meters) rises above the vast, empty Toovii plateau. Though open to the south, Taiohae's deep harbor offers excellent anchorage and cruising yachts are often seen here. A nominal "water fee" is charged.

SIGHTS

Vestiges of an **old prison** can still be seen in Taiohae. Many stone and woodcarvers continue to work on Nuku Hiva, making wooden *tikis,* bowls, ukuleles, ceremonial war clubs, etc. Some items are on display at the Banque Socredo. Other woodcarvings may be viewed in the **Catholic cathedral** (1974) at Taiohae. Ask to see the small collection of artifacts at the Bishop's residence.

For a good view of Taiohae Bay hike up to **Muake** (864 meters) on the Taipivai road. From there lifts are possible with market gardeners headed for the agricultural station on the **Toovii Plateau** to the west.

Taipivai is a five-hour, 17-km walk from Taiohae. Herman Melville spent a month here in 1842. The huge *tohua* of Vahangekua at Taipivai is a whopping 170 by 25 meters. Great stone *tikis* watch over the *meae* of Paeke, also near Taipivai. Vanilla grows wild. At **Hooumi,** a fine protected bay near Taipivae, is a truly magical little church.

Above **Hatiheu** on the north coast are two more *tikis* and a reconstructed *meae.* Anaho, 45 minutes east of Hatiheu on foot, is one of the most beautiful of Nuku Hiva's bays with a fine **white beach** and good snorkeling. Unfortunately, it's infested with *nono* sand flies. Even better white-sand beaches face Haatuatua and Haataivea bays beyond Anaho. No one lives there, though wild horses are seen.

At Hakaui, west of Taiohae, a river rushes down a steep-sided valley. Fantastic 350-meter **Vaipo Waterfall,** highest in the territory, drops from the plateau at the far end of the valley, four km from the coast. It's a two-hour walk from Hakaui to the waterfall. A boat from Taiohae to Hakaui costs f.12,000, plus f.3000 for a guide. A switchback trail also crosses the 535-meter ridge from Taiohae to Hakaui.

PRACTICALITIES

Accommodations
The **Keikahanui Inn** (B.P. 21, Taiohae; tel. 92-03-82) on the west side of Taiohae Bay is run by American yachties Rose and Frank Corser (ask to see Maurice's log books). They have three screened Polynesian bungalows with private bath: f.7000 s, f.9500 d, f.12,000 t with Continental breakfast. Meals in the dining room are f.2000 each. The Corsers give much lower rates to locals, so you might try bargaining for a 50% reduction. You can buy Fatu Hiva *tapa* at the Inn. Frank and Rose have co-authored a *Tahiti Traveler's Guide.*

The **Hotel Moana Nui** (Marcelline Kautai, B.P. 9, Taiohae; tel. 92-03-30) in the middle of Taiohae has seven rooms with private bath. Bed and breakfast is f.2500 pp, meals f.2500 each.

Chez Fetu Peterano (B.P. 22, Taiohae; tel. 92-03-66) near the wharf in Taiohae provides rooms in the owner's house at f.2000 pp with breakfast. You can cook.

In Hatiheu **Chez Yvonne Katupa** offers

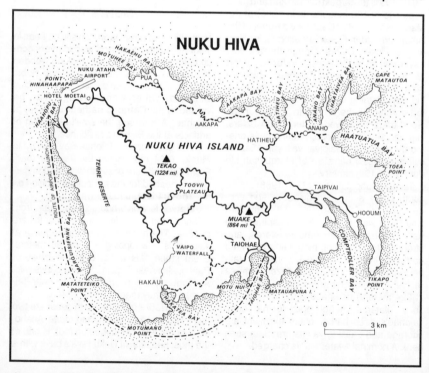

NUKU HIVA

Hakaui on Nuku Hiva's south coast, home of the Taioa tribe

three bungalows without cooking facilities or hot water at f.1400 pp, breakfast included. A small restaurant nearby serves fried fish for f.700, lobster for f.1500.

Chez Clarisse Omitai also provides accommodations (f.1000 pp) in Hatiheu. At Taipivai camp on football field.

Chez Marie Foucaud, on a white-sand beach at Anaho Bay, has four bungalows at f.1800 pp including breakfast, other meals f.1000.

The **Hotel Moetai Village** (Guy Millon, tel. 92-04-91) near Nuku Ataha Airport has six bungalows with private bath: f.2500 s, f.3500 d for bed and breakfast, other meals f.2000.

Services

Madame Debora Kimitete (B.P. 38, Taiohae; tel. 92-03-72) operates the Syndicat d'Initiative information office opposite the wharf at Taiohae. She sells excellent topographical maps of the main islands for f.1200 each. Taiohae has a Banque Socredo branch (tel. 92-03-63). Don't have your mail sent c/o poste restante at the local post office as it will be returned via surface after 15 days. Instead have it addressed c/o the Keikahanui Inn.

Get bread at Ropa's Bakery and supplies from Maurice McKitrick's store (tel. 92-03-91). Yachties who figure they'll need fuel when they get to the Marquesas should write a letter to Maurice and ask him to order an extra drum or two from Papeete. Things to bring to trade with the locals include perfume, earrings, reggae tapes, T-shirts, and surfing magazines, for which you'll receive *tapas,* tye-dyed *pareus,* and all the fruit you can carry. A small crafts center is on the ocean side near Maurice's store. War clubs, wooden bowls, and ukuleles are the most popular items. Take care with the drinking water at Taiohae.

Getting Around

The airport *truck* is the only one on Nuku Hiva, though you can hitch fairly easily. Several people in Taiohae arrange horseback riding to Taipivai for about f.4000 pp.

Airport

Nuku Ataha Airport (NHV) is in the "Terre-Deserte" at the northwest corner of Nuku Hiva. A restaurant and hotel are near the terminal. To reach Taiohae (60 km), take a *truck* from the terminal to Haahopu Bay (f.250, 15 minutes), then the launch *Atea* to Taiohae (f.800, two hours).

HIVA OA

Measuring 40 by 19 km, 315-sq-km Hiva Oa (population 1671 in 1988) is the second largest of the Marquesas. The administrative headquarters for the Marquesas group switched back and forth several times: Taiohae was the center until 1904, then it was Atuona until 1944, when Taiohae once more took over. The town may be the center of the southern cluster of the Marquesas but it's quieter still than Taiohae. Mt. Temetiu (1,276 meters) towers above Atuona to the west.

Atuona was made forever famous when Paul Gauguin came to live here in 1902. Despite the attentions of his 14-year-old mistress, Vaeoho, he died of syphilis a year later at age 55 and is buried in the cemetery above the town. When Tioka, Gauguin's neighbor, found him stretched out with one leg hanging over the side of his bed, he bit him on the head as the Marquesans do to see if he really was dead. No, there was no doubt. *"Ua mate Koke!"* he cried, and disappeared. Gauguin was constantly in conflict with the colonial authorities who disapproved of his heavy drinking sessions with the locals. Just a week before his death, Gauguin was summarily convicted of "libel of a *gendarme* in the course of his official duties," fined, and sentenced to three months in prison.

The famous Belgian *chanson* singer Jacques Brel and companion Maddly Bamy came to the Marquesas in 1975 aboard his 18-meter yacht, the *Askoy II*. Jacques decided to settle at Atuona and sold his boat to an American couple. Maddly, who had been a dancer on her native Guadeloupe, gave dancing lessons to the local girls, while Jacques ran an open-air cinema. His plane, nicknamed "Jojo," was kept at Hiva Oa airport for trips to Papeete, 1,500 km southwest. The album *Brel 1977* under the Barclay label includes one of his last songs, "Les Marquises." In 1978 chain-smoker Brel died of lung cancer and was buried in Atuona cemetery near Gauguin.

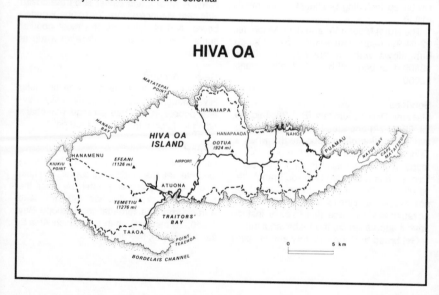

HIVA OA

MATATEPAI POINT

HANAIAPA

HANAUI BAY

HIVA OA ISLAND

HANAPAAOA

NAHOE

OOTUA (924 m)

PUAMAU

NATUU BAY

CAPE MATAFENUA

HANAMENU

EFEANI (1126 m)

AIRPORT

KIUKIU POINT

ATUONA

TEMETIU (1276 m)

TRAITORS' BAY

TAAOA

POINT TEAEHOA

BORDELAIS CHANNEL

0   5 km

Marquesan model Tohotaua served as the model for "Girl with a Fan."
The photo was taken by Gauguin's friend Louis Grelet.

SIGHTS

The view of Atuona from the **graveyard** is good (take the first left fork in the road as you climb the hill), but the beach at Atuona is poor. A **lighthouse** on the point looks across Taaoa or "Traitors'" Bay. Polynesian ruins may be found up the Vaioa River just west of Atuona.

For better swimming take the road five km south along the bay to **Taaoa.** A big *meae* (temple) is found a km up the river from there.

A second village, **Puamau,** is on the northeast coast, about 30 km from Atuona over a winding road. It's a good eight-hour walk from Atuona to Puamau, up and down all the way. Five huge stone *tikis* and Meae Takaii can be seen in the valley behind Puamau, a 10-minute walk from Chez Bernard. One stands over two meters high.

At **Hanaiapa** ask for William who keeps a yachties' log. He's happy to have his infrequent visitors sign. **Hanamenu** in the northwest corner of Hiva Oa is now uninhabited

but dozens of old stone platforms can still be seen. If you'd like to spend some time here as a hermit ask for Ozanne in Atuona who has a house at Hanamenu he might be willing to rent. To the right of Ozanne's house is a small, crystal-clear pool.

PRACTICALITIES

Accommodations

The **Mairie d'Atuona** (tel. 92-73-32) rents out five pleasant bungalows behind the Town Hall at f.1500-1800 pp. The food served is good (ask for *popoi*—fermented breadfruit). You'll be awakened in the very early morning by noisy roosters, dogs, people.

Chez Jean Saucourt (tel 92-73-33) at Atuona has one bungalow with cooking facilities, f.3000 d, f.3500 t.

Gabriel Heitaa (B.P. 52, Atuona; tel. 92-73-02) has a two-room bungalow at Atuona, f.2000 pp including breakfast. Airport transfers are f.1000 pp roundtrip.

The tomb of Gauguin at Atuona. Gauguin's wish that his ceramic figure of Oviri, goddess of death, mourning, and destruction, be erected over his tomb has finally been granted, if only in the form of a copy. The name Oviri also means "the savage."

The budget traveler's best friend, **Philippe Robard** (B.P. 46, Atuona; tel. 92-74-73),

takes guests in his large bungalow four km southwest of Atuona for f.400 pp. Cooking facilities are available and vegetables can be purchased from Philippe.

In Puamau stay at **Chez Bernard Heitaa**. The two rooms with cooking facilities and shared bath are f.1500 pp, or f.3000 pp including all meals.

Services

The Banque Socredo branch (tel. 92-73-54) is next to the post office at Atuona. Of the five small stores in Atuona, only Duncan's (the blue one) sells propane; diagonally across the street from Duncan's is a hardware store. The snack bar in Atuona charges f.400 for a Coke. To rent a six-passenger Land Rover from Atuona to Puamau will run you f.10,000. Inquire at Atuona Town Hall. Yachts anchor behind the breakwater in Tahauku Bay, two km east of the center of town. The copra boats also tie up here. A shower stall and laundry tub are provided on the wharf.

Airport

The airstrip (AUQ) is on a 441-meter-high plateau 13 km northeast of Atuona. It's a two-hour walk from the airport to Atuona (or you can hitch).

OTHER ISLANDS

UA HUKA

Goats and wild horses range across the plateaus and through the valleys of 81-sq-km Ua Huka (population 539 in 1988). Mt. Hitikau (884 meters) rises northeast of Hane village. The tiny island of Teuaua off the southwest tip of Ua Huka is a breeding ground for millions of *kaveka* (sternas). Vaipaee is the main village of the island, although the clinic is at Hane.

Archaeological excavations dated a coastal site on Ua Huka to 300 A.D. which is the oldest in Tahiti-Polynesia; the island was probably a major dispersal point for the an-

cient Polynesians. Small *tikis* may be visited in the valley behind Hane. In Vaipaee is a small **museum** of local artifacts. Woodcarvers are active on the island.

Accommodations

Several of the residents provide room and board for visitors. **Joseph Lichtle** at Vaipaee has a three-bedroom house with cooking facilities, f.2500 pp meals included. Joseph also has five bungalows ensconced on the white sands of Haavei Beach (same price). Joseph and Laura are reputedly the best cooks in the Marquesas. Their son Leon, mayor of Ua Huka, is extremely helpful. Rent a horse from Joseph for f.1500 a day.

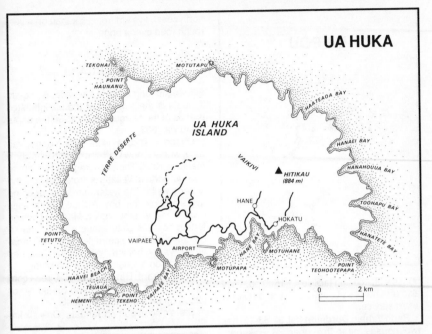

Laura Raioha, nicknamed "Tati Laura," rents out four rooms in her house with cooking facilities at Vaipaee (f.1500 s, f.2500 d). Also in Vaipaee, Miriama Fournier has three rooms with cooking facilities (f.1000 pp, meals f.500).

In Hane **Jean and Celina Fournier** offer four rooms with shared bath and no cooking at f.2000 s, f.3000 d. Food is available at their restaurant. Also in Hane, **Madame Vii Fournier** rents rooms in a two-bedroom house with cooking facilities at f.15,000 a month.

Getting There
The airstrip (UAH) is on a hilltop between Hane and Vaipaee, closer to the latter. Ships tie up to a wharf at Vaipaee.

UA POU

This island lies about 40 km south of Nuku Hiva. Several jagged volcanic plugs loom behind Hakahau, the main village on the northeast coast of 120-sq-km Ua Pou. One of these sugarloaf-shaped mountains inspired Jacques Brel's song "La Cathedrale." Mt. Oave (1,203 meters), highest point on Ua Pou, is often cloud-covered. The population of 1,918 (1988) is almost the same as Nuku Hiva. In 1988, 500 French foreign legionnaires rebuilt the breakwater at Hakahau.

A track goes right around the island. The road leads south from Hakahau to a beach beyond Hohoi. On 112-meter-high Motu Oa off the south coast millions of seabirds nest. The villages of Hakatao and Hakamaii on the west coast are only reachable on foot, hoof, or sea. In Hakahetau village are two new churches, one Catholic, the other Protestant. The first stone church in the Marquesas was erected at Hakahau in 1859.

Accommodations
Chez Yvonne et Jules Hituputoka (tel. 92-53-33) at Hakahau is a three-room guest-

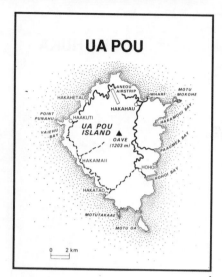

UA POU

UA POU ISLAND

OAVE
(1203 m)

0   2 km

north coast, five km from Hakahau on a very rough road over a ridge.

TAHUATA

Fifteen km long by nine km wide, 61-sq-km Tahuata is the smallest of the six inhabited islands of the Marquesas. In 1988 the population was 633.

On the west coast is the main village, Vaitahu, where a new Catholic church was completed in 1988. The anchorage at Hana moe noa just north of Vaitahu is protected from the ocean swells. The water here is clear as no rivers run into this bay. Archaeological sites exist in the Vaitahu Valley. Hapatoni village farther south is picturesque with a tamanu-bordered road and petroglyphs in the Hanatahau Valley behind. White-sand beaches are found on the north side of the island.

Chez Naani Barsinas is a three-room house, f.1500 pp for bed and breakfast, or f.2500 pp for a bed and all meals.

There's no airport on Tahuata. Only six km

house with cooking facilities, f.1500 pp. They also rent horses at f.3000 a day and operate a taxi service.

Rene Vahiau Dordillon (tel. 92-53-15) has two houses near the wharf at Hakahau. A room with cooking facilities is f.1500 s, f.2500 d.

Other people in Hakahau with rooms at f.1500 pp include **Julienne Pahuaivevau** (tel. 92-53-80), **Marguerite Kaiha-Schaffer** (tel. 92-53-97), and **Rosalie Tata** (tel. 92-53-11). Rosalie also operates a restaurant.

Services
The Banque Socredo branch (tel. 92-53-63), post office, gendarmerie, and six or seven stores are at Hakahau. A boutique sells some local carvings and beautiful hand-painted *pareus.* Four woodcarvers work in the village—just ask for *les sculpteurs.* If you're buying, shop around at the beginning of your stay as many items are unfinished and there'll be time to have something completed for you; the same carvings cost three times as much on Tahiti. On the right just past the bakery (great baguettes!) is the home of Jacob Teikitutoua, who makes ukuleles.

Ua Pou's Aneou airstrip (UAP) is on the

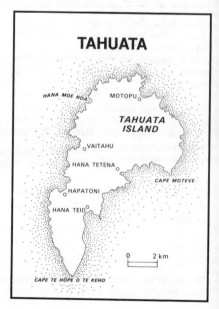

TAHUATA

TAHUATA ISLAND

HANA MOE NOA   MOTOPU

VAITAHU

HANA TETENA

CAPE MOTEVE

HAPATONI

HANA TEIO

0   2 km

CAPE TE HOPE O TE KEHO

south of Hiva Oa across Bordelais Channel, to charter an eight-passenger boat between the islands is f.8800 (one hour). Small boats leave Hiva Oa for Tahuata almost daily, so ask around at the harbor on Takauku Bay near Atuona. Take supplies with you.

FATU HIVA

Fatu Hiva was the first of the Marquesas to be visited by Europeans (Mendana called in 1595). Thor Heyerdahl spent one year in 1937-38 with his young bride Liv on this southernmost island, and wrote a book called *Fatu Hiva,* describing their attempt "to return to a simple, natural life." Fatu Hiva (80 sq km) is far wetter than the northern islands and the vegetation is lush. Mt. Tauaouoho (960 meters) is the highest point. *Tapa* cloth is still made and painted on Fatu Hiva. Hats and mats are woven from pandanus. Monoi oils are made from coconut oil, gardenia, jasmine, and sandalwood.

the Cannilie Kai *at Bay of Virgins, Fatu Hiva*

This is the most remote of the Marquesas and no French officials are present. With 497 (1988) inhabitants, Fatu Hiva has only two villages, Omoa and Hanavave. It takes about five hours to walk the 17-km trail linking the two, up and down over the mountains amid breathtaking scenery. Surfing onto the rocky beach at Omoa can be pretty exciting! Hanavave on the Bay of Virgins offers one of the most fantastic scenic spectacles in all of Polynesia, with *tiki*-shaped cliffs dotted with goats. Yachts usually anchor in the Bay of Virgins (from Jan. to Sept.); the swell can be uncomfortable at times but the holding is good in about six fathoms.

Many local families take paying guests and camping is possible. In Omoa, **Joseph Tetuanui** and **Kehu Kamia** rent rooms at f.1000 pp, plus another f.1000 for all meals. **Francois Peters** and **Jean Bouyer** charge f.3000 pp inluding all meals. Mr. Peters has a room for f.10,000 pp a month. A bakery and four or five small stores are also in Omoa.

In Hanavave, **Veronique Kamia** has two rooms at f.2000 pp including meals. She also makes *tapa* cloth and sandalwood oil. - **Jacques Tevenino** and **Daniel Pavaouau** rent rooms at f.1500 pp or f.35,000 a month. **Tutai Kohueinui** charges f.1000 pp, while **Lionel Cantois** and **Ahutoui Tevenino** are f.2000 pp.

If you plan on staying a while get some free anti-elephantiasis pills at a clinic. Fatu Hiva doesn't have any *nonos,* but lots of mosquitos. Horses and canoes are for hire in both villages. There's a speedboat or "bonitier" once a week from Fatu Hiva to Atuona (f.3000 OW). It takes just over three hours and carries eight people, mail, and video cassettes.

MOTANE

Motane (Mohotani) is an eight-km-long island rising to 520 meters about 18 km southeast of Hiva Oa. The depredations of wild sheep on Motane turned the island into a treeless desert. When the Spaniards "discovered" it in 1595 Motane was well-wooded and populated, but today it's uninhabited.

EIAO

Uninhabited Eiao and Hatutu islands, 85 km northwest of Nuku Hiva, are the remotest of the Marquesas. Eiao is a 40-sq-km island, 10 km long and 576 meters high, with landings on the northwest and west sides. The French once used Eiao as a site of deportation for criminals or "rebellious" natives. Wild cattle, sheep, pigs, and donkeys forage across Eiao, ravaging the vegetation, and suffering from droughts.

Hatutu, the northernmost of the Marquesas, measures 6.4 sq km. Thousands of birds nest here.

Marquesan artifacts

BOOKLIST

GUIDEBOOKS

Bisignani, J.D. *Hawaii Handbook*. Chico, CA: Moon Publications; 788 pages, fully indexed. Joe takes you beyond the glitz and high-priced hype of Hawaii, and leads you on a genuine island experience.

Bruce, Erroll. *Deep Sea Sailing*. London: Stanley Paul, 1953. The classic text on ocean cruising. Study it beforehand if you're thinking of working as crew on a yacht.

Danielsson, Bengt. *Tahiti, Circle Island Tour Guide*. Singapore: Les Editions du Pacifique, 1986. A kilometer-by-kilometer ride around the island with *the* expert.

Davock, Marcia. *Cruising Guide to Tahiti and the French Society Islands*. Stamford, CT: Wescott Cove Publishing, 1985. A large-format, spiral-bound guide for yachties.

Fisher, Dr. Jon. *The Last Frontiers on Earth*. Loompanics Unlimited, Box 1197, Port Townsend, WA 98368. This little book and Dr. Fisher's other work, *Uninhabited and Deserted Islands,* are essential reading for anyone considering relocating in Polynesia.

Hermann-Auclair, Helene, and Alain Durand. *A Tahiti en Polynesie a l'Ile de Paques*. Paris: Hachette, 1985. The main French-language guide to the area.

Hinz, Earl R. *Landfalls of Paradise: The Guide to Pacific Islands*. Western Marine Enterprises, 4051 Glencoe Ave., Suite 14, Marina del Rey, CA 90292-5607; $39.95. The only genuine cruising guide to all 32 island groups of Oceania.

Lucas, Allan. *Cruising in Tropical Waters and Coral*. International Marine Publishing, 21 Elm St., Camden, ME 04843. A how-to book for sailors in paradise.

Stanley, David. *South Pacific Handbook*. Chico, CA: Moon Publications. Covers the entire region in the same manner as the book you're reading. There's also a *Micronesia Handbook*.

Street, Donald. *The Ocean Sailing Yacht*. New York: Norton, 1973. A complete handbook on the operation of a cruising yacht.

DESCRIPTION AND TRAVEL

Bovis, Edmond de. Robert D. Craig, trans. *Tahitian Society Before the Arrival of the Europeans*. Honolulu: University of Hawaii Press, 1980. These observations of a French naval officer on the history, customs, religion, and government of Tahiti, were written in 1850.

Childress, David Hatcher. *Lost Cities of Ancient Lemuria and the Pacific*. Adventures Unlimited Press, Box 22, Stelle, Illinois 60919. The Indiana Jones of Pacific archaeology takes you on a mysterious journey to the pyramids of paradise.

Danielsson, Bengt. *Forgotten Islands of the South Seas*. London: Allen and Unwin, 1957. A fascinating tale of life and love in the Marquesas Islands.

————. *From Raft to Raft*. New York: Doubleday and Co., 1960. The story of one of the greatest sea adventures of modern times: Eric de Bisschop's raft voyage from Tahiti to South America and back, as told by one of the survivors.

Dodd, Edward. *Polynesia's Sacred Isle*. New York: Dodd, Mead and Co., 1976. An excellent account of Raiatea, its culture and history, based on the author's own researches, together with a vivid account of his many sojourns on the island.

Ellis, William. *Polynesian Researches*. Rutland, VT: Charles E. Tuttle Co., 1969. An early missionary's detailed observations of Tahiti during the years 1817-1825.

Eskridge, Robert Lee. *Manga Reva, The Forgotten Islands*. Honolulu: Mutual Publishing, 1986. The autobiography of a wandering American painter in the Gambiers in 1927.

Finney, Ben R. *Hokule'a: The Way to Tahiti*. New York: Dodd, Mead, 1979. The story of the *Hokule'a's* 1976 voyage from Hawaii to Tahiti.

Hatt, John. *The Tropical Traveler*. Pan Books, 1985. Over a thousand tips covering every aspect of tropical travel.

Heyerdahl, Thor. *Fatu Hiva, Back to Nature*. New York: Doubleday, 1974. In 1936 Heyerdahl and his wife Liv went to live on Fatu Hiva. This book describes their year there.

————. *Kon Tiki*. Translated by F.H. Lyon. Chicago: Rand McNally, 1950. Convinced that the mysterious origin of the Polynesians lies in the equally mysterious disappearance of the pre-Incan Indians of Peru, the author finds that only by repeating their feat of sailing some 6500 km across the Pacific in a balsa-raft can he substantiate his theory.

Kyselka, Will. *An Ocean in Mind*. Honolulu: University of Hawaii Press, 1987. Analyzes the learning techniques of Nainoa Thompson, who successfully navigated the re-created traditional Polynesian sailing vessel, *Hokule'a*, during its second roundtrip journey between Hawaii and Tahiti in 1980, without the use of modern navigational equipment.

Martini, Frederic. *Exploring Tropical Isles and Seas*. Englewood Cliffs, New Jersey: Prentice-Hall, 1984. A fine introduction to the natural environment of the islands.

Stevenson, Robert Louis. *In the South Seas*. New York: Scribner's, 1901. The author's account of his travels through the Marquesas, Tuamotus, and Gilberts by yacht in the years 1888-90.

Thompson, Reverend Robert. Robert D. Craig, ed. *The Marquesas Islands*. Honolulu: University of Hawaii Press, 1980. Thompson's account, written in 1841, is a valuable record of the Marquesas just before their rapid decline.

GEOGRAPHY

Couper, Alastair, ed. *The Times Atlas of the Oceans*. New York: Van Nostrand Reinhold, 1983. A superb study of the oceans of the world in their contemporary context.

Fosberg, F.R., ed. *Man's Place in the Island Ecosystem*. Honolulu: Bishop Museum Press, 1963. A series of papers presented at a symposium.

Freeman, Otis W., ed. *Geography of the Pacific*. New York: John Wiley, 1951. Although somewhat dated, this book does provide a wealth of background information on the islands.

NATURAL SCIENCE

Bruner, Phillip L. *Field Guide to the Birds of French Polynesia*. Honolulu: Bishop Museum Press, 1972.

DeLuca, Charles J., and Diana MacIntyre DeLuca. *Pacific Marine Life: A Survey of Pacific Ocean Invertebrates*. Rutland, VT: Charles E. Tuttle Co., 1976. An informative 82-page pamphlet.

Dupont, John E. *South Pacific Birds*. Greenville, Delaware: Museum of Natural History, 1975. A beautifully illustrated field guide.

Hargreaves, Bob, and Dorothy Hargreaves. *Tropical Blossoms of the Pacific*. Hargreaves Company, Inc., Box 895, Kailua, HI 96734. A handy 64-page booklet with color photos to assist in identification; a matching volume is titled *Tropical Trees of the Pacific*.

Hinton, A.G. *Shells of New Guinea and the Central Indo-Pacific*. Australia: Jacaranda Press, 1972. A photo guide to identification.

Mayr, Ernst. *Birds of the Southwest Pacific.* Rutland, VT: Charles E. Tuttle Co., 1978. A reprint of the 1945 edition.

Merrill, Elmer D. *Plant Life of the Pacific World.* Rutland, VT: Charles E. Tuttle Co., 1981. First published in 1945, this handy volume is a useful first reference in a field very poorly covered.

Nelson, Bryan. *Seabirds: Their Biology and Ecology.* New York: A & W Publishers, 1979. A fully illustrated manual.

Pratt, Douglas. *A Field Guide to the Birds of Hawaii and the Tropical Pacific.* New Jersey: Princeton University Press, 1986. The best of its kind—essential reading for birders.

Tinker, Spencer Wilkie. *Fishes of Hawaii: A Handbook of the Marine Fishes of Hawaii and the Central Pacific Ocean.* Hawaiian Service, Inc., Box 2835, Honolulu, HI 96803; $25. A comprehensive, indexed reference work.

HISTORY

Bellwood, Peter. *Man's Conquest of the Pacific.* New York: Oxford University Press, 1979. One of the most extensive studies of the prehistory of Southeast Asia and Oceania ever published.

————. *The Polynesians, Prehistory of an Island People.* London: Thames and Hudson, 1978. A well-written account of the archaeology of Polynesian expansion.

Buck, Peter H. *Vikings of the Pacific.* Chicago: University of Chicago Press, 1959. A popular narrative of Polynesian migrations.

Clark, Thomas Blake. *Omai, First Polynesian Ambassador to England.* Honolulu: University of Hawaii Press, 1969. Catches the atmosphere of the cultural impact of Polynesia on the West, in that pristine dawn, before the counter-impact of the West on Polynesia.

Danielsson, Bengt. *What Happened on the Bounty.* London: Allen and Unwin, 1963. A reappraisal of Capt. Bligh whom Hollywood has unfairly cast as a tyrant. The subsequent fate of the mutineers is also given in depth.

Howarth, David. *Tahiti: A Paradise Lost.* New York: Penguin Books, 1985. A readable history of European exploration in the Society Islands.

Howe, K.R. *Where the Waves Fall.* Honolulu: University of Hawaii Press, 1984. This South Seas history from first settlement to colonial rule maintains a steady and sympathetic focus on the islanders themselves.

Jennings, Jesse D., ed. *The Prehistory of Polynesia.* Cambridge: Harvard University Press, 1979. A comprehensive work on the subject.

Langdon, Robert. *The Lost Caravel.* Sydney: Pacific Publications, 1975. The author proposes that Spanish castaways from Magellan's fleet gave a totally new direction to Polynesian culture, an audacious theory which has met with little approval among professional anthropologists and historians.

————. *Tahiti, Island of Love.* Australia: Pacific Publications, 1979. A popular history of Tahiti since the European discovery in 1767.

Moorehead, Alan. *The Fatal Impact.* New York: Harper & Row, 1966. European impact on the South Pacific, as illustrated in the cases of Tahiti, Australia, and Antarctica.

Newbury, Colin. *Tahiti Nui: Change and Survival in French Polynesia, 1767-1945.* Honolulu: University of Hawaii Press, 1980. Describes major events, while providing many details of the social and economic processes.

Oliver, Douglas L. *The Pacific Islands.* Honolulu: University of Hawaii Press, 1989. A new edition of the classic 1951 study of the history and economies of the entire Pacific area.

MARITIME HISTORY

Beaglehole, J.C. *The Exploration of the Pacific.* Stanford: Stanford University Press,

1966. A history of European exploration from Magellan to Capt. Cook.

Buck, Peter H. *Explorers of the Pacific.* Honolulu: Bishop Museum Press, 1953. A concise summary of the European discoveries.

Dole, Paul W. *Seventy North to Fifty South: Captain Cook's Last Voyage.* Englewood Cliffs, NJ: Prentice-Hall, Inc., 1969. A modern annotation of Cook's final journal.

Friis, Herman R. *The Pacific Basin: A History of Its Geographical Exploration.* New York: American Geographical Society, 1967. A specialized work.

Oliver, Douglas L. *Return to Tahiti: Bligh's Second Breadfruit Voyage.* Honolulu: University of Hawaii Press, 1988. Offers insights on the inhabitants of Tahiti and their customs at the time of European contact.

Sharp, Andrew. *The Discovery of the Pacific Islands.* Oxford: Clarendon Press, 1960. A sort of dictionary of the achievements of 122 European explorers and discoverers, listing which island or island group each found.

PACIFIC ISSUES

Ali, Ahmed, and Ron Crocombe, eds. *Politics in Polynesia.* Suva: University of the South Pacific, 1983. A country by country survey of political trends and developments in the area.

Bulletin of Concerned Asian Scholars. 3239 9th St., Boulder, CO 80302-2112, USA. The Volume 18, Number Two, 1986, issue is devoted entirely to the anti-nuclear movement in the Pacific.

Danielsson, Bengt and Marie-Therese. *Poisoned Reign, French nuclear colonialism in the Pacific.* Penguin Books, 1986. An updated version of *Moruroa Mon Amour,* first published in 1977.

Hayes, Peter, Lyuba Zarsky, and Walden Bello. *American Lake, Nuclear Peril in the Pacific.* Australia: Penguin Books, 1986. How the nuclear build-up in the cause of "peace" fuels the threat of war.

Robie, David. *Eyes of Fire: The Last Voyage of the Rainbow Warrior.* New Society Publishers, 4527 Springfield Ave., Philadelphia, PA 19143. Robie was aboard the Greenpeace protest vessel sunk at Auckland by French terrorists. His photos and firsthand account tell the inside story.

SOCIAL SCIENCE

Danielsson, Bengt. *Love in the South Seas.* Honolulu, Mutual Publishing, 1986. Sex and family life of the Polynesians based on early accounts as well as observations by the noted Swedish anthropologist.

———. *Work and Life on Raroia.* Danielsson spent 18 months on this atoll observing Tuamotu life.

Howell, William. *The Pacific Islanders.* New York: Scribner's, 1973. An anthropological study of the origins of Pacific peoples.

Levy, Robert. *Tahitians: Mind and Experience in the Society Islands.* Chicago: University of Chicago Press, 1973. Levy's study, based on several years of field work on Tahiti and Huahine, includes an intriguing examination of the *mahu* (transvestite) phenomenon.

Marshall, Don. *Raivavae.* New York: Doubleday and Co., 1961. The author, who is a professional anthropologist, did field work on this high island in the Austral group in 1957-58, to find out what was left of the old orgiastic pagan religion and sexual rites.

Oliver, Douglas L. *Ancient Tahitian Society.* Honolulu: University of Hawaii Press, 1975. Sets out to describe what Tahitian society was like immediately before, and immediately after, contact with peoples of literate, industrial societies.

———. *Native Cultures of the Pacific Islands.* Honolulu: University of Hawaii Press, 1988. Intended primarily for college-level courses on precontact anthropology, history, economy, and politics of the entire region; an abridged version of Oliver's *Oceania* listed above.

————. *Oceania; The Native Cultures of Australia and the Pacific Islands.* Honolulu: University of Hawaii Press, 1988. A massive, two-volume, 1,264-page anthropological survey.

————. *Two Tahitian Villages.* Honolulu: University of Hawaii Press, 1983. What is learned about this developing Polynesian society is useful to the study of other human societies.

LANGUAGE

Anisson du Perron, Jacques, and Mai-Arii Cadousteau. *Dictionaire Moderne, Tahitien-Francais et Francais-Tahitien.* Papeete: Stepolde, 1973.

Tryon, Darrell T. *Conversational Tahitian.* Canberra: Australian National University Press, 1970.

————. *Say It In Tahitian.* Sydney: Pacific Publications, 1977. For lovers of the exotic, an instant introduction to spoken Tahitian.

LITERATURE

Andersen, Johannes C. *Myths and Legends of the Polynesians.* Rutland, VT: Charles E. Tuttle Co., 1969. A massive compilation of Polynesian mythology; fully indexed.

Day, A. Grove. *The Lure of Tahiti.* Honolulu: Mutual Publishing, 1986. Fifteen choice extracts from the rich literature of "the most romantic island in the world."

————. *Pacific Literature: One Hundred Basic Books.* Honolulu: University Press, 1971. Reviews the most outstanding books to come out of the Pacific experience over the past 400 years.

Hall, James Norman, and Charles Bernard Nordhoff. *The Bounty Trilogy.* New York: Grosset and Dunlap, 1945. Retells in fictional

form the famous mutiny, Bligh's escape to Timor, and the mutineers' fate on Pitcairn.

Hall, James Norman. *The Forgotten One and Other True Tales of the South Seas.* Honolulu, Mutual Publishing, 1987. Hall arrived on Tahiti in 1920 collaborated with Charles Nordhoff in such famous works as *The Mutiny of the Bounty* (1930) and *Hurricane* (1936). He died at his home in Arue in 1951.

Loti, Pierre. *The Marriage of Loti.* Honolulu: University of Hawaii Press, 1976. This tale of Loti's visits to Tahiti in 1872 helped create the romantic myth of Polynesia in contemporary Europe.

Maugham, W. Somerset. *The Moon and Sixpence.* Story of a London stockbroker who leaves his job for Tahiti and ends up leading an artist's primitive life that isn't as romantic as he hoped.

Melville, Herman. *Typee, A Peep at Polynesian Life.* Evanston, IL: Northwestern University Press, 1968. In 1842 Melville deserted from an American whaler at Nuku Hiva, Marquesas Islands. This semifictional work tells of Melville's four months among the Typee people. A sequel, *Omoo*, relates his observations on Tahiti at the time of the French takeover.

Michener, James A. *Return to Paradise.* New York: Randon House, 1951. Essays and short stories. Michener's, *Tales of the South Pacific*, the first of over 30 books, won the Pulitzer Prize for fiction in 1948. A year later it appeared on Broadway as the long-running musical *South Pacific*.

Stone, William S. *Idylls of the South Seas.* Honolulu: University of Hawaii Press, 1971. Stone uses the same narrator, Tetua, to recount ten myths and legends of Tahiti.

THE ARTS

Barrow, Terence. *The Art of Tahiti.* London: Thames and Hudson, 1979. A concise, well-illustrated survey of works of art from the Society, Austral, and Cook islands.

Danielsson, Bengt. *Gauguin in the South Seas.* New York: Doubleday, 1966. Danielsson's fascinating account of Gauguin's ten years in Polynesia.

Gauguin, Paul. *Noa Noa.* A Tahitian journal kept by this famous artist during his first two years in the islands.

Guiart, Jean. *The Arts of the South Pacific.* New York: Golden Press, 1963. A well-illustrated coffee table size art book. Consideration is given to the cultures which produced the works.

Linton, Ralph, and Paul S. Wingert. *Arts of the South Seas.* New York: Museum of Modern Art, 1946. Although a little dated, this book provides a starting point for the study of the art of Polynesia.

REFERENCE BOOKS

Carter, John, ed. *Pacific Islands Yearbook.* Sydney: Pacific Publications; US$29.95. Despite the name, a new edition of this authoritative sourcebook has come out about every three years since 1932. The information is heavily slanted toward official bureaucratic structures and overseas trade statistics, but the history sections are quite good.

Dickson, Diane, and Carol Dossor. *World Catalogue of Thesis on the Pacific Islands.* Honolulu: University of Hawaii Press, 1970.

Fenton, Thomas P., and Mary J. Heffron, eds. *Asia and Pacific: A Directory of Resources.* Maryknoll: Orbis Books, 1986. A complete survey of organizations, books, periodicals, pamphlets, articles, audiovisuals, and other resources relating to Pacific issues. Complete names and addresses plus five indexes make this work an invaluable contact point.

Gould, Donald P., and Katherine Gould. *Directory of Travel Information Sources for the Pacific Islands.* Pilot Books, 103 Cooper St., Babylon, NY 11702, USA. This amazing 78-page booklet catalogs virtually everything in

print relating to travel in the Pacific islands, and then some.

Oceania, A Regional Study. Washington, DC: U.S. Government Printing Office, 1985; extensive bibliography and index. This 572-page volume forms part of the area handbook series sponsored by the U.S. Army and intended to educate American officials. A comprehensive, uncritical source of background information.

Silveira de Braganza, Ronald, and Charlotte Oakes, eds. *The Hill Collection of Pacific Voyages.* San Diego: University Library, 1974. A descriptive catalog of antique books about the Pacific.

Taylor, Clyde R. *A Pacific Bibliography: Printed Matter Relating to the Native Peoples of Polynesia, Melanesia and Micronesia.* Oxford: Clarendon Press, 1965. Extensive.

The Far East and Australasia. London: Europa Publications. An annual survey and directory of Asia and the Pacific. Provides abundant and factual political, social, and economic data; an excellent reference source.

PERIODICALS

Atoll Research Bulletin. A specialized journal issued by The Smithsonian Institution, Washington, DC. An inexhaustable source of fascinating information (and maps) on the most remote islands of the Pacific.

Conde Nast's Traveler. Box 52469, Boulder, CO 80321-2469 (12-issue subscription $15). A glossy but incisive travel magazine.

Islands Business. Box 12718, Suva, Fiji Islands (annual airmailed subscription US$38 to North America, US$50 to Europe, A$32 to Australia, NZ$40 to New Zealand). A monthly news magazine with the emphasis on political, economic, and business trends in the South Pacific. Since the Rubuka coups they've mellowed.

Journal of Pacific History. Australian National University, GPO Box 4, Canberra, ACT 2601 (twice annual subscription US$30). The volume XXI 3-4 1986 issue includes several scholarly articles on recent events in Polynesia. Outstanding.

Journal of the Polynesian Society. Department of Anthropology, University of Auckland, Private Bag, Auckland, New Zealand. Established in 1892, this quarterly journal contains a wealth of specialized material on Polynesian culture.

Pacific Islands Monthly. Box 22250, Honolulu, HI 96822 (annual subscription A$24 to Australia, US$45 to North America, and A$64 to Europe). Founded in Sydney by R.W. Robson in 1930, PIM is the grand-daddy of regional magazines. Since being absorbed into the media empire of Rupert Murdoch in 1987, however, it has gained in gloss and lost in substance. Incredibly, in 1988 they moved their editorial offices to Fiji where press censorship is in force, so disregard their coverage of that country.

Pacific Magazine. Box 25488, Honolulu, HI 96825 (every other month; US$12 annual subscription). This business-oriented magazine keeps you up to date on what's happening in the American territories in the Pacific. An excellent means of keeping in touch with the region.

Pacific News Bulletin. Box A391, Sydney South, NSW 2000, Australia (monthly; A$7.50 a year in Australia, A$13.50 a year elsewhere).

Realites du Pacifique Editions de l'Echiquier, 43 rue de l'Arbre-Sec, 75001 Paris. This serious bimonthly newsletter (in French) carries analytic features on the situation in the French Pacific territories. Overseas Subscriptions are US$60, within France 500 FF.

Skin Diver. Box 3295, Los Angeles, CA 90078 (annual subscription $20). This monthly magazine carries frequent articles on Polynesian dive sites and facilities.

The Surf Report. Box 1028, Dana Point, CA 92629 ($30 a year). A monthly summary of worldwide surfing conditions with frequent feature articles on the islands.

Third World Resources. 464 19th St., Oakland, CA 94612 (two-year subscription $25). A quarterly review of books, articles, and organizations involved with development issues in the Third World.

Tok Blong SPPF. South Pacific Peoples Foundation of Canada, 409-620 View St., Victoria, BC V8W 1J6, Canada ($10 a year). A quarterly of news and views of the Pacific islands.

Wellington Pacific Report. Box 9314, Wellington, New Zealand (NZ$15 in N.Z., NZ$25 elsewhere). Owen Wilkes' incisive monthly newsletter with startling revelations of covert U.S. activities in the Pacific.

FREE CATALOGS

Books, Maps & Prints of Pacific Islands. Colin Hinchcliffe, 12 Queens Staith Mews, York, Y01 1HH, England. An excellent source of antique books, maps, and engravings.

Books & Series in Print. Bishop Museum Press, Box 19000-A, Honolulu, HI 96817-0916. An indexed list of publications on the Pacific available from the Bishop Museum.

Defense Mapping Agency Catalog of Maps, Charts, and Related Products: Part 2—Hydrographic Products, Volume VIII, Oceania. Defense Mapping Agency Combat Support Center, ATTN: DDCP, Washington, DC 20315-0010. This complete index and order form for nautical charts of Polynesia is the only catalog listed here which is not free (send US$2.50).

Hawaii and the Pacific. University of Hawaii Press, 2840 Kolowalu St., Honolulu, HI 96822. Lists many new and current titles on Tahiti-Polynesia.

Hawaii and Pacific Islands. The Book Bin, 351 NW Jackson St., Corvallis, OR 97330. A complete mail-order catalog of hundreds of rare books on the Pacific.

International Marine Books. International Marine Publishing Co., Route 1, Box 220, Camden, ME 04843. Books for the sailor.

Moon Publications Adventure Travel Handbooks Catalog. Moon Publications, 722 Wall St., Chico, CA 95928. The entire Moon series of guides to the Pacific and western U.S. described in detail.

Societe des Oceanistes Catalogue. Musee de l'Homme, 75116, Paris, France. Many scholarly works (in French) on Polynesia are available from this body.

Tales of the Pacific. Mutual Publishing, 2055 N. King St., Suite 201, Honolulu, HI 96819. The classics of Pacific literature available in cheap paperback editions.

AN IMPORTANT MESSAGE

Authors, editors, and publishers wishing to see their publications listed here should send review copies to:

David Stanley
722 Wall St.,
Chico, CA 95928, USA.

GLOSSARY

ahimaa—Tahitian underground or earth oven; called an *umu* in Samoa

ahu—Polynesian stone temple platform

aparima—a Tahitian hand dance

archipelago—a group of islands

arii—a Polynesian high chief

Arioi—a pre-European religious society which traveled among the Society Is. presenting ceremonies and entertainments

atoll—a low-lying, ring-shaped coral reef enclosing a lagoon

bareboat charter—chartering a yacht without crew or provisions

barrier reef—a coral reef separated from the adjacent shore by a lagoon

beche de mer—sea cucumber; trepang; an edible sea slug; in Tahitian *rori*

blackbirder—European recruiter of island labor during the 19th century

breadfruit—a large round fruit with starchy flesh grown on an *uru* tree *(Artocarpus altilis)*

cassava—manioc; a starchy edible root

ciguatera—a form of fish poisoning caused by microscopic algae

coir—coconut husk sennit

confirmation—A confirmed reservation exists when a supplier acknowledges, either orally or in writing, that a booking has been accepted.

copra—dried coconut meat used in the manufacture of coconut oil, cosmetics, soap, and margarine

coral—a hard calcareous substance of various shapes comprised of the skeletons of tiny marine animals called polyps

coral bank—a coral formation over 150 meters long

coral head—a coral formation a few meters across

coral patch—a coral formation up to 150 meters long

cyclone—Also known as a hurricane (in the Caribbean), tornado (in the U.S.), or typhoon (in the Pacific). A tropical storm which rotates around a center of low atmospheric pressure; it becomes a cyclone when its winds reach 64 knots. In the Northern Hemisphere cyclones spin counterclockwise, while south of the equator they move clockwise. The winds of cyclonic storms are deflected toward a low-pressure area at the center, although the "eye" of the cyclone may be calm.

direct flight—a through flight with one or more stops but no change of aircraft, as opposed to a non-stop flight

dugong—a large plant-eating marine mammal; called a manatee in the Caribbean

EEZ—Exclusive Economic Zone; a 200-nautical-mile offshore belt of an island nation or seacoast state which controls the mineral exploitation and fishing rights

endemic—something native to a particular area and existing only there

fafa—a "spinach" of cooked taro leaves

farani—French; *francais*

FIT—foreign independent travel; a custom-designed, prepaid tour composed of many individualized arrangements

fringing reef—a reef along the shore of an island

gendarme—a French policeman on duty only in rural areas in France and French overseas territories

guano—manure of sea birds, used as a fertilizer

lagoon—an expanse of water bounded by a reef

leeward—downwind; the shore (or side) sheltered from the wind; as opposed to "windward"

le truck—a truck with seats in back used for public transportation

maa Tahiti—Tahitian food

mahimahi—dorado, Pacific dolphin (no relation to the mammal)

mama ruau—actually "grandmother," but also used for the Mother Hubbard long dress introduced by missionaries

mana—authority, prestige, virtue, "face," psychic power, a positive force

manahune—a commoner or member of the lower class in pre-Christian society

mangrove—a tropical shrub with branches that send down roots forming dense thickets along tidal shores

manioc—cassava, tapioca, a starchy root crop

mahu—male transvestite, sometimes also homosexual

maohi—a native of Tahiti-Polynesia

marae—a Tahitian temple or open-air cult place, called **meae** in the Marquesas

Melanesia—the high island groups of the western Pacific (Fiji, New Caledonia, Vanuatu, Solomon Islands, Papua New Guinea)

Micronesia—chains of high and low islands mostly north of the Equator (Carolines, Gilberts, Marianas, Marshalls)

monoi—perfumed coconut oil

motu—a reef islet on an atoll

Oro—the Polynesian god of war

ORSTOM—Office de la Recherche Scientifique et Technique d'Outre-Mer

otea—a ceremonial dance performed by men and women in two columns

overbooking—the practice of confirming more seats, cabins, or rooms than are actually available to ensure against no-shows

pa—ancient stone fortress

PADI—Professional Association of Dive Instructors

pandanus—screw pine with slender stem and prop roots. The sword-shaped leaves are used for plaiting mats and hats. In Tahitian, *fara*.

pareu—a Tahitian sarong-like wraparound skirt or loincloth

pass—a channel through a barrier reef, usually with an outward flow of water

passage—an inside passage between an island and a barrier reef

pelagic—relating to the open sea, away from land

peretane—Britain, British

pirogue—outrigger canoe, in Tahitian *vaa*

poe—a sticky pudding made from bananas, papaya, pumpkin, or taro mixed with starch, baked in an oven, and served with coconut milk

poisson cru—raw fish marinated in lime, in Tahitian **ia ota**

Polynesia—divided into Western Polynesia (Tonga and Samoa) and Eastern Polynesia (Tahiti-Polynesia, Cook Is., Hawaii, Easter I., and New Zealand)

pupu—traditional dance group

raatira—chief, dance leader

reef—a coral ridge near the ocean surface

scuba—self-contained underwater breathing apparatus

sennit—braided coconut-fiber rope

shoal—a shallow sand bar or mud bank

shoulder season—a travel period between high/peak and low/off-peak

subduction—the action of one tectonic plate wedging under another

subsidence—geological sinking or settling

tahua—in the old days a skilled artisan; today a sorcerer or healer

tamaaraa—a Tahitian feast

tamure—a new name for Ori Tahiti, a very fast erotic dance

tapa—bark cloth, called **ahu** in old Tahitian

tapu—taboo, sacred, set apart, forbidden, a negative force

taro—a starchy tuber *(Colocasia esculenta),* a staple food of the Pacific islanders

tavana—the elected mayor of a commune (from the English "governor")

tifaifai—a patchwork quilt based on either European or Polynesian motifs

tiki—a human-like sculpture used in the old days for religious rites and sorcery

tinito—Chinese

toere—a hollow wooden drum hit with a stick

tradewind—a steady wind blowing toward the equator from either northeast or southeast, depending on the season

trench—the section at the bottom of the ocean where one tectonic plate wedges under another

tridacna clam—eaten everywhere in the Pacific, its size varies between 10 cm and one meter

tropical storm—a cyclonic storm with winds of 35 to 64 knots

tsunami—a fast-moving wave caused by an undersea earthquake

vigia—a mark on a nautical chart indicating a dangerous rock or shoal

windward—the point or side from which the wind blows, as opposed to "leeward"

zories—rubber sandals, thongs, flip-flops

CAPSULE TAHITIAN VOCABULARY

ahiahi—evening
aita—no
aita e peapea—no problem
aita maitai—no good
aito—ironwood
amu—eat
ananahi—tomorrow
arearea—fun, to have fun
atea—far away
atua—god
avae—moon, month
avatea—midday (from 1000-1500)

e—yes, also *oia*
e aha te huru?—how are you?
e hia?—how much?

faraoa—bread
fare—house
fare iti—toilet
fare moni—bank
fare rata—post office
fenua—land
fetii—parent, family
fiu—fed up, bored

haari—coconut palm
haere mai io nei—come here
haere maru—go easy, take it easy
hauti—play, make love
he haere oe ihea?—where are you going?
hei—flower garland, lei
here hoe—number-one sweetheart
himene—song, from the English "hymn"
hoa—friend

ia orana—good day, may you live, prosper
i nanahi—yesterday

ino—bad
ioa—name
ite—know

maeva—welcome
mahana—sun, light, day
mahanahana—warm
maitai—good, I'm fine, also a cocktail
manava—conscience
manu—bird
manuia—to your health!
mao—shark
maruru—thank you
maururu roa—thank you very much
miti—salt water
moana—deep ocean
moemoea—dream
moni—money

nana—goodbye
naonao—mosquito
nehenehe—beautiful
niau—coconut palm frond
niu—coconut tree

ora—life, health
ori—dance
oromatua—the spirits of the dead
otaa—bundle, luggage
oti—finished

pahi—boat, ship
pape—water, juice
parahi—goodbye
pia—beer
pohe—death
poipoi—morning
popaa—foreigner, European
potii—teenage girl, young woman

raerae—effeminate
roto—lake

taata—human being, man
tahatai—beach
tamaa maitai—bon appetit
tamarii—child
tane—man, husband
taofe—coffee
taote—doctor
taravana—crazy

tiare—flower
toetoe—cold
tupapau—ghost

ua—rain
uaina—wine
uteute—red

vahine—woman, wife
vai—water
veavea—hot

NUMBERS

hoe 1	ahuru ma vau 18
piti 2	ahuru ma iva 19
toru 3	piti ahuru 20
maha 4	piti ahuru ma hoe 21
pae 5	piti ahuru ma piti 22
ono 6	piti ahuru ma toru 23
hitu 7	toru ahuru 30
vau 8	maha ahuru 40
iva 9	pae ahuru 50
ahuru 10	ono ahuru 60
ahuru ma hoe 11	hitu ahuru 70
ahuru ma piti 12	vau ahuru 80
ahuru ma toru 13	iva ahuru 90
ahuru ma maha 14	hanere 100
ahuru ma pae 15	tauatini 1,000
ahuru ma ono 16	ahuru tauatini 10,000
ahuru ma hitu 17	mirioni 1,000,000

CAPSULE FRENCH VOCABULARY

bonjour—good day
bonsoir—good evening
salut—hello
Je vais à...—I am going to...
Où allez-vous?—Where are you going?
Jusqu'où allez-vous?—How far are you going?
Où se trouve...?—Where is...?
C'est loin d'ici?—Is it far from here?
Je fais de l'autostop.—I am hitchhiking
A quelle heure?—At what time?
horaire—timetable
hier—yesterday
aujourd'hui—today
demain—tomorrow
Je désire, je voudrais...—I want...
J'aime...—I like...
Je ne comprends pas.—I don't understand
une chambre—a room
Vous êtes très gentil.—You are very kind.
Où habitez vous?—Where do you live?
Il fait mauvais temps.—It's bad weather.
gendarmerie—police station
Quel travail faites-vous?—What work do you do?
la chômage, les chômeurs—unemployment, the unemployed
Je t'aime.—I love you.
une boutique, un magasin—a store
du pain—bread
du lait—milk
du vin—wine
casse croute—sandwich
conserves—canned foods
fruits de mer—seafood
café très chaud—hot coffee
de l'eau—water
plat du jour—set meal
Combien ça fait?—How much is it?
   Combein ça coûte?
   Combien? Quel prix?
auberge de jeunesse—youth hostel
la clef—the key
la route, la piste—the road
la plage—the beach
la falaise—cliff
cascade—waterfall

grottes—caves
Est-ce que je peu camper ici?—May I camp here?
Je voudrais camper.—I wish to camp.
le terrain de camping—campsite
Devrais-je demander la permission?—Should I ask permission?
s'il vous plaît—please
oui—yes
merci—thank you
cher—expensive
bon marché—cheap
merde—shit

un	1
deux	2
trois	3
quatre	4
cinq	5
six	6
sept	7
huit	8
neuf	9
dix	10
onze	11
douze	12
treize	13
quatorze	14
quinze	15
seize	16
dix-sept	17
dix-huit	18
dix-neuf	19
vingt	20
vingt et un	21
vingt-deux	22
vingt-trois	23
trente	30
quarante	40
cinquante	50
soixante	60
soixante-dix	70
quatre-vingts	80
quatre-vingt-dix	90
cent	100
mille	1,000
dix mille	10,000
million	1,000,000

INDEX

Page numbers in *italics* indicate information in maps, illustrations, photos, charts, etc.

PLEASE HELP US

Well, you've heard what *we* have to say, now we want to hear what *you* have to say! How did the book work for you? Your experiences were unique, so please share them. Let us know which businesses deserve a better listing, what we should warn people about, and where we're spot on. It's only with the help of readers like yourself that we can make *Tahiti-Polynesia Handbook* a complete guide for *everyone*. The address is:

David Stanley
c/o Moon Publications
722 Wall Street
Chico, CA 95928 USA

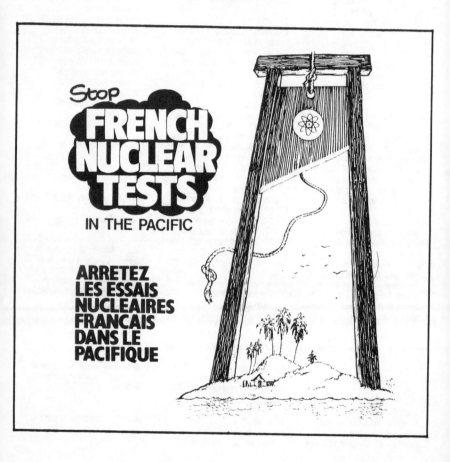

ABOUT THE AUTHOR

During the late '60s David Stanley got involved in Mexican culture by spending a
year in several small towns near Guana-
juato. Later he studied at the universities of
Barcelona (Spain) and Florence (Italy), before settling down to get an honors degree
(with distinction) in Spanish literature from
the University of Guelph (Canada). Since
then he's backpacked through 123 countries, including a three-year journey from
Tokyo to Kabul. Although Dr. Livingston
proved elusive, Stanley managed to link up
with "Gypsy Bill" Dalton in 1977 and together
they wrote the first edition of the *South
Pacific Handbook*. Since then David has
mixed island hopping with computer print-
outs, while Bill settled into the sedentary
world of publishing. (The name "Moon" originated on a moonlit Goa beach in 1973, when
Dalton had a vision which inspired him to

David Stanley atop Tahiti's Mt. Aorai

become a publisher/author.) Stanley's no part-time writer who earns his income in another
field; his full time and attention are devoted to his books. He lives like a hermit crab, shedding
one shell for the next. His only home still fits on his back.

TRAVEL BOOKS
BY DAVID STANLEY:

Alaska-Yukon Handbook
Eastern Europe on a Shoestring
Finding Fiji
Micronesia Handbook
South Pacific Handbook
Tahiti-Polynesia Handbook

YOUR CAT CAN SAVE A DROWNING DOLPHIN WITHOUT EVEN GETTING HER PAWS WET.

Both cats and humans are faced with a choice.

We can keep buying tuna fish and tuna-flavored products.

Or we can save the dolphins.

Hundreds of thousands of dolphins are being intentionally slaughtered by the Pacific tuna fleet. They set their nets on dolphin families to catch tuna swimming below.

Baby dolphins, pregnant dolphins, and mothers nursing their young are most vulnerable. Because dolphins breathe air just like the rest of us.

Trapped in the nets, unable to surface, they drown.

Millions of Americans are joining a national boycott of all canned tuna products.

We'd like your cat to join the boycott, too.

After all, millions of pounds of tuna are sold to cat food makers. And they need to feel the pressure along with the other big canners.

Together, we can force the tuna fleets to change their fishing methods. So they catch as many fish. But stop killing the dolphins.

In fact, you can help us apply all kinds of pressure.

We're working very hard to strengthen the federal law that's supposed to protect the dolphins. This law is now being violated by the tuna fleets.

Videotapes taken undercover and shown on national news confirm that hundreds of thousands of dolphins are being massacred off the Pacific coast.

It's the biggest kill of marine mammals in the world today. And only your cat — and you — can stop it.

Of course, not every cat will *volunteer* to rescue dolphins from drowning.

In that case, just explain that you're the one who buys the food.

And a hundred thousand dead dolphins is too high a price to pay.

Please boycott all brands of tuna cat food.

Robert Mosbacher
Secretary of Commerce
Commerce Building
14th Street NW
Washington, DC 20230

We can't allow the massacre of dolphins to go on. It's time to enforce the federal Marine Mammal Protection Act and bring the dolphin kill down to zero. Future generations won't forgive inaction.

NAME_____

ADDRESS_____

CITY_____STATE____ZIP_____

(we'll forward this portion to Sec. Mosbacher)

I've joined the tuna boycott as of today. Here's my contribution to your fight to rescue the 75,000 to 150,000 dolphins now killed each year. [ ] $10 [ ] $15 [ ] $25 [ ] $50 [ ] $150 [ ] more. Keep me posted.

EARTH ISLAND INSTITUTE
DOLPHIN PROJECT
300 Broadway, Suite 28
San Francisco, CA 94133
ATTN: David Brower

(415) 788-3666

Did You Enjoy This Book?

Then you may want to order other MOON PUBLICATIONS guides.

Like the guide you're holding in your hands, you'll find the same high standard of quality in all of our other titles, with informative introductions, up-to-date travel information, clear and concise maps, beautiful illustrations, a comprehensive subject/place-name index, and many other useful features. All Moon Publications guides come in this compact, portable size, with a tough Smyth-sewn binding that'll hold up through years of hard traveling.

The Pacific/Asia Series

TAHITI-POLYNESIA HANDBOOK   by **David Stanley**

Legendary Tahiti, isle of love, has long been the vision of "La Nouvelle Cythere," the earthly paradise. All five French Polynesian archipelagoes are covered in this comprehensive new guidebook by Oceania's best-known travel writer. Leap from the lush, jagged peaks of Moorea and Bora Bora to the exotic reefs of Rangiroa and Paul Gauguin's lonely grave on Hiva Oa. Rub elbows with the local elite at the finest French restaurants and save francs by sleeping in a lagoonside tent, then take in the floor show at a luxury resort for the price of a drink. This handy book shows you how to see Polynesia in style for under $50 a day. Color and b/w photos, illustrations, 29 maps, 6 charts, booklist, glossary, index. 250 pages.   **$9.95**

MICRONESIA HANDBOOK:
Guide to the Caroline, Gilbert, Mariana, and Marshall Islands
by **David Stanley**

Midway, Wake, Saipan, Tinian, Guam—household words for Americans during WWII, yet the seven North Pacific territories between Hawaii and the Philippines have received little attention since. Enjoy the world's finest scuba diving in Belau, or get lost on the far-flung atolls of the Gilberts. With insight into island culture, leads on the best diving locales and other recreation, and creative accommodation and dining suggestions, *Micronesia Handbook* cuts across the plastic path of packaged tourism and guides you on a real Pacific adventure all your own. 8 color pages, 77 b/w photos, 68 illustrations, 69 maps, 18 tables and charts, index. 300 pages.   **$9.95**

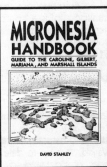

SOUTH PACIFIC HANDBOOK   by **David Stanley**
Here is paradise explored, photographed, and mapped—the original comprehensive guide to the history, geography, climate, cultures, and customs of the 16 territories in the South Pacific. A finalist for the prestigious Thomas Cook Travel Guide Award in 1986. No other travel book covers such a phenomenal expanse of the Earth's surface, and no other traveler knows the South Pacific like David Stanley. 12 color pages, 195 b/w photos, 121 illustrations, 35 charts, 138 maps, booklist, glossary, index. 588 pages. **$14.95**

HAWAII HANDBOOK   by **J.D. Bisignani**
This definitive travelers' resource to the magnificent archipelago takes you beyond the glitz and high-priced hype and leads you to a genuine Hawaiian experience. It offers a comprehensive introduction to the islands' geography, history, and culture, as well as inside tips on the best sights, entertainment, services, food, lodging, and shopping. This is also the guide for the outdoor enthusiast, with extensive listings for land and water sports of every sort. 12 color pages, 318 b/w photos, 132 illustrations, 74 maps, 43 graphs and charts, Hawaiian and pidgin glossaries, appendix, booklist, index. 788 pages. **$15.95**

MAUI HANDBOOK: Including Molokai and Lanai   by **J.D. Bisignani**
Maui is one of the most enchanting and popular islands in all of Oceania. Luxuriate on glistening beaches, swim and snorkel in reef-protected waters, dive into the mysteries of a submerged volcanic crater, or challenge the surf at world-famous beaches. Discover unspoiled Molokai, where ethnic Hawaiians still work the land, and sail the "Lahaina Roads" to Lanai for beauty and solitude. Bisignani offers "no fool-'round" advice on these islands' full range of accommodations, eateries, rental cars, shopping, tours, and transport, plus a comprehensive introduction to island ways, geography, and history. 8 color pages, 60 b/w photos, 72 illustrations, 34 maps, 19 charts, booklist, glossary, index. 350 pages. **$10.95**

KAUAI HANDBOOK   by **J.D. Bisignani**
From its dazzling chain of uncrowded beaches to its highest peak, Hawaii's "Garden Island" bows to no other for stunning scenery. Kauai is where Hawaiians come when they want to get away from it all. *Kauai Handbook* introduces you to the island's history, culture, and natural features, and takes you into a world away from the hustle and crowds of Waikiki. With up-to-date facts on accommodations, dining, shopping, entertainment, and services, plus detailed coverage of outdoor recreation, *Kauai Handbook* is the perfect antidote to the workaday world. Color and b/w photos, 21 maps, 11 tables and charts, 54 illustrations, Hawaiian and pidgin glossaries, booklist, index. 225 pages. **$9.95**

BLUEPRINT FOR PARADISE: How to Live on a Tropic Island
by **Ross Norgrove**

This one-of-a-kind guide has everything you need to know about moving to and living comfortably on a tropical island. Derived from personal experiences, Norgrove concisely explains: choosing an island, designing a house for tropical living, transportation, installing electrical and water systems, adapting to the island lifestyle, successfully facing the elements, and much more. Norgrove also addresses the special concerns of "snowbirds"—those Northerners who escape to an island getaway each year to leave winter far behind. Whether you're an armchair Robinson Crusoe dreaming of faraway beaches, or your gear is packed and you're ready to leave the mainland behind, you'll find *Blueprint for Paradise* as entertaining as it is practical. 8 color pages, 40 b/w photos, 3 maps, 14 charts, appendices, index. 202 pages. **$14.95**

INDONESIA HANDBOOK   by **Bill Dalton**

This one-volume encyclopedia explores island-by-island Indonesia's history and geography, her people, languages, crafts and artforms, her flora and fauna, ancient ruins, dances, and folk theater. It's a gypsy's manual packed with money-saving tips, pointing the way to Indonesia's best-value eating and accommodations, and guiding you through the cities, mountains, beaches, and villages of this sprawling, kaleidoscopic island nation. The *Sunday Times* of London called this "one of the best practical guides ever written about any country." 30 b/w photos, 143 illustrations, 250 maps, 17 charts, booklist, extensive Indonesian vocabulary, index. 1,050 pages.   **$17.95**

BALI HANDBOOK   by **Bill Dalton**

Since the early 20th century, foreigners have been drawn to Bali, an island so lovely that Nehru called it "the morning of the world." They're seldom disappointed, for Bali's theater-stage scenery, its spectacular music and dance, its highly developed handicrafts, its baroque temples, its tropical climate, glorious beaches, and colorful religious festivals have no equal. This comprehensive, well-informed guide has detailed travel information on bargain accommodations, outstanding dining, volcano climbing, surfing and diving locales, performing arts, and advice on exploring beyond the crowded southern beach resorts. Color and b/w photos, illustrations, 35 maps, glossary, booklist, index.
400 pages.   **(Available Fall 1989) $12.95**

NEW ZEALAND HANDBOOK   by Jane King

New Zealand is nature's improbable masterpiece, an entire world of beauty and wonder jammed into three unforgettable islands. Pristine fjords, icy waterfalls, smoldering volcanos, lush rainforests, and tumbling rivers, all bordered by sun-drenched beaches and an aquamarine sea. New Zealand's got it all. This information-packed guide introduces you to the people, places, history, and culture of this extraordinary land, and leads you to reasonably priced accommodations, restaurants, entertainment, and outdoor adventure—all the best that only New Zealand can offer. 8 color pages, 99 b/w photos, 146 illustrations, 82 maps, booklist, index. 512 pages.   **$14.95**

SOUTH KOREA HANDBOOK   by Robert Nilsen

A land of haunting beauty, rich culture, and economic promise, South Korea neatly weaves the warp and woof of tradition and modernity. This definitive guide to the once-hidden "Hermit Kingdom" leads you into the heart of Seoul...and beyond to the heart and soul of the country, with an emphasis on exploring and understanding the many facets of Korean society. Whether you're visiting on business or searching for adventure, *South Korea Handbook* is an invaluable companion. 8 color pages, 78 b/w photos, 93 illustrations, 109 maps, 10 charts, Korean glossary with useful notes on speaking and reading the language, booklist, index. 548 pages.   **$14.95**

JAPAN HANDBOOK   by J.D. Bisignani

This comprehensive guide dispels the myth that Japan is too expensive for the budget-minded traveler. The theme throughout is "do it like the Japanese" and get the most for your time and money. *Japan Handbook* is a cultural and anthropological encyclopedia on every facet of Japanese life, an indispensable tool for understanding and enjoying one of the world's most complex and intriguing countries. 8 color pages, 200 b/w photos, 92 illustrations, 112 maps and town plans, 29 charts, appendix on the Japanese language, booklist, glossary, index. 504 pages.   **$12.95**

The Americas Series

ARIZONA TRAVELER'S HANDBOOK   by Bill Weir

Arizona, the sunniest state in the Union, is a land of dazzling contrasts, packed with as much history and natural beauty as one state can hold: giant saguaro cactus and shimmering aspen, ancient pueblos and sophisticated cities, the lofty peaks of the San Francisco Range, and of course, the magnificent Grand Canyon. This meticulously researched guide contains a comprehensive introduction, motel, restaurant, and campground listings, trail maps and descriptions, and travel and recreation tips —everything necessary to make Arizona accessible and enjoyable. 8 color pages, 250 b/w photos, 81 illustrations, 53 maps, 4 charts, booklist, index. 448 pages.   **$11.95**

UTAH HANDBOOK   by Bill Weir

Three states rolled into one, Utah has the pristine alpine country of the Rockies, the awesome canyons of the Colorado Plateau, and the remote mountains of the Great Basin. Take in cosmopolitan Salt Lake City, ski Utah's "greatest snow on earth," and explore the spectacular rock formations in Zion, Bryce, Capitol Reef, Canyonlands, and Arches national parks. Or choose among the many national monuments and other special areas for outstanding scenery, geology, Indian lore, and pioneer history. Weir gives you all the carefully researched facts and background to make your visit a success. 8 color pages, 102 b/w photos, 61 illustrations, 30 maps, 9 charts, booklist, index. 468 pages.   **$11.95**

NEVADA HANDBOOK   by Deke Castleman

Nevada—born of Comstock silver, and prospering from casino gold. Fastest-growing and second-most-visited, Nevada is also the wildest state in the Union, indoors and out. You can get married on a whim and divorced in a flash, freely partake of the world's oldest profession, protest nuclear testing and dumping, and turn your hands black feeding one-armed bandits. Basque ranchers and cowboy poets, tuxedoed high-rollers and topless showgirls, nine residents per square mile and 30 million visitors—Nevada has it all, and then some. *Nevada Handbook* puts it all into perspective and makes it manageable and affordable. Color and b/w photos, illustrations, 40 maps, charts, booklist, index. 300 pages.   **(Available Fall 1989) $10.95**

NEW MEXICO HANDBOOK by **Stephen Metzger**
New Mexico is a haunting and magical land of gorgeous moun-
tains, fertile river valleys, broad expanses of high desert, and
breathtakingly beautiful skies. This guide takes you from prehistoric
Indian ruins to 16th-century Spanish settlements, to ghost towns
and 20th-century artists' colonies. Explore the badlands where
Billy the Kid roamed, wander through the stark redrock plains of
Navajo country, ski the high peaks of the southern Rockies. *New
Mexico Handbook* offers a close-up and complete look at every
aspect of this wondrous state, including its geology, history, culture, and recreation. Color and b/w photos, illustrations, 40 maps,
charts, booklist, index. 400 pages.
(Available Fall 1989) $11.95

BRITISH COLUMBIA HANDBOOK by **Jane King**
British Columbia is snowcapped mountains and shimmering
glaciers, dense green forests and abundant wildlife, mirror-perfect
lakes and mighty rivers teeming with salmon and trout, thriving
cosmopolitan cities and fun-filled resorts. *British Columbia
Handbook* introduces you to the province's colorful history, geography, flora and fauna, and more. With an emphasis on outdoor
adventures, this guide covers mainland British Columbia,
Vancouver Island, the Queen Charlotte Islands, and the Canadian
Rockies, and includes attractions, good-value restaurants, entertainment, transportation, and accommodations from tentsites to
luxury hotels. Color and b/w photos, illustrations, 60 maps, charts,
booklist, index. 396 pages.   **$11.95**

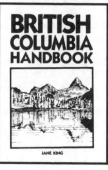

WASHINGTON HANDBOOK   by **Dianne J. Boulerice Lyons**
Few states are as geographically diverse and rich in recreational
opportunities as Washington. Volcanos, deserts, rainforests,
islands, glaciers, lakes, rivers, and seashore offer such outdoor diver-
sions from mountain climbing to clam digging, cycling to sun wor-
shipping. Seattle and other cities offer such urban delights as
award-winning restaurants, world-class shopping, and myriad cultural and historical attractions. *Washington Handbook* covers
sights, shopping, services, and transportation, hot spots for hiking,
boating, fishing, windsurfing, birdwatching, and other outdoor
recreation, and has complete listings for restaurants and accommodations. Color and b/w photos, illustrations, 81 maps, charts,
booklist, index. 425 pages.   **$11.95**

BACKPACKING: A HEDONIST'S GUIDE
by **Rick Greenspan and Hal Kahn**
Imagine yourself hanging out in an alpine meadow high up in your favorite mountains, enjoying
the sunset and reflecting that the strenuous hike ended at the second most beautiful campsite
in the world; that the bubble-and-fly bagged a panful of trout; that the bread rose,and the
brandy chocolate warmed your very soul. If this sounds enticing, then *Backpacking: A
Hedonist's Guide* is for you. This humorous, handsomely illustrated how-to-guide will convince
even the most confirmed naturophobe that it's safe, easy, and enjoyable to leave the smoggy
security of city life behind—in style. 90 illus., annotated booklist, index. 200 pages.   **$7.95**

ALASKA-YUKON HANDBOOK: Including the Canadian Rockies
by **Deke Castleman & David Stanley**

Alaska occupies a special place in the geography of the imagination; its mystery and magnetism have compelled adventurers northward for over a hundred years. *Alaska-Yukon Handbook* guides you to North America's tallest mountains, wildest rivers, greatest glaciers, largest wilderness parks, and most abundant wildlife. Castleman and Stanley provide the inside story, with plenty of well-seasoned advice to help you cover more miles on less money, tips on working in Alaska, plus what the Alaskans themselves do for recreation and where they take visitors for fun. 8 Color pages, 26 b/w photos, 92 illustrations, 90 maps, 6 charts, booklist, glossary, index. 398 pages.   **$10.95**

GUIDE TO CATALINA: and California's Channel Islands
by **Chicki Mallan**

Twenty-six miles across the sea from Los Angeles, Santa Catalina Island offers a world of vacation opportunities right in Southern California's back yard. A complete guide to these remarkable islands, from the windy solitude of the Channel Islands National Marine Sanctuary to bustling Avalon, *Guide to Catalina* covers hiking and birdwatching; the best locations for scuba diving and snorkeling, fishing, swimming, and tidepooling; and activities for children. Boaters will especially appreciate the comprehensive listing of marinas and other boating facilities in the area. 8 color pages, 105 b/w photos, 65 illustrations, 40 maps, 32 charts, booklist, index. 262 pages.   **$8.95**

GUIDE TO THE YUCATAN PENINSULA: Including Belize
by **Chicki Mallan**

Explore the mysterious ruins of the Maya, plunge into the color and bustle of the village marketplace, relax on unspoiled beaches, or jostle with the jet set in modern Cancun. Mallan has gathered all the information you'll need: accommodations and dining for every budget, detailed transportation tips, plans of archaeological sites, and accurate maps to guide you into every corner of this exotic land. The new section on Belize helps open up this delightful, little-known Caribbean getaway just over the border from Mexico. 8 color pages, 154 b/w photos, 55 illustrations, 57 maps, 70 charts, appendix, booklist, Mayan and Spanish glossaries, index. 400 pages.   **$11.95**

The International Series

EGYPT HANDBOOK   by **Kathy Hansen**

Land of ancient civilizations, diverse cultures, and sharp contrasts, Egypt presents a 5,000-year-old challenge to all comers. *Egypt Handbook* leads you through the labyrinth of sprawling Cairo, along the verdant Nile, across the desert, and into the far oases. With a deeper appreciation for Egypt's profound cultural legacy than any other guidebook, *Egypt Handbook* helps the traveler to unravel the complexities of the "Gift of the Nile," from prehistory to the present. An invaluable companion for intelligent travel in Egypt. Color and b/w photos, illustrations, over 40 detailed maps and site plans to museums and archaeological sites, Arabic glossary, booklist, index. 500 pages.
(Available Fall 1989) $14.95

IMPORTANT ORDERING INFORMATION

PRICES: All prices are subject to change. We always ship the most current edition. We will let you know if there is a price increase on the book you ordered.

SHIPPING & HANDLING OPTIONS:
  1) Domestic UPS or USPS 1st class (allow 10 working days for delivery): $3.00 for the 1st item, 50¢ for each additional item.
  Exceptions:
  - **Indonesia Handbook** shipping is $4.00 for the 1st item, $1.00 for each additional copy.
  - **Moonbelts** are $1.50 for one, 50¢ for each additional belt.
  - Add $2.00 for same-day handling.
  2) UPS 2nd Day Air or Printed Airmail requires a special quote.
  3) International Surface Bookrate (8-12 weeks delivery): $3.00 for the 1st item, $1.00 for each additional item.

FOREIGN ORDERS: All orders which originate outside the U.S.A. **must** be paid for with either an International Money Order or a check in U.S. currency drawn on a major U.S. bank based in the U.S.A.

TELEPHONE ORDERS: We accept Visa or Mastercard payments. **Minimum Order is U.S. $15.00.** Call in your order: (916) 345-5473. 9:00 a.m.—5:00 p.m. Pacific Standard Time.

How did you hear about Moon guides?_____

Are Moon guides available at your local bookstore?_____

If not, please list name of store and we will follow up:_____

_____

_____

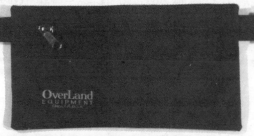

MOONBELTS. A new concept in moneybelts. Made of heavy-duty Cordura nylon, the **Moonbelt** offers maximum protection for your money and important papers. This pouch, designed for all-weather comfort, slips under your shirt or waistband, rendering it virtually undetectable and inaccessible to pickpockets. Many thoughtful features: 1-inch-wide nylon webbing, heavy-duty zipper, and a 1-inch high-test quick-release buckle. No more fumbling around for the strap or repeated adjustments, this handy plastic buckle opens and closes with a touch, but won't come undone until you want it to. Accommodates travelers cheques, passport, cash, photos. Size 5 x 9 inches. Available in black only. **$8.95**

ORDER FORM
(See important ordering information on opposite page)

Name: _____ Date: _____

Street: _____

City: _____

State or Country: _____ Zip Code: _____

Daytime Phone: _____

Quantity	Title	Price

Taxable Total	
Sales Tax (6%) for California Residents	
Shipping & Handling	
TOTAL	

Ship to: ❏ address above ❏ other _____

_____

_____

Make checks payable to:

Moon Publications, Inc., 722 Wall Street, Chico, California, 95928, USA

We Accept Visa and MasterCard

To order: Call in your Visa or Mastercard Number, or send a written order with your Visa or Mastercard number and expiration date clearly written.

Card Number: ❏ Visa ❏ MasterCard

❏❏❏❏ ❏❏❏❏ ❏❏❏❏ ❏❏❏❏

expiration date: _____

Card Name:

❏ same as above ❏ other _____

signature _____

33-6

WHERE TO BUY THIS BOOK

Bookstores and Libraries:
Moon Publications, Inc., guides are sold world-wide. Please write sales manager Donna Galassi for a list of wholesalers and distributors in your area that stock our travel handbooks.

Travelers:
We would like to have Moon Publications' guides available throughout the world. Please ask your bookstore to write or call us for ordering information. If your bookstore will not order our guides for you, please write or call for a free catalog.

MOON PUBLICATIONS, INC.
722 WALL STREET
CHICO, CA 95928 USA
tel: 916/345-5473

THE METRIC SYSTEM

Since this book is used by people from all around the world, the metric system is employed throughout. Here are the equivalents:

1 inch =	2.54 centimeters (cm)
1 foot =	.304 meters (m)
1 mile =	1.6093 kilometers (km)
1 km =	.6214 miles
1 fathom =	1.8288 m
1 chain =	20.1168 m
1 furlong =	201.168
1 acre =	.4047 hectares (ha)
1 sq km =	100 ha
1 sq mile =	59 sq km
1 ounce =	28.35 grams
1 pound =	.4536 kilograms (kg)
1 short ton =	.90718 metric ton
1 short ton =	2000 pounds
1 long ton =	1.016 metric tons
1 long ton =	2240 pounds
1 metric ton =	1000 kg
1 quart =	.94635 liters
1 US gallon =	3.7854 liters
1 Imperial gallon =	4.5459 liters
1 nautical mile =	1.852 km

To avoid confusion, all clock times follow the 24-hour airline timetable system, i.e., 0100 is 1:00 a.m., 1300 is 1:00 p.m., 2330 is 11:30 p.m. From noon to midnight, merely add 12 onto regular time to derive airline time. Islanders operate on "coconut time": the coconut will fall when it's ripe.

To compute Centigrade temperatures, subtract 32 from Fahrenheit and divide by 1.8. To go the otherway, multiply Centigrade by 1.8 and add 32. Unless otherwise indicated, north is at the top of all maps in this book. When using official topographic maps you can determine the scale by taking the representative fraction (RF) and dividing by 100. This will give the number of meters represented by one centimeter. For example, a map with a RF of 1:10,000 would represent 100 m for every cm on the map.

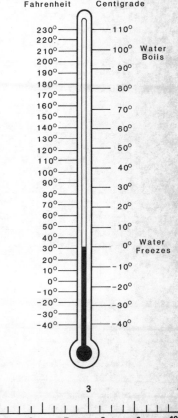

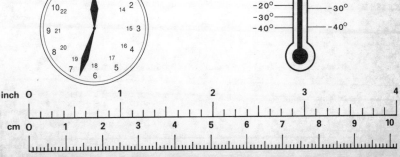

1989

JANUARY

S	M	T	W	T	F	S
1	2	3	4	5	6	7
8	9	10	11	12	13	14
15	16	17	18	19	20	21
22	23	24	25	26	27	28
29	30	31				

FEBRUARY

S	M	T	W	T	F	S
			1	2	3	4
5	6	7	8	9	10	11
12	13	14	15	16	17	18
19	20	21	22	23	24	25
26	27	28				

MARCH

S	M	T	W	T	F	S
			1	2	3	4
5	6	7	8	9	10	11
12	13	14	15	16	17	18
19	20	21	22	23	24	25
26	27	28	29	30	31	

APRIL

S	M	T	W	T	F	S
						1
2	3	4	5	6	7	8
9	10	11	12	13	14	15
16	17	18	19	20	21	22
23	24	25	26	27	28	29
30						

MAY

S	M	T	W	T	F	S
	1	2	3	4	5	6
7	8	9	10	11	12	13
14	15	16	17	18	19	20
21	22	23	24	25	26	27
28	29	30	31			

JUNE

S	M	T	W	T	F	S
				1	2	3
4	5	6	7	8	9	10
11	12	13	14	15	16	17
18	19	20	21	22	23	24
25	26	27	28	29	30	

JULY

S	M	T	W	T	F	S
						1
2	3	4	5	6	7	8
9	10	11	12	13	14	15
16	17	18	19	20	21	22
23	24	25	26	27	28	29
30	31					

AUGUST

S	M	T	W	T	F	S
		1	2	3	4	5
6	7	8	9	10	11	12
13	14	15	16	17	18	19
20	21	22	23	24	25	26
27	28	29	30	31		

SEPTEMBER

S	M	T	W	T	F	S
					1	2
3	4	5	6	7	8	9
10	11	12	13	14	15	16
17	18	19	20	21	22	23
24	25	26	27	28	29	30

OCTOBER

S	M	T	W	T	F	S
1	2	3	4	5	6	7
8	9	10	11	12	13	14
15	16	17	18	19	20	21
22	23	24	25	26	27	28
29	30	31				

NOVEMBER

S	M	T	W	T	F	S
			1	2	3	4
5	6	7	8	9	10	11
12	13	14	15	16	17	18
19	20	21	22	23	24	25
26	27	28	29	30		

DECEMBER

S	M	T	W	T	F	S
					1	2
3	4	5	6	7	8	9
10	11	12	13	14	15	16
17	18	19	20	21	22	23
24	25	26	27	28	29	30
31						

1990

JANUARY

S	M	T	W	T	F	S
	1	2	3	4	5	6
7	8	9	10	11	12	13
14	15	16	17	18	19	20
21	22	23	24	25	26	27
28	29	30	31			

FEBRUARY

S	M	T	W	T	F	S
				1	2	3
4	5	6	7	8	9	10
11	12	13	14	15	16	17
18	19	20	21	22	23	24
25	26	27	28			

MARCH

S	M	T	W	T	F	S
				1	2	3
4	5	6	7	8	9	10
11	12	13	14	15	16	17
18	19	20	21	22	23	24
25	26	27	28	29	30	31

APRIL

S	M	T	W	T	F	S
1	2	3	4	5	6	7
8	9	10	11	12	13	14
15	16	17	18	19	20	21
22	23	24	25	26	27	28
29	30					

MAY

S	M	T	W	T	F	S
		1	2	3	4	5
6	7	8	9	10	11	12
13	14	15	16	17	18	19
20	21	22	23	24	25	26
27	28	29	30	31		

JUNE

S	M	T	W	T	F	S
					1	2
3	4	5	6	7	8	9
10	11	12	13	14	15	16
17	18	19	20	21	22	23
24	25	26	27	28	29	30

JULY

S	M	T	W	T	F	S
1	2	3	4	5	6	7
8	9	10	11	12	13	14
15	16	17	18	19	20	21
22	23	24	25	26	27	28
29	30	31				

AUGUST

S	M	T	W	T	F	S
			1	2	3	4
5	6	7	8	9	10	11
12	13	14	15	16	17	18
19	20	21	22	23	24	25
26	27	28	29	30	31	

SEPTEMBER

S	M	T	W	T	F	S
						1
2	3	4	5	6	7	8
9	10	11	12	13	14	15
16	17	18	19	20	21	22
23	24	25	26	27	28	29
30						

OCTOBER

S	M	T	W	T	F	S
	1	2	3	4	5	6
7	8	9	10	11	12	13
14	15	16	17	18	19	20
21	22	23	24	25	26	27
28	29	30	31			

NOVEMBER

S	M	T	W	T	F	S
				1	2	3
4	5	6	7	8	9	10
11	12	13	14	15	16	17
18	19	20	21	22	23	24
25	26	27	28	29	30	

DECEMBER

S	M	T	W	T	F	S
						1
2	3	4	5	6	7	8
9	10	11	12	13	14	15
16	17	18	19	20	21	22
23	24	25	26	27	28	29
30	31					

1991

JANUARY

S	M	T	W	T	F	S
		1	2	3	4	5
6	7	8	9	10	11	12
13	14	15	16	17	18	19
20	21	22	23	24	25	26
27	28	29	30	31		

FEBRUARY

S	M	T	W	T	F	S
					1	2
3	4	5	6	7	8	9
10	11	12	13	14	15	16
17	18	19	20	21	22	23
24	25	26	27	28		

MARCH

S	M	T	W	T	F	S
					1	2
3	4	5	6	7	8	9
10	11	12	13	14	15	16
17	18	19	20	21	22	23
24	25	26	27	28	29	30
31						

APRIL

S	M	T	W	T	F	S
	1	2	3	4	5	6
7	8	9	10	11	12	13
14	15	16	17	18	19	20
21	22	23	24	25	26	27
28	29	30				

MAY

S	M	T	W	T	F	S
			1	2	3	4
5	6	7	8	9	10	11
12	13	14	15	16	17	18
19	20	21	22	23	24	25
26	27	28	29	30	31	

JUNE

S	M	T	W	T	F	S
						1
2	3	4	5	6	7	8
9	10	11	12	13	14	15
16	17	18	19	20	21	22
23	24	25	26	27	28	29
30						

JULY

S	M	T	W	T	F	S
	1	2	3	4	5	6
7	8	9	10	11	12	13
14	15	16	17	18	19	20
21	22	23	24	25	26	27
28	29	30	31			

AUGUST

S	M	T	W	T	F	S
				1	2	3
4	5	6	7	8	9	10
11	12	13	14	15	16	17
18	19	20	21	22	23	24
25	26	27	28	29	30	31

SEPTEMBER

S	M	T	W	T	F	S
1	2	3	4	5	6	7
8	9	10	11	12	13	14
15	16	17	18	19	20	21
22	23	24	25	26	27	28
29	30					

OCTOBER

S	M	T	W	T	F	S
		1	2	3	4	5
6	7	8	9	10	11	12
13	14	15	16	17	18	19
20	21	22	23	24	25	26
27	28	29	30	31		

NOVEMBER

S	M	T	W	T	F	S
					1	2
3	4	5	6	7	8	9
10	11	12	13	14	15	16
17	18	19	20	21	22	23
24	25	26	27	28	29	30

DECEMBER

S	M	T	W	T	F	S
1	2	3	4	5	6	7
8	9	10	11	12	13	14
15	16	17	18	19	20	21
22	23	24	25	26	27	28
29	30	31				

1992

JANUARY

S	M	T	W	T	F	S
			1	2	3	4
5	6	7	8	9	10	11
12	13	14	15	16	17	18
19	20	21	22	23	24	25
26	27	28	29	30	31	

FEBRUARY

S	M	T	W	T	F	S
						1
2	3	4	5	6	7	8
9	10	11	12	13	14	15
16	17	18	19	20	21	22
23	24	25	26	27	28	29

MARCH

S	M	T	W	T	F	S
1	2	3	4	5	6	7
8	9	10	11	12	13	14
15	16	17	18	19	20	21
22	23	24	25	26	27	28
29	30	31				

APRIL

S	M	T	W	T	F	S
			1	2	3	4
5	6	7	8	9	10	11
12	13	14	15	16	17	18
19	20	21	22	23	24	25
26	27	28	29	30		

MAY

S	M	T	W	T	F	S
					1	2
3	4	5	6	7	8	9
10	11	12	13	14	15	16
17	18	19	20	21	22	23
24	25	26	27	28	29	30
31						

JUNE

S	M	T	W	T	F	S
	1	2	3	4	5	6
7	8	9	10	11	12	13
14	15	16	17	18	19	20
21	22	23	24	25	26	27
28	29	30				

JULY

S	M	T	W	T	F	S
			1	2	3	4
5	6	7	8	9	10	11
12	13	14	15	16	17	18
19	20	21	22	23	24	25
26	27	28	29	30	31	

AUGUST

S	M	T	W	T	F	S
						1
2	3	4	5	6	7	8
9	10	11	12	13	14	15
16	17	18	19	20	21	22
23	24	25	26	27	28	29
30	31					

SEPTEMBER

S	M	T	W	T	F	S
		1	2	3	4	5
6	7	8	9	10	11	12
13	14	15	16	17	18	19
20	21	22	23	24	25	26
27	28	29	30			

OCTOBER

S	M	T	W	T	F	S
				1	2	3
4	5	6	7	8	9	10
11	12	13	14	15	16	17
18	19	20	21	22	23	24
25	26	27	28	29	30	31

NOVEMBER

S	M	T	W	T	F	S
1	2	3	4	5	6	7
8	9	10	11	12	13	14
15	16	17	18	19	20	21
22	23	24	25	26	27	28
29	30					

DECEMBER

S	M	T	W	T	F	S
		1	2	3	4	5
6	7	8	9	10	11	12
13	14	15	16	17	18	19
20	21	22	23	24	25	26
27	28	29	30	31		